THE SECRET GOSPEL OF JESUS

THE SECRET GOSPEL OF JESUS

Unveiling the Mystery of the
Sator Square and Decoding
the Hidden Rules

Bert P. Regan

Speraro
Ottawa, Canada

Speraro

Library and Archives Canada 2024

ISBN (ePub)	978-1-990395-01-7
ISBN (paperback) Large edition	978-1-990395-03-1
ISBN (hardcover)	978-1-990395-02-4

Thank you for visiting the website of the author: bertpregan.com

Cover original idea: R.P./Speraro/Cover and text design: New Design Dimension/Heather Morin)/Cover image: Adapted from *chillchill_lanla/Shutterstock.com/* Graphic elements in Figures in Chap. 11 and 12 added by Speraro.

Unless otherwise indicated, scripture taken from the NEW AMERICAN STANDARD BIBLE®, Copyright © 1960, 1962, 1968, 1971, 1973, 1975, 1977, 1995 by Lockman Foundation. Used by permission.

All quotations from the Church Fathers are taken from: New Advent org. online version, with permission from Kevin Knight – New Advent.

The words in italics (other than foreign words and titles) have been added to the text by the author for emphasis.

Printed in Canada

(1-2)

Disclaimer: The content presented in the book is based on the author's perspective, research and interpretation of the subject matter. This book represents the personal views and opinions of the author and does not necessarily reflect the positions or opinions of any organization, institution, or other individual.

*In memory of my beloved father
Gabriel who despite his early death
remains forever etched in my heart.*

I desire to speak five words with my mind so that I may instruct others

FIRST EPISTLE OF PAUL TO THE CORINTHIANS 14:19

ACKNOWLEDGMENTS

I would like to express my deepest gratitude to my wife Jocelyne for her patience and her unwavering support from the beginning of this lengthy project, as well as my daughter Roxanne, my sweet angel, for all her help and guidance along the way. Without their love and support, I would not have been able to complete this book.

I would like to thank Dr. Isaac for reviewing parts of this book. His comments and expertise were greatly appreciated. I would also like to thank Clare for translating an early version of the manuscript and for her judicious comments and ability to find the right words during the revision process.

Finally, I am grateful to Mark, Andrzej, Paul, Serge, François and Guy who were present at an opportune moment in my journey.

ABBREVIATIONS

CCC   Catechism of the Catholic Church.

G   Strong's Greek number from James Strong, *Strong's Exhaustive Concordance of the Bible*, Updated and Expanded Edition (Massachusetts: Hendrickson Publishers, 2009)

H   Strong's Hebrew number from James Strong, *Strong's Exhaustive Concordance of the Bible*, Updated and Expanded Edition (Massachusetts: Hendrickson Publishers, 2009)

S. Th.   *Summa Theologiae*

CONTENTS

PREFACE

When I was young, I wanted to be a Roman Catholic priest. That turned out to be a short-lived aspiration. By my mid-teens, I had become a non-practicing Christian. I still believed in Jesus Christ, but in my own way.

In adulthood, I developed a passion for archeology and religion from a historical perspective. Therefore, I came to believe that religion was made up of a structured collection of beliefs, practices and rites designed by haughty, shrewd individuals to control others and serve their own agenda. That does not paint a pretty picture, does it? I have come a very long way since then, mainly because of the profound, life-altering experience I had one September evening in 2011.

While I was on my computer, staring at an image of a first-century artifact, I suddenly had an experience that could be described as a personal revelation. In religious circles, the phenomenon is known as a "conversion." Although I could have written an entire tome about this intense experience and though it is the profound source and the light that has guided my writing, it is not what this book is about.

The artifact had caught my attention a few weeks before, when I watched a television documentary entitled *Decoding the Ancients: The Roman Army's Secret Christians*.[1] The documentary summarized the primary research on the artifact, including the possibility that it was of Christian origin, but I had no idea about its origin and meaning and I began to explore it.

As I deepened my research, the discoveries kept coming. I am a pragmatic person, so I realized that if I was going to share my findings publicly, which I felt moved to do, I would have to thoroughly, logically substantiate every claim I made—or risk having the book dismissed out of hand! I am confident that, like me, you will find both the form and content of the archeological wonder astounding. I hope you will also find my evidence conclusive.

Now for a bit of history, to give you an idea of the magnitude of what I have discovered.

CHRISTIAN DIVERSITY

Whenever I pass a church, I find myself scanning its name and Christian denomination. If you have ever done the same, I am sure you would have noticed the large variety of Christian groups. In fact, it would take several pages to list them all.

Christianity remains the religion with the greatest number of adherents in the world today, most of whom belong to one of three main branches: Catholicism, Protestantism, and Orthodox Christianity. These three branches have many offshoots, professing distinctive doctrines. There are also several smaller Christian denominations, some of which, like Mormonism and the Jehovah's Witnesses, have millions of members. Thus, it appears that Christianity could be classified throughout its history as a *divided* religion.

A bewildering number of Christian groups with a variety of beliefs, rituals, and interpretations have flourished since the beginning of Christianity. Some Christian factions continue to be born and rapidly proliferate, while others decline and fade away.

History shows that many Christians have fought for their convictions to the extreme extent of being willing to die or even kill to preserve their faith, even if their actions have sometimes targeted other Christian groups. Many followers sincerely believe that their group possesses the Christian truth, and often loudly proclaim that others' truth is false. Which group possesses the *real* truth? This is certainly not new; people having been asking the same question since the first few decades after the death of Jesus.

The Heretics

Shortly after that pivotal event, Christian disciples[2] left Palestine and scattered across the entire Eastern Mediterranean, as far as the city of Rome, to form Christian communities, and various Christian ideologies spread throughout this vast territory. Seeing that neither the end of the world nor the arrival of a new age was imminent, a rudimentary form of Christian organization called the "nascent Church" or "early Church" was created to counter this rapid proliferation of ideologies. This organization soon realized the importance of solidifying its structure and promoting its doctrines to protect and propagate the authentic Gospel of Christ, the truth that it upheld.

In the early centuries, several schools of thought, such as Marcionism, Docetism, and Gnosticism, emerged and developed, with beliefs that were not at all pleasing to the early Church. The number of followers, the origin and the exact names of these groups are often questioned even today.[3] Given that the vast majority of the leaders of these rebel groups already belonged to the early Church, they were a major threat to orthodoxy and therefore could do a great deal of damage with their false doctrines. Many of these groups are considered to be offshoots of the early Church. According to the nascent Church, they altered the truth and misled the faithful by preaching a distorted message. In *Against Heresies*, Bishop Irenaeus of Lyon explained that at first glance, the ideologies of these offenders seemed to follow orthodoxy, but after careful scrutiny, they clearly contradicted the only truth.[4]

To flourish, and more importantly, to survive, the nascent Church had to eliminate the doctrines of the offenders before they expanded further. To achieve this, it actively sought out and assessed the other Christian groups that were inconsistent with its established Christian orthodoxy. In addition to destroying offending documents, the nascent Church used a strategy that later proved to be quite effective: isolating each offender from the orthodox organization and grouping them all under a single term, the heretics. The Church subsequently assigned negative characteristics to members of this large group, including that they were "possessed by the devil, the devil's interpreter, the Antichrist, the false prophet and the blasphemer."[5]

Some authors, especially from the contemporary era, tend to portray the leaders of the early Church as intolerant, malicious, and opportunistic individuals who used their political and social power to preach their ideas against those of the well-intentioned, oppressed heretics.

Indeed, the bishops of the early Church had some theological control and were able to exert pressure on people of their respective communities during the second and third centuries. However, the organizational structure of the Church in that period was quite rudimentary and fragmented, until the arrival of Emperor Constantine around the year A.D. 312.[6] In addition, during this period, disputes among Christian groups were mainly kept on an ideological level.

Above all, the early Church was mostly made up of individuals who acted with conviction and sincerity, with the goal of protecting the faith, and they were often willing to risk their own lives.[7] They were profoundly convinced that they held the truth and were following the path of Christ.

CHRISTIAN UNIFICATION
UNDER A POWERFUL INSTRUMENT

Even though there was a diversity of Christian ideologies, many Fathers of the Church, such as Ignatius of Antioch, Irenaeus of Lyon, Tertullian of Carthage, and Clement of Alexandria, were convinced that the early Church had a distinctive and indestructible instrument that established the credibility of its orthodoxy.

At the end of the second century, Irenaeus of Lyon boldly stated that this instrument of universal faith—that made it easy to distinguish between truth and falsehood—was recognized by the entire Christian population, even by barbarians who did not have access to written texts like the Bible.[8]

A Secret Apostolic Instrument

The unshakable, even absolute force of this persuasive instrument stems from its origin and its method of transmission. It was originally instituted by Jesus Christ, and subsequently transferred to the apostles, then transmitted to generations of bishops through apostolic succession. As such, the early Church openly proclaimed that it was the only organization that possessed, and used, this authentic and well-established instrument as the absolute truth. The Catholic Church continues to make this claim to this day.

Despite its immense value, the apostolic content and the form of the enigmatic instrument have never been disclosed. If this divine instrument, transmitted among bishops, really exists, then why must it remain an internal secret instead of being publicly shared?

Evidently, the Church's secrecy arouses suspicion. For some scholars, this undisclosed instrument is pure fiction. Did the Church use this instrument to support its customized doctrines or to maintain its power? The Protestant Reformation, which began in the 16th century, voiced such concerns.

Is the instrument concrete or intangible? Does it contain oral or written content? How did the Church preserve the authenticity of the content?

A Real and Tangible Instrument

My research leads me to believe that this powerful instrument does in fact exist—it is known as the *Sator Square*. The instrument appears to be neither subterfuge nor fiction. It is a tangible artifact that holds secret, pragmatic content. I believe that the secret of the Sator Square remained under wraps for two millennia. The Church may well have intentionally protected it by conforming to a law of silence or secret discipline called the *Disciplina arcani* in Latin.

If truth be told, I was not looking for this secret; it rather subtly presented itself to me. Once I realized the significance of the Sator Square, I understood the repercussions of my discovery. My enlightened quest is leading me to a risky and controversial place that I really did not want to go. Given my knowledge of this field, I know that many people are resistant to these kinds of discoveries, and they utterly repudiate them without consideration. I have no doubt about the fate that could befall this book. I am aware that some parts will probably be misrepresented and challenged on their details.

I sincerely believe that I have presented clear and specific facts, along with numerous references to support my position. Nevertheless, while writing, I often felt unable to express the full breadth and depth of this discovery. Even though I have included a lot of unprecedented material, the book cannot and does not claim to reveal the entirety of the secret, mystical message and its full meaning.

It is absolutely not my intention to criticize the Catholic Church, any Christian group in particular, or any individual. I have explained the reason why I decided to reveal my discovery in the conclusion. I do not claim to hold the truth. I can only humbly share my comprehension of my discovery. If my findings, supported by data, do not suit you, I respect that.

My goal is not to convince, but to bear witness to the Gospel, as will be revealed in this book. We will see that there is only one truth, which lends itself to many interpretations. The interpretations do not destroy Christianity; they bring it alive.

While I stand behind the information concerning the artifact that I have presented in this book, as a Roman Catholic, I will defer to the Church's official interpretation of the content of the Sator Square— whether or not it is identical to mine.

PART I

THE SATOR SQUARE AND

ITS HIDDEN ORIGIN

1

AN UNUSUAL ARTIFACT

One of the most mysterious archeological discoveries found to date is the enigmatic artifact known as the Sator Square. It has also been referred to as the Rotas Square and the Magic Square. As we will see, this artifact is in fact the unifying instrument mentioned in the preface.

The Sator Square consists of a series of letters organized in the shape of a square. The letters were painted or engraved on various supports such as stones or amulets. Some of the oldest of these artifacts were discovered in the city of Pompeii, buried beneath the ashes from the eruption of Mount Vesuvius, in A.D. 79. Many other Magic

Squares have been identified in different parts of the world.

While numerous researchers have studied the origin and meaning of the artifact, their findings are inconclusive. The Sator Square remains one of the greatest secrets of the past two millennia.

THE PALINDROME

Two types of artifacts have been found since the 19th century. The first is the Sator Square. It is composed of the following five Latin words, each five letters long:

SATOR, AREPO, TENET, OPERA, ROTAS (see Figure 1.1).

The arrangement of the letters is particularly unusual, as the artifact forms a palindrome, which is a word or phrase that can be read from left to right or right to left, like the word "kayak."

In fact, the Sator Square is a palindromic square, as each of the five words can also be read from top to bottom and bottom to top. For instance, the word SATOR is found four times in a Sator Square, from top to bottom, bottom to top, left to right and right to left.

Over the years, a second type of palindromic square has also been found, the Rotas Square, which includes the following five words in sequential order:

ROTAS, OPERA, TENET, AREPO, SATOR
(see Figure 1.2).

Figure 1.1 Sator Square	Figure 1.2 Rotas Square

S	A	T	O	R
A	R	E	P	O
T	E	N	E	T
O	P	E	R	A
R	O	T	A	S

R	O	T	A	S
O	P	E	R	A
T	E	N	E	T
A	R	E	P	O
S	A	T	O	R

Generally, the Rotas Squares are considered older than the Sator Squares. Some believe that the Rotas Squares came from a non-Christian source and were later changed to Sator Squares by Christians to emphasize the word *Sator* or "sower," a name that is often attributed to Jesus Christ and to God.

While most of the artifacts are painted or engraved on stone, some have been found on coins, amulets, and talismans, and as illustrations in ancient manuscripts. They are generally not hidden in obscure locations or confined spaces; they are commonly exposed to public view. The fact that they spread around the world over almost two millennia signals their importance.

Numerous characteristics were attributed to the artifacts. For instance, some believed that they would reveal the location of a treasure hidden by the Templars, eliminate bad spells, ward off demons, or extinguish fire. Some even thought that the artifacts had medicinal properties, such as the ability to cure snake bites or help with childbirth.[1] It is evident that these artifacts have attracted a lot of interest over a very long time.

For the purposes of this book, I use the term "Rotas Square" when referring specifically to that arrangement of letters on the artifact; I use "Sator Square" to refer to the Sator Square or to represent the artifact in general. The term Magic Square will also be used as a general reference to the artifact.

THE GEOGRAPHIC LOCATION

The artifact can be found in various locations around the world. Currently, approximately fifteen Rotas Squares have been discovered in different countries, including the following:

- The oldest Rotas Squares were found in one of the most famous archeological sites in the world: Pompeii. During excavations of the site in 1936, the Italian archeologist Mateo Della Corte found a Rotas Square inscribed on one of the columns that surround the Large Palestra near the Amphitheater. The Palestra is an outdoor courtyard that is thought to have been used by youth for physical and military training. At least one other Rotas Square was also found in Pompeii, inscribed on a wall of a residence.[2]

- Two Rotas Squares are located in England: one was found engraved on the wall of a Roman house in the town of Cirencester, which dates back to the third century A.D.[3] The second was discovered in Manchester on a container, likely an amphora from the second century A.D.

- A Rotas Square was discovered on a second or third-century tile in a Roman residence in the ancient city of Aquincum, whose ruins are located in present-day Budapest, Hungary.[4]

- Several Rotas Squares were discovered at the site of Dura-Europos, a city on the Euphrates

River in Syria. Three of them were unearthed during excavations in the 1930s in the ancient pagan temple of Artemis Azzanathkona. The Rotas Square inscriptions are dated between 200 and 256 A.D. At that time, towards the end of the Roman occupation, the city was a garrison site. The temple was used by the empire's army and possibly by its administrators.

Photo 1: Replica of the Rotas Square in Manchester, England, written on Roman pottery sherds from the second century A.D. *Photo credit: Courtesy of Manchester Museum, The University of Manchester*

The Sator Squares—often considered the most recent Magic Squares—are mostly concentrated in France, including the ancient village of Oppède le Vieux and the Jarnac, Loches and Rochemaure communes, as well as in the cities of Rome, Siena and Bolzano and the Brusaporto commune in Italy. They have also been found in Santiago de Compostela, Spain and in Germany. The aforementioned lists only represent a few of the numerous artifacts that have been discovered.

THE THREE CATEGORIES OF RESEARCH

There have been many studies in the last few centuries aimed at deciphering the Sator Square. According to some, it is an intellectual exercise that consists of creating a perfect palindrome, or simply a Roman word game,[5] whose rules remain obscure.

The failure to uncover its meaning is evidently not due to a lack of effort. In fact, the Sator Square is so puzzling that it has generated a substantial amount of research. Renowned author Rose Mary Sheldon has compiled one of the most comprehensive directories concerning research on the Magic Squares in *"The Sator Rebus: An Unsolved Cryptogram?"* She lists several hundred investigations, conducted over a period of almost 150 years, which attempt to demystify this ancient artifact. While her work remains a key tool for advanced research on the subject, she recognizes that theories are numerous and that new ones are constantly emerging.[6]

All of the research can be grouped under three non-exclusive categories: 1. studies on the overall meaning of the artifact, 2. studies on its origin, and 3. studies on the five words of the palindrome.

The Overall Meaning

Some believe that the Sator Square contains coded information that is embedded in the cryptogram.

In 1926, Felix Grosser, a priest from the city of Chemnitz, Germany, created an anagram with the letters of the Sator Square.[7] An anagram consists of letters that are rearranged to form words or phrases. Using the letters of the Magic Square, Grosser formed a cross symbol with two words, *pater noster* (Our Father), which cross at the letter "N." However, he was unable to use all 25 letters of the Sator Square.

He believed that the four remaining letters (two As and two Os) represented Alpha and Omega. He referred to two excerpts from the book of

Revelation, namely "I am the Alpha and the Omega, says the Lord God, who is and who was and who is to come, the Almighty" (1:8) and "I am the Alpha and the Omega, the first and the last, the beginning and the end" (22:13). To respect these New Testament passages, Grosser placed a letter "A" at the beginning and a letter "O" at the end of each *pater noster* (see Figure 1.3).[8]

Figure 1.3 Felix Grosser's *Pater Noster*

```
            A
            P
            A
            T
            E
            R
A P A T E R N O S T E R O
            O
            S
            T
            E
            R
            O
```

Grosser's discovery did not meet with universal agreement. For example, William Baines expressed reservations about the discovery by successfully reproducing results similar to Grosser's, using other five-letter Magic Squares.[9] Despite these reservations, Grosser's discovery is likely to be part of the solution to the message.

Several other authors, probably influenced by Grosser, have attempted to decrypt the secret message using anagrams. Some managed to do so using all 25 of the Sator Square's letters. Others have even generated satanic sentences like the following:

Retro Satana, toto opere asper!

Satan, oro te, pro arte a te spero !

Or praise, like:

Oro te, pater, oro te, pater, sanas !

O pater ores, pro aetate nostra!

In fact, with some imagination, and preferably with the use of a computer, it might be possible to form several other anagrams from the letters of the Sator Square. Others have attempted to make smaller anagrams using only a few letters from the artifact. However, most of these methods seem completely random and are not systematic. In my view, all of these attempts to form anagrams from the letters of the Sator Square seem to provide incomplete or irrelevant information. However, it should be noted that Grosser's theory was well received, likely due to the importance of "Our Father" to Christians.

Other studies that seek to decipher the overall meaning of the artifact employ numerology, more specifically gematria. This method, used by the Jews and Greeks, assigns a numerical value to each letter and then interprets words and sentences according to their numerical values. Gematria reveals the order and coordination that were established through God's creation. People who perceive certain elements of the divine order through gematria are said to manifest wisdom. It is highly likely that the creator of the Magic Square intended to use gematria to demonstrate the divine nature of the artifact.

The Origin

The next category of studies focuses on the origin of the Sator Square. These studies suggest a wide range of potential origins: Christian (e.g., Orthodox and Gnostic), Hebrew, Mithraic, the Greek philosophical school (e.g., Stoicism and Epicureanism), or Greek mythology.

Theories that support a Christian origin for the artifact are often based on the following four main points, some of which have been subject to debate:

1. Grosser's *Pater Noster*, which is currently the most recognized, though still disputed theory.

2. Some people have observed that it is possible to form a cross in the center of the Sator Square with the word *tenet* written both horizontally and vertically. However, many scholars specify that the cross symbol was commonly used by groups other than the Christians, even before Jesus' time. Others also seem to be convinced that the cross symbol was not used by the Christians until the fourth century. If this is true, it also refutes Grosser's theory of a cross symbol made up of two words, *Pater Noster*.

3. The word "Sator" is known as a metaphor for Jesus Christ. However, the word also represents other deities, such as God himself, Zeus, Jupiter[10] and Saturnus-Aion.[11]

4. Many Sator Squares are located in or near Christian establishments. Others were found in proximity to information of a Christian nature, such as the amulet housed in one of the Staatliche (State) Museums in Berlin, which

contains the Greek word *ichthus*, meaning "Jesus Christ Son of God Savior," written with the Magic Square.[12]

The Five Words of the Palindrome

This last research category encompasses several studies that attempted to solve the Sator Square based on an in-depth analysis of the five Latin words found in the palindrome: SATOR, AREPO, TENET, OPERA and ROTAS. The common meaning associated with each of these five words is as follows:

- **Sator** represents "the sower" or "the creator," which is a metaphor for God or Jesus Christ.[13] Other gods, like Zeus, were also designated using this word.

- **Arepo** has no known meaning, but it could represent a person's name. This word presents a major obstacle to understanding the five-word message.

- **Tenet** means he/she holds/maintains.

- **Opera** designates "effort" or "work."

- **Rotas** refers to "wheels."

Thus, some researchers have created the following sentences with the five words:

> With his plow, the Sower holds carefully his wheels.

> The Sower carefully leads his plow in the field.

Or

> The Sower Arepo holds his wheels with effort.

> The Sower Arepo holds his wheels with care.

The message in these sentences is unclear. Who is Arepo? In fact, the enigmatic word "Arepo" seems to confuse researchers. In their attempt to understand and explain the five words, some experts have suggested that the Magic Square was written using the boustrophedon method,[14] which consists of writing lines alternatively, the first from left to right, the second from right to left, and so on, reproducing the movements of an ox during plowing. This old method of writing eliminates the problematic word "Arepo" and results in the following sentence:

> The great Sower holds in his hand all works.[15]

The meaning could ultimately be the famous saying that you get what you deserve. Nevertheless, these sentences could be seen as vague and insignificant.

In the end, when I looked at the studies from all three categories, I found them to be inconclusive. The fact that many contemporary researchers still believe that Grosser's theory of the *Pater Noster* solves the Sator Square mystery clearly underlines the inability to decrypt the secret of the artifact.

John Cullen's Two Sentences

One day while researching the artifact, I came across the book *Sator Enigma, Ancient Roman Mystery Solved*. To my surprise, I quickly realized that the book's prolific author, John T. Cullen, had actually discovered the meaning of the five words of the Sator Square. Cullen's brilliant explanation of the five words offers a fresh perspective. He proposes that the five words, joined together, represent not one sentence, but two sentences:

God [the sower] holds the plow, but you turn the furrows.[16]

This message was intended for everyone, considering the importance of agriculture in the lives of people in the first century A.D. Cullen further specifies that the plower must turn at the end of the straight line to dig another furrow.[17] In the first century A.D., turning with the plow was a very difficult and meticulous task for laborers. After turning, the plowers had to make sure they were in the right position to dig another long, narrow groove to maximize productivity and to hope for a fruitful harvest. For context, German theologian Joachim Jeremias specified that Jewish sowers from that period had to channel all their energy and focus into the task along the route.[18] In addition to discovering the two sentences, Cullen believes that the artifact has its origins in a period well before the time of Jesus Christ. According to him, Christians took ownership of the non-Christian Magic Square in the third century.[19] While Cullen's two sentences represent a remarkable advancement in uncovering the mystery of the artifact, his findings on its origin and meaning appear inconclusive. Moving forward, Cullen's two sentences will serve as the starting point of my in-depth analysis of the origin and meaning of the artifact. I will also present other crucial discoveries. The Sator Square has many secrets to reveal.

2

SEARCHING FOR THE ORIGIN

As we saw in the previous chapter, researchers believe that the secret meaning of the Sator Square was lost over the past two thousand years. In fact, the key to the cryptogram exists and I have every reason to believe that it is being guarded to this day by a select few individuals who are intentionally concealing it from the public eye. This book will finally bring to light the secrets behind the Sator Square.

To unlock these secrets, we must first uncover the origin of the artifact. To do this, let's begin with John Cullen's discovery of the two sentences made from the five words of the Sator Square:

God [the sower] holds the plow, but you turn the furrows.

These two sentences are far from innocuous; they have a much deeper meaning, one that discloses the true origin of the Magic Square.

Part I examines the sentences and identifies key themes, then matches the themes to theories that pinpoint the Sator Square's origin. The results of the analysis are presented in Chapter 4.

Before beginning the analysis, let us highlight a few salient points. Firstly, the word *Sator* or "sower" is often used as a metaphor for the divine power. The metaphor is most notably used in the famous "Parable of the Sower" contained in the first three gospels of the New Testament,[1] which are also known as the Synoptic Gospels. For the purposes of my analysis, the word "sower" will represent God. Note that Cullen's first sentence uses the term "sower" instead of "sowers," to indicate that there is *only one* God.

Secondly, the two sentences are authoritative; someone is communicating instructions on how to sequentially perform tasks. In other words, there is a division of labor: I [God] do this and you do that.

Lastly, it is safe to say that the creator of the Sator Square speaks in the name of God. The designer of the artifact can only be one of God's messengers from the line of prophets, angels, or even God himself, considering that the two sentences reveal God's activities (i.e., God holding the plow).

EXTRACTING THE SEVEN KEY THEMES

Now that we have covered the basic elements, let us identify the key themes of the two sentences.

Theme 1: Initial Grace Is Offered to Everyone

What is striking about the two sentences is that they display God's willingness to establish a close relationship with every human being, despite His transcendence.

The word "you" in the second sentence directly addresses every reader. God is not calling out to anyone in particular—the invitation is extended to all of humanity.[2] In essence, God is addressing everyone, no matter their culture, race, sexual orientation, gender or religion.

This help, or divine gift, is often called the "grace" of God, a concept frequently found in the Bible. In Christianity, this grace is often referred to as "initial grace," "operating grace" or "prevenient grace" because it is offered at the beginning of the spiritual path.

Theme 2: Initial Grace Is Free

Initial divine assistance is offered freely. There are no preconditions—such as meritorious work or offerings—required by God to hold the plow.

Theme 3: Grace Is Constantly Present

The verb "hold" in the second sentence is in the present tense. It conveys an action that is not time-bound, indicating that God is present at any time. God never lets us go—he holds the plow all along the way. His divine action is also accomplished when a human being turns, finds a furrow and continues to walk. There is an overarching sense of hope in suggesting that God, in His great kindness, will hold the plow of the person who has accepted His offer—even if the person takes the wrong furrow.

Imagine that you are working under very difficult conditions in the fields on hard and stony soils and under oppressive heat. You are plowing a furrow and getting ready to turn at the end of the row towards the next furrow. Although you are exhausted and your muscles are aching, you take a deep breath to make a last-ditch effort to turn. Then, you suddenly hear " ... a word behind you, 'This is the way, walk in it,' whenever you turn to the right or to the left." (Isa. 30:21).

Theme 4: Once Initial Grace is Accepted, God Guides and Provides Advice

The first sentence indicates that God (the sower) is controlling the plow. By way of illustration, when laborers push their plow in the field, they are not obligated to maintain their walking speed or balance the load if, for instance, they are faced with bumpy terrain. When holding the plow, they are free to maneuver it as they wish, like a captain holding the wheel of a boat and tilting it a bit more towards the left or right. The laborer can speed up, slow down, abruptly push harder, stop, or even resist.

Further, the two sentences demonstrate that a person who accepts God's initial grace is figuratively embarking on the plow. The person assents to being guided by God, the controller of the plow. From that starting point, the person's decisions and actions in the new journey are greatly affected by God.

Theme 5: Freedom to Believe

The two sentences illustrate human free will to believe or not believe in God. It is the person's prerogative to accept the divine invitation. Before participating in the activity, the individual must first believe in God and the divine process.

Theme 6: Freedom to Work

Once the person has gone through the intellectual process and made the choice to believe, the person has the freedom to perform the physical act of working or "turning."

Although God controls the plow, the human being seems to have a certain kind of control by being able to turn the plow towards the good or bad furrow. This represents the moral responsibility of choosing between right and wrong. Making a wise and responsible choice initially requires the opportunity for the person to make a decision. Therefore, the second sentence demonstrates that the person has the freedom to work (to turn).

While we are on the topic of moral responsibility, it is important to note that this moral decision is usually decisive and leads to future repercussions. Yet despite the ethical dimension in the two sentences, there is no mention of any direct consequences, reward or punishment.

Further, there is no mention of a destination or outcome. Considering that the sentences are set in an agricultural environment, we can imply that the desired outcome is to have a fruitful harvest—figuratively representing eternal salvation. This highlights the importance of the participant's faith in God, which is the hope that God, who holds the plow, will bring the participant to their destination.

As we have seen, the concepts of ethics and salvation are evident in the Sator Square. There is a clear link between God, morality and salvation. In our search for the origin of the Sator Square, we can immediately eliminate a polytheist origin—the belief in multiple deities—as the artifact shows that there is only one God. In addition, in the polytheist Hellenic world, moral issues belong to the domain of philosophy, not religion.[3]

Theme 7: Human Freedom Cooperates with the Grace of God for Salvation

The final theme that can be extracted from the two sentences is that both the grace of God *and* human effort are necessary for success. The interrelationship between the two wills is crucial; they must be entirely and perfectly synchronized.

This interaction between the two wills seems to be lacking in Cullen's explanations. Moreover, the message of the Sator Square is not about fatality—as Cullen believes[4]—rather it is about the grace of God. Contrary to fate, grace is a divine gift given to human beings. This free grace, which is mainly provided for the salvation of sinners, demonstrates God's love.

A clear message arises from the sentences: nothing is possible without God, because He is in control of the plow. Human effort is also a necessary component for a fruitful harvest. The divine will and the human will need to be in unison, signifying a pure message of unity and love.

Two paramount principles emerge from these seven key themes: the grace of God and human free will. These principles affirm that the Sator Square undeniably has Christian roots.

Christian Debates on the Grace of God and Human Free Will

From the beginning of Christianity, the principles of the grace of God and free will have been dominant topics of discussion. In fact, they are closely connected to several Christian doctrines. Together, they produce a paradoxical effect, being both a source of divergent opinion, division and war, and at the same time, a source of convergence, unity, inspiration and hope for billions of followers.

Divine grace and free will have generated disagreements and major, vigorous debates within the Catholic Church itself, which came to a head during two periods of Christian history. The first intense ideological debate took place in the fifth century between Augustine of Hippo and the Pelagians. The second began in the 16th century, this time between Protestant reformers and members of the Roman Catholic Church.[5] These discussions are still going on today.

THE POSITION OF JOHN CASSIAN

The fifth-century Christian debate concerned two diametrically opposed positions: that of Augustine, Bishop of Hippo, who believed that human salvation could only be obtained through the grace of God, and the position of the Pelagians, who maintained that salvation was basically acquired through human freedom to act.

In the midst of the stormy debate, a third group known as "semi-Pelagians" and led by the monk John Cassian, supported the concept of cooperation of the wills. According to this concept, human freedom and the grace of God must cooperate fully for human beings to have any hope of salvation. Cassian's position could incorrectly be seen as being between the two extremes, or similar to that of the Pelagians due to its name. In reality, Cassian's position was very similar to that of Augustine.[6]

When John Cassian moved from the Christian East to the Christian West around A.D. 415 and founded a monastery and a convent in Marseille, he brought vast monastic experience and an array of knowledge of traditions acquired in Bethlehem, Constantinople and Egypt, mainly through the deeply honored Desert Fathers and Mothers.

Cassian wrote two notable works: the *Institutes* and *Conferences,* which are widely used by monastic orders like the Benedictines.

In *Conference 13*, written around the year 426, Cassian stated his position on the cooperation between divine and human will. Interestingly, the themes from Cassian's *Conference 13* share striking similarities with the seven key themes extracted from the artifact (see Table 2.1). Further, Cassian's agricultural analogies are similar to the ones contained in the message in the Sator Square, including the following:

For a man should consider and with a most careful scrutiny weigh the fact that he could not by his own strength apply those very efforts which he has earnestly used in his desire for wealth, unless the Lord's protection and pity had given him strength for the performance of all agricultural labours; and that his own will and strength would have been powerless unless Divine compassion had supplied the means for the completion of them (Chapter 3).

For when he says: I laboured, he shows the effort of his own will; when he says: yet not I, but the grace of God, he points out the value of Divine protection; when he says: with me, he affirms that it cooperates with him... (Chap 13.)[7]

In Cassian's passages, we see the two paramount principles emerge again: the grace of God and free will and their interaction. Cassian's perspective and similarity in themes may be an indicator—or at least a clue—in uncovering who created the Sator Square. Although Cassian had a sizeable network of ecclesiastical contacts, particularly in Rome,[8] introducing his vision concerning grace and free will would have been perceived as a direct attack on the Catholic Church, as his perspective differed from that of the redoubtable and highly esteemed Augustine of Hippo.

TABLE 2.1 Similarities between the seven key themes of the Sator Square and those of Conference 13

The Seven Key Themes	Similar Themes Found in Conference 13 of Cassian
Grace of God	
1) Initial (Operating) Grace Is Offered to Everyone	Ch. 7: "He wills all men to be saved" "calls all without any exception"
2) Initial Grace Is Free	Ch. 1, 3, 9 and 13: "gift"; Ch. 13: "free grace"
3) Grace Is Constantly Present (Omnipresence)	Ch. 3 and 7: "begin … continues… complete it", "day by day"; Ch. 6: "always"; Ch. 7: "is at hand every day"
4) Once Initial Grace Is Accepted, God Guides and Provides Advice	Ch. 8: "He inspires", "create occasions"; Ch.9: "Direct my way"; Ch. 11: "He meets, guides, and strengthens us"; Ch. 17: "our Helper"
Human Free Will	
5) Freedom To Believe	Ch. 7: "Come to me"; Ch. 9: "If you be willing and hearken unto Me"; Ch. 18: "Unless you believe"

| 6) Freedom To Work or to Turn | Ch. 3: "does not grant these rich crops to idle husbandmen who do not till their fields by frequent ploughing"; Ch. 3 and Ch. 7: "Turn from your evil ways"; Ch. 13: "not idle or careless, but working and making an effort" |

Interaction Between Free Will and Grace of God

| 7) Human Freedom Cooperates with the Grace of God for Salvation | Ch. 11: "the grace of God and free will seem opposed to each other, but really are in harmony"; Ch. 13: "the grace of God always co-operates with our will" |

Augustine is one of the most influential theologians in the development of Western Christianity. He clarified several doctrines such as the primacy of grace, which earned him the title "Doctor of Grace." Augustine's perspective on the primacy of grace leaves little place for human will in the process of salvation.

In A.D. 528, the Council of Orange condemned semi-Pelagianism, declaring it a heresy. Cassian's great courage and compulsive need to express his disagreement came from his conviction that Augustine's position was inconsistent with the apostolic tradition. In other words, Cassian intervened because he felt the need to protect that tradition.

Even though he occasionally referred to the Scriptures, Cassian vehemently asserted that his way was the right way of "walking according to the tradition."[9] According to him, monachism was born in the time of the apostles.[10] The monks obeyed, preserved and protected that very ancient apostolic tradition.[11]

Cassian's successor, Vincent of Lérins, was even more direct. Around A.D. 434, a year before Cassian's death, Vincent delivered a scathing indictment of Augustine's theory by characterizing it as a novelty, and he asked:

> How is it then, that certain excellent persons, and of position in the Church, are often permitted by God to preach novel doctrines to Catholics? [12]

To say that someone was preaching a novelty was a harsh accusation, which in the past had often been used by the Church and even Augustine himself to condemn a heretic group.[13] Vincent of Lérins wanted to remind the Church of the importance of keeping the deposit of faith pure[14] and immune from Augustine's novelties.

In summary, Table 2.1 demonstrates that John Cassian's themes in *Conference 13* have similarities with the seven themes taken from the artifact. The important takeaway is that Cassian based his position on the *tradition*, which in my view will be a key component to understanding the true origin of the Sator Square.

THE POSITION OF THE EASTERN ORTHODOX CHURCH

John Cassian was not alone in defending this position. It was also strongly supported by the Eastern Orthodox Church, which confirmed that Cassian's explanations faithfully and correctly reflected the Christian tradition.

The eminent twentieth-century Orthodox theologian Vladimir Lossky, for example, explained the position of the Eastern Orthodox Church on the cooperation of grace and free will as follows:

> For it is not a question of merits but a co-operation, of a synergy of the two wills, divine and human, a harmony in which grace bears ever more and more fruits, and is appropriated—"acquired"—by the human person.[15]

The word "synergy" comes from the Greek word *synergia*, which means to cooperate or work together. According to Lossky, analyzing the two wills—divine and human—separately, instead of together in close synergy, had been unique to the West since the debate between Augustine and the Pelagians. The Eastern Orthodox Church supported synergy; it stated that human beings worked together with divine grace to ensure human salvation.

Walking with God on the long road of life leads the Christian to sanctification or a divinization, a concept that Eastern Orthodox Christians call *theosis*. Both energies resulting from human and divine will are required to complete the process of Christian perfection. The passage "For we are God's fellow workers [*synergoi (G4904)*]" (1 Cor. 3:9) by the Apostle Paul is frequently quoted to express the cooperation between the two wills. Divine grace is often called the power of the Holy Spirit or the power of Christ.[16]

Thus, the cooperation of divine and human will that Cassian spoke of is not a novelty; in fact, it comes from synergy, a concept that was already well established and very much present at the beginning of Christianity.

Integration and the Rate of Participation

Since human beings are created in the image and likeness of God, their mission is to restore their relationship with God to become more like God. The mission is nothing less than the raison d'être of every human being. Jesus Christ helps every human being fulfill this mission.

There is another Christian concept, similar to synergy, according to which Christians must become fully integrated in Christ to achieve their sanctification. The need for a close relationship between human beings and divinity is unequivocally stated in the epistles of Paul. Paul repeatedly quotes the expressions "*in* Christ Jesus"[17] and "God who is at work *in* you" (Phil. 2:13) to represent the union of the human and the divine.

Thus, to obtain their salvation, Christians must be completely integrated with the divine. The new life "in Christ" starts at baptism. This life allows the faithful to metaphorically become one of the members of the mystical body of Jesus Christ (1 Cor. 12:27). This image is often depicted by representing the Catholic Church as the body of Christ encompassing its Christian members. The use of the word "integration" in this book will signify to be "in Christ."

Integration for salvation requires 100% from God and 100% from the person—rather than 50% from each.

At a first glance, the two sentences of the Sator Square seem to suggest that two people each have a different job: one person holds the plow and the other person turns. After careful consideration, I came to the following realization:

The two sentences of the Sator Square illustrate the principle of integration in Jesus Christ, to be "in Christ."

When I visualized the agricultural activity of plowing, I realized that the two sentences describe not simply two people, but specifically one entity. Indeed, the actions of holding and turning the plow are performed by only one person: the person who is sowing.

Considering that the sower is a metaphor for God or Jesus Christ, the Sator Square unveils that as soon as a faithful person freely agrees to walk with God, the person becomes tightly intertwined with

God to form a single entity. Finally, the divine request made to humans in the Sator Square is not only a call to follow and to turn, but above all, a call to integrate into the divine power.

By being "in Christ," the faithful person becomes the sower (or Sator) who sows the word (Mk. 4:14), and is one of the "partakers of the divine nature" (2 Pet. 1:4). Each human being can thus hope to regain their relationship with God. The above detail is of tremendous significance. It is amazing to realize that the Magic Square illustrates the Christian principle of integration, stated during the same period as, and perhaps even much earlier than, the New Testament.

The Obscure Tradition

In summary, the seven key themes taken from the Sator Square are strongly present in the positions taken by John Cassian and the Eastern Orthodox Church on the relationship between the grace of God and free will for eternal salvation. Both Cassian and the Eastern Orthodox Church relied on the tradition to bolster their respective positions. Many undoubtedly saw Cassian[18] as a witness to a solid and deep-rooted tradition. Also, the Eastern Orthodox Church stated that it kept and preserved the fidelity of the tradition of Jesus Christ that was given to the apostles.[19]

It is not clear what this tradition is. If Cassian and the Eastern Orthodox Church both rely on the "tradition" and endorse similar themes to the Magic Square, then did the creator of the artifact also rely on the same tradition to create the artifact? Or, did Cassian and the Eastern Orthodox Church rely *directly* on the artifact to support their position? If this is the case, then the Magic Square *is* the Eastern tradition.

LATIN MAGIC SQUARES IN THE CHRISTIAN EAST

It may seem peculiar to claim that the Magic Square is the Eastern tradition, given that the artifact is written in Latin. During the fourth and fifth centuries, one could reasonably expect the Desert Fathers and Mothers, John Cassian and members of the Eastern Orthodox Church to speak Coptic, or Greek, but not Latin. So why would they all want to protect the Magic Square, when it is written in Latin?

In fact, French Jesuit archeologist Guillaume de Jerphanion indirectly supports my statement from an archeological point of view when he points out that the Latin Magic Squares entered Egypt in Late Antiquity.[20] The Desert Fathers and Mothers, who greatly influenced the writings of John Cassian, were present in Egypt during this time.

In addition, the city of Faras in the Nubian Desert south of Egypt is home to five inscriptions found in a tomb which now serves as a Christian chapel: one inscription is the famous letter that Jesus wrote to King Abgar. Another, which consists of the five words of the Sator Square, has a Coptic title: "Name of Christ's verses."[21] It is important to note that the following versions of the Magic Square were found in the Christian East:

- Some Latin Magic Squares were found unaltered (see Photo 2.)

- Some Latin inscriptions are very similar to the five Latin words from the Magic Square. For example, a painting in Cappadocia (Turkey) illustrates three shepherds who bear the names Sator, Arepo and Teneton.[22]

- Transpositions of the Latin Magic Square's letters have been found in different languages. Here, transposition consists of exchanging each Latin letter of the Magic Square with the equivalent letter in Greek or the Coptic language.[23] Some Rotas Squares found in Dura-Europos (Syria) were written with five words in Greek. For instance, the five Latin letters *R O T A S* were switched to the corresponding five Greek letters: *P O T A Σ* and *P O T A C*. Other archeological discoveries in Egypt show transpositions of the Latin Magic Square letters into Coptic letters.[24]

Photo 2: This Eastern Rotas Square written in Latin was discovered in the city of Dura-Europos (Syria). *Photo credit: Yale University Art Gallery*

These three versions demonstrate the undeniable importance Eastern Christians attached to the need to preserve, at all costs, the initial version of the five Latin words of the Magic Square.

With this in mind, let us return to John Cassian. Some Byzantine manuscripts mention "Cassian the Roman."[25] The motive for this remains obscure[26] and begs the following questions: was Cassian actually born in Rome, or was he born in another city of the vast Roman Empire? I propose that he earned this nickname simply because he spoke Latin[27] and because he protected the Latin Square. Christine Mohrmann, a specialist in early Christian Latin, mentions that the Latin language was closely associated with the city of Rome.[28]

While Greek was the dominant language during this period, Latin was often learned, even in the Christian Hellenic world. For instance, the monk Evagrius Ponticus—who greatly influenced Cassian—reportedly translated texts into Latin.[29] Even though John Cassian was born in Israel and lived for many years in Egypt, he chose to write his books in Latin while living in Marseille. During his stay in the Eastern regions, his knowledge of Latin allowed him to explain the secrets of the Sator Square to the Greeks and the Copts.

At this point, it is becoming increasingly conceivable that the Eastern Christians directly used the Magic Square as their Eastern tradition.

3

ANTE- AND POST-NICENE POSITIONS

I n A.D. 324, following victories at the battle of the Milvian Bridge and in other heroic battles, Constantine the Great became the sole emperor of both the Western and Eastern Roman Empire. Christians, long persecuted by the Empire, were now under Emperor Constantine's protection and support.

The emperor, seeking to cement his power and strengthen the foundations of his immense realm, and aware of the rifts within the Christian religion, brought the different Churches together in Nicaea in AD 325.

AFTER CONSTANTINE

The First Council of Nicaea was a major turning point for Christianity. Several significant positions emerged after the Council that relate to the seven key themes of the Sator Square.

One of the post-Nicene positions that we explored in the last chapter was John Cassian's theory, which is similar to the seven themes and is based on the tradition. If his position is actually derived from the true tradition, then why did the Catholic Church condemn Cassian? What exactly does the Catholic Church perpetuate as tradition?

On our quest to find the origin of the Sator Square, it would be beneficial to compare other positions adopted *after* the First Council of Nicaea—such as Augustine's position, and more recent ones like those of Thomas Aquinas and the Modern Catholic Church—with the seven themes of the Sator Square.

The Position of Augustine of Hippo

The fifth-century Bishop Augustine of Hippo claims to be following a tradition. He repeatedly invokes tradition as the main argument in his refutations against the heretics.[1]

Knowing the differences between Augustine's position and that of the semi-Pelagians, we can ask ourselves whether Augustine, faithful Father of the Catholic Church, preserves the same tradition as Cassian. Appendix I-A answers that question by providing a closer look at what Augustine preaches about the seven themes through his position on the *initium fidei* and the two doctrines of original sin and predestination.

Conformity With the Predetermined Plan of the Sator Square

Both Augustine's perspective and his contentious debates with other parties about the seven themes lead me to believe that the Sator Square serves as a plan that must be scrupulously followed to preserve Christian orthodoxy.

As we have seen, the Pelagian position downplays the role of God's grace and amplifies that of human free will in the process of salvation.[2] It undeniably goes against the two sentences of the Sator Square. Divine power, represented by the plow bearer, is present throughout the journey. Pelagianism was vehemently rejected and deemed heretical by all the other Christians because it did not respect this blueprint.

With respect to the semi-Pelagians, however, I discovered that the position advocated by Cassian is in fact clearly indicated in the Sator Square. Recall that according to the semi-Pelagians, grace seems to be offered to everyone and the freedom to consent and participate appears to be required to make the journey.

Above all, Augustine wants to reflect the utmost importance of God's grace in the process of salvation, as do the two sentences of the Magic Square. In the artifact, divine grace is present at all stages: it invites the person, holds the plow and guides the person to salvation.

In addition to this operating grace, Augustine believes that divine grace also features cooperating (subsequent) grace.

> He operates, therefore, without us, in order that we may will, but when we will, and so will that we may act, He cooperates with us.[3]

By emphasizing divine grace instead of human freedom, Augustine wants to demonstrate the core point of his thinking:[4] Ultimately, human beings have nothing to be proud of and are not in a position to make any demands. Simply put, God does not owe anything to anyone. No human being can claim salvation because of a lifelong belief or hard work. Salvation is neither retribution nor remuneration; God has no debts or obligations to pay.

Judgment Day is in the hands of the divine; humans can only hope for salvation. As Paul put it:

> Yes, for our sake it was written, because the plowman ought to plow in hope .... (1 Cor. 9:10).

The two sentences of the Sator Square are consistent once again in not promising any set divine retribution. Yet they also reveal information that gives the faithful reasons to hope. I will expand on this later in the book.

My "Brothers"

In the end, both Augustine and Cassian respect a common blueprint, which is identical to that of the Sator Square. Monachism specialist A. M. C. Casiday observes that Augustine's and Cassian's positions on grace and free will are similar in several aspects and that they contain fewer contradictions than some authors suggest.[5]

In addition to passages drawn from the Scriptures, Augustine and Cassian use tradition to support their respective positions. They both basically respect the information in the two sentences of the Sator Square, but each has his own interpretation of its contents.

Augustine does not refer to Cassian and the semi-Pelagians as heretics, but rather as "brothers."[6] To Augustine, the word "brother" means that Cassian does indeed respect the blueprint and follows the same path as he does, although Cassian's interpretation is outdated and incomplete.

In fact, Augustine finds that Cassian's position is at a lower level than his in the process of understanding the concept.[7] Augustine is not the first nor the last to use the rather sympathetic term "brothers" to designate members of other Christian groups that in my view follow the teachings drawn from the Sator Square but interpret them differently. As we will see, well before Augustine, the Apostle Paul used the term in a similar context to designate other Christian members.

What I find remarkable about this debate is that Augustine admits that his first interpretation of the *initium fidei* or "beginning of faith," as explained in Appendix I-A, was incomplete and similar to that of the semi-Pelagians.

> ... I myself also was convinced when I was in a similar error, thinking that faith whereby we believe in God is not God's gift, but that it is in us

from ourselves, and that by it we obtain the gifts of God, whereby we may live temperately and righteously, and piously in this world. For I did not think that faith was preceded by God's grace.[8]

Augustine states that he corrected his own error and therefore, in his debates with the semi-Pelagians, he is presenting his new interpretation based on previous Christian writings.

In contrast with Cassian's position, which seems quite direct in comparison to the sentences of the Sator Square, Augustine's position relies on two contentious doctrines—original sin and predestination. Are these doctrines indicated in the two sentences of the Sator Square?

A close look at the artifact reveals no traces related to original sin. Nothing in it seems to illustrate the inability of human beings to choose good. If Augustine looked closely at the structure of the two sentences of the Sator Square, "I do this and you do that," he would discern that the divine power drives the human will to answer the call.

With respect to predestination, as previously specified, the invitation is extended to all of humanity, because no limitations are indicated. While the message of the artifact is encrypted, there is no indication that the Sator Square is addressed only to those chosen by God.

Finally, there is little information in the Square that supports the two doctrines outlined by Augustine. He defends his position on these points by referring to the Scriptures and to Christian writings.

Does Augustine break with the tradition? Not in his view or that of his followers. He states a position that respects tradition and delves more deeply into it.

Therefore, Augustine extrapolates from—or deepens—the existing tradition. In my view, it is important to clarify that the verb "extrapolate" in this book refers to an extension of the limited information provided by the Sator Square. The primary purpose of the book is to examine the information in the Sator Square, not to analyze whether the doctrines are true or false.

To Cassian and Vincent of Lérins, the doctrines outlined by Augustine contradict tradition because they remove the universality of God's gift and basically view the human race as entirely corrupt. This remains a question of interpretation that was dealt with later by the Roman Church (see

Appendix I-C). Heresy, like the devil, is in the details!

So there is a very strong correlation between the tradition mentioned by both parties and the information in the two sentences embedded in the artifact.

The Position of Thomas Aquinas

Augustine and Thomas Aquinas are among the greatest pioneers in the development of Catholic Church doctrines. In the 13th century, eight hundred years after Augustine, Thomas Aquinas, a monk in the Dominican order who was also called Doctor of the Church, wrote an extensive theological work entitled *Summa Theologica*, in which he clarified the relationship between divine grace and free will and their interaction. His position is outlined in Appendix I-B.

It would be very difficult to ignore the close linkages between what is written on the artifact and what Thomas tells us. We can easily assume that, like Cassian, Thomas's eyes were riveted on the Magic Square when developing his position.

The Position of the Catholic Church

The Catholic Church has also expressed its position through various ecumenical councils, as detailed in Appendix I-C. The institution's position follows a tradition that is similar to that of Augustine and Thomas and its position aligns with the seven themes found in the Sator Square.

In summary, all the previously mentioned Christian authors, as well as the Catholic Church—with the exception of the Pelagians—agree on the themes and topics that are indicated in the Sator Square. Also, all of these themes and topics that are found scattered throughout the Bible are presented in a concise form in the artifact.

We can see that the Christian authors and the Catholic Church have divergent views on information that contradicts the artifact or on information that is not explicitly stated in it. This leads me to make the following statement:

The Sator Square must be the Christian tradition.

Therefore, it is clear that extreme caution had to be exercised by Christian authors when stating a doctrine, to ensure that it fully respected the plan set out in the Christian tradition, which I believe is the Sator Square.

DIGGING DEEPER

My analysis in the previous section suggests that, at least since the First Council of Nicaea, Christian orthodoxy must have relied on the unique content of the Magic Square to support its dogmatic assertions. As such, if the Church took possession of the artifact from a non-Christian entity, as some believe,[9] we can conclude that this appropriation did not occur any time *during or after* the Council of Nicaea of A.D. 325.[10]

Consequently, to discover the origin of the Magic Square, we must look further back in Christian history to determine whether Christians also relied on the artifact *before* the Council of Nicaea. Let us look at the period between the beginning of Christianity and the year 325 to find out whether the ante-Nicene Church Fathers and the New Testament texts mentioned the seven key themes of the Sator Square.

The Position of the Ante-Nicene Church Fathers

It is difficult to find a passage in Christian documentation prior to the Council of Nicaea that brings together all seven key themes; however, the themes can be found scattered throughout many of the texts written by the ante-Nicene Church Fathers. Some of these will be mentioned in future chapters and Appendix II-A provides examples.

The Position of Jesus in the Four Gospels

If the information in the Sator Square derives from the teachings of Jesus, then it is fundamental that the seven themes align with the words of Jesus in the four canonical gospels. This is demonstrated in Appendix II-B. In short, the words of Jesus that are cited are fully consistent with the themes that were extracted from the Sator Square. The fact that his words appear in each of the four canonical gospels of the New Testament emphasizes the importance and the authenticity of these themes in his teachings. However, no complete or even summary explanation of the themes appears in the gospels. The dispersal of the message in the New Testament is not random; on the contrary, it seems to be deliberate.

The Position of All the Authors of New Testament Books (Excluding the Four Gospels)

The seven key themes are also included in other New Testament books. Biblical references related to the seven themes are listed in Appendix II-C.

Apart from the four canonical gospels, it is the epistles of Paul in the New Testament that reference all the extracted themes related to the process of salvation. Among other things, Paul talks about synergy, integration in Jesus Christ and the lack of a guarantee that human beings will achieve their ends. Again, the themes are spread throughout his epistles.

Even today, the Apostle Paul provides a great deal of useful information that Christian writers use extensively to support their statements. Thus, some may believe that the Christian writers mentioned in the previous chapters (e.g., Irenaeus, Origen, Augustine, Thomas) base their position on the epistles of Paul. However, Christian authors like John Cassian have repeatedly revealed that they are not referring solely to the epistles of Paul—they are primarily using another source called "tradition."

4

THE TRUE ORIGIN REVEALED

My analysis reveals that the message in the Sator Square is remarkably consistent, not only with the information espoused by the Church in the period after the Council of Nicaea, but also with the information it conveyed before the Council. Therefore, this message has been passed down throughout Christian history. My analysis also shows that the message coincides with the teachings of Jesus Christ in New Testament writings. At this point, I can make the following assertion:

> *There is no evidence that the Church seized the Magic Square from another entity. My research leads me to believe that the artifact originates from Jesus' teachings; it has been Christian since the earliest days of Christianity.*

Indeed, it is difficult to support the idea that at some point, the early Church seized the artifact, because:

- no one else has claimed to be the author.
- the early Church was able to decode it while more than 150 years of subsequent modern studies have been unsuccessful.[1]
- the information exactly matches Jesus' words in the New Testament.
- the message coincides precisely with the teachings transmitted by the Church throughout its history.

In addition, the Church could neither change the content of the Magic Square to make it conform to its doctrines, nor adapt its doctrines to the message on a supposedly foreign artifact.

Transforming a Rotas Square into a Sator Square involves a simple 90-degree rotation of the Rotas Square, which does not affect the arrangement of the letters; all the extracted messages in the artifact remain precisely the same, whether it is a Rotas or a Sator Square. Consequently, this rotation undoubtedly rests on the importance placed on the first of the five words read horizontally (either "Rotas" or "Sator"), which differentiates the type of artifact. The reason behind the rotation will be explained later in the book.

At the end of the day, it seems that those who preach orthodoxy in general rely on certain guiding principles to direct them during discussions of divine grace and free will. As previously seen, the points the parties agree on are consistent with the excerpted themes of the Sator Square, while the points of contention are not as well articulated or are simply absent from the Magic Square.

To justify their positions, the parties frequently refer to the tradition given directly to the apostles by Jesus of Nazareth. This tradition establishes the important principles of salvation.

My research suggests that the Magic Square is not only a Christian tradition; it appears to be the divine apostolic tradition.

The Catholic Church has always claimed to possess and protect the divine apostolic tradition.[2] My analysis seems to show that this is utterly and undeniably true.

To make it easier to understand the divine apostolic tradition, the ideas related to the tradition and the secret language that the Church has most likely used for a very long time to protect the artifact will be explained in part II of this book.

CHRISTIANS IN POMPEII

The fact that the artifact seems to be of Christian origin means that there were Christians living in Pompeii in the first century A.D, as two Rotas Squares were discovered in the ancient city. Many other clues also point to the presence of Christians in Pompeii:

- A charcoal graffito with the word Christianos adorned a wall in the atrium of a house.[3]

- Another house has the words "Sodom and Gomorrah" written on a dining room wall.[4]

- Several cross symbols were discovered in Pompeii, including one in a bakery.[5]

- A cross and an altar were discovered in the House of the Bicentenary in Herculaneum.[6]

Around the year A.D. 60, during his journey to Rome, Paul landed in the port city of Puteoli, less than 50 kilometers (30 miles) from Pompeii. He spent seven days there with some Christian brethren (Acts 28:13-14). This demonstrates that there were Christians in the surrounding region.

However, the late second-century Christian author Tertullian, from the city of Carthage, believes otherwise. According to him, there were no Christians in the city of Pompeii "in the days when the fire" wiped out the city.[7] His statement implies that there were indeed Christians in Pompeii at some point; either long before or immediately before the eruption of Vesuvius in August 79.

The Two Sinful Cities

It is quite probable that the destruction of Pompeii and Herculaneum in A.D. 79 was considered a divine punishment, similar to that suffered by the cities of Sodom and Gomorrah. The Old Testament says that prior to the destruction of these cities, God sent angels to save the righteous people (Lot and his family) living in Sodom (Gn. 19:15). Likewise, Tertullian implies that Christians were spared the divine punishment inflicted on the cities of Pompeii and Herculaneum. I doubt the veracity of Tertullian's statement, which was made 120 years after the eruption of Vesuvius.[8]

Although they were present in Pompeii, which had about 25,000 inhabitants,[9] Christians were relatively few in number, roughly between 100 and 200 people.[10] Therefore, the Christians in Pompeii used the Rotas Square as the Christian tradition that came directly from the teachings of Jesus Christ.

ARGUMENTS FAVORING THE ARTIFACT'S NON-CHRISTIAN ORIGIN

Three main arguments are invoked to deny the Christian origin of the Magic Square, all of which are based on situations that occurred in the period before the Council of Nicaea. I will present a counter-argument for each, in support of the artifact's Christian origin. The first argument, which we have just refuted, is that there were no Christians in Pompeii. The other two arguments, that the cross was not a Christian symbol in the early centuries A.D. (Chapter 10), and that during the same period, Greek, not Latin, was the dominant language for Christians, even in Western Christianity (Chapter 14), will be covered later on in the book.

PART II

UNVEILING THE SECRETS

OF THE TRADITION

5

THE HIDDEN SIDE
OF THE TRADITION

I f my research suggests that the two sentences
of the Sator Square have been venerated since
the beginning of Christianity, then why does the
Church not mention the artifact? What does the
artifact represent for the Church?

When the Christian writers we discussed earlier
mention the seven key themes found in the two
sentences of the Sator Square, they often specify
that the themes come from tradition. What exactly
does tradition mean?

COMMON TRADITION

In an ever-evolving world, tradition may seem archaic, outdated, and of no great interest. It is often perceived as an obstacle to modernization or globalization. However, there are some individuals who are heavily reliant on their traditions and feel they must protect and defend them against threats such as suppression by cultural homogenization.

Most people are familiar with the word, but the concept of tradition may seem vague and intangible, even though it can be expressed through concrete actions.

Tradition could be defined as a set of practices, beliefs and customs from the past; however, it encompasses a multitude of concepts and definitions.

The traditions that I call "common" are passed down from generation to generation in various communities at the national, regional, local or family level. Common traditions often provide a feeling of comfort and belonging that helps people find their place in society in comparison with others. Some people use traditions like a mirror that reflects their image or their true identity.

To illustrate the idea of a common tradition, let us use a fictional family that includes a young man named Victor. Victor's family has an annual tradition in which his father blesses the family before carving the Thanksgiving turkey.

The Thanksgiving tradition is comprised of different aspects: national (celebrating an official holiday), religious (blessing the family and thanking God), historical (acknowledging the roots from which the tradition arose) and familial (gathering yearly as a family to eat dinner and to celebrate).

In general, traditions seem immutable and firmly anchored over several generations. They often nurture feelings of safety, devotion, and loyalty.

In reality, the vast majority of traditions change over time and across generations; they are *living* traditions. In continuing with our example, the following three fictional events have affected the tradition in Victor's family over time:

During the first event, after tasting Aunt Anna's incredible cognac gravy, the family decides that henceforth all their Thanksgiving meals will include the delicious gravy. It was not previously part of the tradition, but on general acceptance, the cognac gravy was added without changing the core of the existing tradition. The recipe complements and broadens the tradition without altering it.

The second event occurs after the death of Victor's father. Instead of asking Victor—as the next-generation father—to give the Thanksgiving blessing, the family decides to respect the principle of gender equality by asking Victor's mother Irma, the eldest person in the family, to perform the ceremonial role. The family adopts the change and carries the tradition forward.

The third event happens many years later. Victor's grandson Max announces that his employer will require him to work on Thanksgiving Day for at least the next few years. This leads to serious discord in the family.

Two camps soon form. The first group supports the idea that tradition can be adapted and that the family gathering should take place on a weekend day close to the official date, when everyone can attend. To the members of this group, the ultimate significance of the tradition is the opportunity for the whole family to gather and celebrate. In defense of this view, a supporter of adaptation says that the date of the Thanksgiving celebration has little importance, since many countries celebrate the holiday on different days and some, like the United

States, have changed the date of the holiday in the past.

The second group firmly holds that the family celebration should occur on the exact date of Thanksgiving, as it has for generations, despite Max's absence. To the members of this group, changing the date would alter the established tradition. One of them says: "We will save Max a piece of turkey with cognac gravy!"

On reflection, is every change in the three events real progress from the initial tradition, or an alteration of the initial tradition that changes it into something else, i.e., a new tradition?

The first two changes are unanimously accepted and integrated into the initial tradition, while during the third event, there is no agreement. The date of the Thanksgiving celebration is a contentious issue; each group refers to the initial tradition but interprets it differently. Either group may firmly believe that it is respecting the initial tradition. The first group may decide to start a new tradition.

As we can see from these three events, the concept of authority is closely tied to tradition. The influence of an individual or a group of people is often the determining factor in establishing and making changes to a tradition.

As a general rule, a common tradition changes and evolves over time. Once accepted, the most recent version of the tradition becomes the truth for all members of the group.

CHRISTIAN TRADITION

While there are similarities with common tradition, the Christian tradition has specific characteristics that must be considered.

The Revelation of the Word of God

God's love for human beings is indisputable. In the Scriptures, God clearly demonstrates a desire to progressively reveal not only the divine plan of salvation for humanity but also the identity of God. Therefore, this "divine Revelation" is gradually understood through God's actions (including the Creation) and God's words (such as the revelations given to different angels, prophets and other intermediaries), as indicated in the Old Testament.

It will certainly come as no surprise to Christians that the Revelation of the Word of God is found in the Scriptures. It is written down, it is tangible, and it serves as the foundation of Christianity. As one of the Catholic faithful, I grasped the significance and role of the Scriptures at a young age.

However, I will admit that Christian tradition seemed like an abstract concept to me. I used to believe that tradition was limited to old rituals handed down orally from generation to generation. Quite frankly, it held little interest for a lay person like me.

Later on, I was surprised to learn that the last three councils of the Roman Catholic Church maintained that the Revelation of the Word of God exists not only in the Scriptures, but also in the tradition.[1] Thus, as per those councils, the Christian traditions are essential, as they contain information that comes from God through His Son Jesus Christ. Let us look more closely at why both the Council of Trent and the Second Vatican Council underscored the importance of this tradition.

THE COUNCIL OF TRENT AND VATICAN II ON TRADITION

The Protestant Reformation movement of the 16th century questions several of the Catholic Church's laws and practices that are based on its traditions. The great reformer Martin Luther denounces, for example, his era's abusive practice of indulgences,[2] which is a concept that is not included in the Bible. Indulgence consists of making a monetary contribution to the Church[3] in exchange for a promise of complete or partial forgiveness of sin during purification in Purgatory, to reduce the person's suffering or that of a loved one. The Reformation movement also challenges the idea of purgatory and the Pope's supremacy.

To the Reformers, the Christian tradition promoted by Catholics is an accumulation of diverse elements with different origins. Some elements do not even appear in the Scriptures, and sometimes they even contradict each other. The Reformers also see the explanations provided by the Church as nebulous and adapted to their own ends and to the requirements of the age.

Luther's barely concealed distrust of the tradition presented by the Catholic Church drives him to proclaim his famous *Sola Scriptura*, stating that "the Scriptures alone" were valid.

With that statement, Luther seems to be categorically rejecting the Catholic tradition as a whole. In fact, Luther and the Reformation movement believe that part of the Catholic tradition is divine, but that it has been significantly altered by the Church. In their view, the authentic part of the divine Revelation can only be found in the Scriptures.[4] Some individuals believe that the Reformation neutralizes tradition or at most accords it a secondary role in comparison to the Scriptures, which they deem to be complete and sufficient.[5]

Reformation advocates accuse Church leaders of having created their own human principles and laws, and of incorporating them into the divine ones. Perhaps they have Paul's warning to the Colossians in mind with respect to this type of practice:

> See to it that no one takes you captive through philosophy and empty deception, according to the tradition of men, according to the elementary principles of the world, rather than according to Christ. (Col. 2:8).

The Unwritten Traditions of the Council of Trent

In the mid-16th century, in response to the Reformation movement, the Church convenes the Council of Trent to counteract the Protestant surge by defending the Church's theory of justification, and by reiterating its support for the apostolic traditions that originate with Jesus Christ.

At the Council of Trent, several participants use the Latin expression *partim-partim* to declare that the Revelation was in part in the written books and partly in the unwritten traditions.

Photo 3: The Council of Trent was held over an 18-year period, from December 13, 1545 to December 4, 1563. *Photo credit: Morphart Creation/Shutterstock.com*

This expression is disturbing, since it suggests that the unwritten traditions contain material that is not in the Scriptures.[6]

The expression *partim-partim* is ultimately replaced by a statement that does not mention any proportion, indicating that both written books and the unwritten traditions hold the truth.[7] These are called the two sources, or *fons* in Latin.

The Sacred Tradition of the Second Vatican Council

The Second Vatican Council takes place in Rome from 1962 to 1965. The Church shows willingness to modernize, to open up to the world and to establish universal reconciliation. The antagonism during the Council of Trent gives way to a rapprochement with the Protestants and other religions, and there is a spirit of optimism in the air.

Nevertheless, two distinct groups form. The conservatives want to keep the Church's foundations stable, thus they promote a virtual *status quo.*

The progressive group, representing the majority of the members present, wants to open the Church to the world and move forward. This group does not demand a formal review of the existing structure and does not question the institution or papal authority.

Unlike the Council of Trent, where the demand for reform comes from Protestants outside the Church, in this case the demands come from *within* the Roman Catholic Church, with its most faithful and high-ranking dignitaries—including Pope John XXIII—applying the pressure.

The Sacred Tradition and Sacred Scripture

A significant change occurs during this council. The names of the two sources that contain the Revelation of the Word of God are suddenly altered. The Council no longer speaks of "written books" and "unwritten traditions," instead, it uses "Sacred Scripture" and "sacred tradition." The Council evidently wants the terms to be more specific. Hence, not all written books contain the Revelation, but only the Sacred Scripture, which includes both the Old and New Testaments. Similarly, not all the *unwritten* traditions contain the Revelation, but only the sacred tradition, also known as the Tradition with a capital "T." The key term "unwritten" will be discussed in the next chapter.

The sacred tradition is still enigmatic to this day. Unlike the content of Sacred Scripture, which presents the Word of God in written form, the content of sacred tradition has never been disclosed.

The Council further mentions that this Tradition is entitled to the same respect as Sacred Scripture.[8]

The sacred tradition and the Sacred Scripture are the Words of God and together they form the "deposit of faith."[9] This apostolic deposit was given to the Catholic Church and remains under its protection. Thus, I can make the following statement:

My research indicates that the Sator Square is most likely contained in the sacred tradition.

This statement is supported by what has I have covered up to this point. Specifically, my analysis in Part I of this book showed that the Sator Square may be the Christian tradition; it contains an apostolic message that comes directly from Jesus. These characteristics are also found in the sacred tradition mentioned by the Council.

Let us go back to the Second Vatican Council, specifically to the beginning of deliberations on the *Dei Verbum* (Dogmatic Constitution on Divine Revelation). The Theological Preparatory Commission, headed by conservative Cardinal Alfonso Ottaviani, presents a draft proposal stating that the Divine Words are found in two distinct sources: the written books and unwritten traditions.[10] He repeats the statement about the two sources (*fons*) that was issued at the Council of Trent. Although the statement about two separate sources *may in fact be true*—and is supported by many theologians and bishops—it remained controversial during Vatican II. The statement erected a barrier to Christian unity and was an indirect threat to the Church. Did the Church fear having to disclose the identity and content of the sacred tradition, which appears to be the Sator Square.

To resolve the issue, the Church seems to have used the dual meaning of the word "source" or *fons* in Latin. The initial debate about the two sources at the Second Vatican Council concerns the primary meaning of the word source, namely a document, a book, a work, an entity, etc. that provides information, as in the expression "cite their sources." Are Sacred Scripture and the sacred tradition two distinct entities? To avoid answering this question directly and above all to close the discussion, the Council quite brilliantly employs the second meaning of the word source, namely "origin," such as the expression "at source" in "we tackled this problem at source." In the final *Dei*

Verbum document, the Second Vatican Council holds that the Sacred Scripture and sacred tradition contain the truth and that both come from the same source or origin, namely from Jesus Christ.[11] Note that the high-ranking dignitaries do not deny that there were in fact two separate entities: the Sacred Scripture and the sacred tradition (which I believe to be the Sator Square); they simply diverted the conversation to avoid having to reveal the content of the sacred tradition.

Fixed Tradition

The sacred tradition, like the Sacred Scripture, comprises a fixed part and a variable part. The rest of this chapter will focus on both the fixed and variable parts of the sacred tradition to better understand where I believe the Sator Square fits.

We saw that God wants to gradually reveal the divine plan of salvation and the identity of God. The Bible shows us that the Revelation of the Word of God occurred over many millennia and was fulfilled in Christ.[12] The Revelation of God is undeniably centered on Jesus Christ, who is the fullness or culmination of the divine Revelation. Basically, this means that after the coming of Jesus Christ, there will be *no further* Revelations of the Word of God.[13]

The Revelation of God was handed down by Jesus to the apostles, and then to future generations of bishops through the content of the sacred tradition. In this particular context, the fixed, authentic and complete apostolic content of the sacred tradition comes from the time of Jesus, almost 2,000 years ago. Contrary to common tradition, Christian tradition, whose source is divine, can be nothing but the pure truth. This divine truth takes its origin from *fixed content*, whatever its form. It is all-powerful and immutable; it cannot be changed unless God wishes to do so.

To further understand fixed tradition, a return to Vincent of Lérins is in order. In the fifth century, under the pseudonym Peregrinus, the ardent semi-Pelagian monk wrote a treatise called the *Commonitory* with the aim of preserving orthodoxy. The document is considered indispensable to studies on the development of Christian doctrines even today. Vincent of Lérins states that this authentic truth, handed down in the form of a divine deposit from Jesus Christ, must be protected.[14] Although the basic content of the Tradition is fixed, the monk does not reveal it. Therefore, based on my research, I can make the following statement:

The content of the Sator Square must be the fixed content of the sacred tradition that comes from Jesus Christ.

Vincent of Lérins also states that the Church received a tradition comprised of "a great amount of matter in a few words."[15] The Sator Square undeniably fits this characteristic, as it contains only five words. Vincent of Lérins appears to subtly inform high-ranking Church dignitaries that he is aware of the Sator Square's secrets and that the position he states in his writings is consistent with the message of the artifact. As a result, I believe that the heart of the sacred tradition—the fixed content given by Jesus Christ—is in fact the unaltered content of the Sator Square. If that is the case, the Church must certainly perceive the immutable character of this divine content, not as a constraint, but as a sign that the Church was entrusted with protecting it. It represents God's love for human beings; this love provides hope for Christians.

Living Tradition

Although the Revelation of God, fulfilled by Jesus Christ, was handed down in its entirety in the sacred tradition and in Sacred Scripture, it is by no means stagnant. While the content of the sacred tradition is fixed and fulfilled, like that of Sacred Scripture, it is not yet completely understood. The content remains veiled and mysterious.[16] Understanding the truth given to us by Jesus Christ is an evolving process that will continue until the Parousia, meaning until the return of Christ at the end of the world. Those who respond to God's call commit to seeking and understanding this truth with the help of the Holy Spirit.[17] While the monk Vincent of Lérins placed a lot of emphasis on the fixed content of the tradition given to us by Christ, he is not an extreme conservative. He does not limit himself to the fixed content of the deposit of faith; he recognizes its evolving and dynamic nature. For him, interpretations of this fixed content are acceptable, as long as the content is not converted into something else; it must be kept intact.[18] Vincent calls this acceptable interpretation of the truth "progress." According to him, we must ensure that an interpretation "is real progress, not alteration of the faith."[19] Vincent reiterates that divine truth "admit[s] no change, no waste of its distinctive property, no variation in its limits."[20] In other words, progress causes the evolution of the fixed divine content given to us through Christ. It becomes part of the fixed content and brings it alive, unlike an alteration that transforms it into something else. By way of analogy, progress is the growth and flowering of a seed sown by God. Alteration is the transformation of the flower, such as by prematurely cutting and drying it to make a popular fragrance. The notion of progress is splendidly expressed in one of Paul's epistles, which states that one must continue building on Christ's foundation and not on some other foundation (1 Cor. 3:10-11). Determining whether something is progress is no small feat. As mentioned in Chapter 3, Augustine's two doctrines (original sin and predestination) do not appear in the content of the Sator Square, nor in my view in the fixed content of the Tradition, but they are tied to this fixed content. To Augustine, both doctrines represent an acceptable advancement of the fixed Tradition, making it a living Tradition. However, in the eyes of Cassian and Vincent of Lérins, the doctrines do not respect the Tradition; they alter it, as a novelty would do.[21] Clearly, interpretation plays a crucial role. Who determines whether an interpretation is considered progress or an alteration? Vincent of Lérins, who has complete faith in the authority of the Church to identify errors or false truths, indirectly asks the Church to revise Augustine's doctrines. Thus, in the fifth century, Vincent acknowledges the Church's authority of interpretation. Fifteen centuries later, the Second Vatican Council reiterates that in matters of Sacred Scripture and sacred tradition, final interpretation authority rests with the Magisterium (all the bishops and particularly the Pope).[22] Living tradition, in addition to encompassing things that are considered true progress in the content of fixed tradition, also refers to all the activities related to disseminating and teaching the divine message, as well as the monuments of Tradition, such as liturgical rites, Christian art and patristic and official Christian documentation.[23]

A Matter of Interpretation

The Word of God in Sacred Scripture and sacred tradition that was entrusted to the Church did not come with a manual of detailed instructions—it must be interpreted. This is not a simple task; the Word of God is often obscure and cloaked in mystery. The Word of God is interpreted from different perspectives (e.g., literal, literary, historical, and theological) comprising several layers of understanding. Often, these interpretations have both a rational basis and a spiritual basis with the dimension of faith. Christian interpretations have faced many challenges and much criticism. They have raised many questions, including the following:

- Universal interpretation: Is it necessary to have a single, universal interpretation of the Word of God for all Christians? Can the divine message have more than one accepted meaning, as long as it follows a certain framework?

- Errors in interpretation: The Catholic Church relies on the help of the Holy Spirit to interpret and actualize the tradition.[24] Is the Church truly infallible? Could the institution correct one of its previous interpretations? It is important to remember that the Revelation progresses over time. As such, any change in interpretation might be viewed as progress as opposed to an error.

- Immutable interpretation: Does the Church truly want the Revelation to progress, or does it prefer an immutable interpretation? Is the fear of making mistakes really justified when it is indicated that the Holy Spirit ultimately ensures that the Revelation—fulfilled by Jesus Christ—progresses?

- Social recognition of the interpretation: Considering that culture largely influences our way of life, is social recognition important in the process of interpreting the Word of God? If so, does that reduce the process to a popularity contest? Must the interpretation constantly change to follow the latest trends?

- Diverse approaches on interpretation: Is everything in the Bible considered divine? Does the Bible contain any errors? Must Christians follow everything that is written in the Bible to the letter? For example, did Jesus Christ specifically exclude all the groups of people listed in the first epistle of Paul to the Corinthians (6:9) from the Kingdom of Heaven? Or was Paul, in drawing up the list, heavily influenced by the perceptions and understanding of the society and culture of his time? His position on slavery is another example, when he says: "All who are under the yoke as slaves are to regard their own masters as worthy of all honor" (1 Tim. 6:1). Instead, should we not try to understand the underlying divine precepts used by Paul to create this list of groups? Should we consider the biblical statements from a restrictive perspective or a more global standpoint with multiple perspectives (e.g., literal, literary and historical)?[25]

Now that we have explored the ambiguities concerning interpretations, let us go back to our fictitious Thanksgiving tradition example, but change one important element. If God had directly specified in the Scriptures, "The father blesses his family before eating turkey at each Thanksgiving celebration," does changing the person giving the blessing from the father to the eldest person in the family alter God's wish? Would this change be considered progress or an alteration of divine truth? Should we continue to assign the role to the father of the family for the sole reason that it is literally written in the Bible? Or does the word "father" have different meanings depending on its historical context? Could it refer to the eldest person in the family or the person who is the family provider? Can we adapt the word "father" to a modern context? Is it important to have consensus on a doctrine within the Church? What about a consensus among believers?

The Interpretation of Tradition Stems From What Source?

In both the fictitious example and the discussion of interpretation, it is worth noting that the assessment of whether the statements represent progress or an alteration of the Word of God is based on *Sacred Scripture*. The critical question is, how can someone assess whether a statement is considered progress or an alteration of the sacred tradition when they do not even know the fixed divine content of that tradition? How can one differentiate between the living part of sacred tradition (extensive additional content that is considered progress) from the fixed part, which could be the fixed divine content of the Sator Square? In fact, according to my research only the people who know the secret message of the artifact have the ability to do so.

RETURN TO THE SOURCE

The various interpretations of the divine content that have been accepted by the Church over the past two millennia may create some disadvantages. Have we lost the true, full meaning of the initial divine message through the years? Do some of these interpretations limit or even prevent the growth of the divine truth?

French theologian Yves Congar, a Dominican friar, asked the same questions. He was part of the group of progressives who contributed significantly to discussions at the Second Vatican Council. Initially, Congar was brushed aside because of his progressive ideas, but he had the support of Pope Jean XXIII, who invited him back to Vatican II as a consultant. His expertise in tradition, reflected in *Tradition and Traditions,* the book he wrote during the same period, contributed greatly to Vatican II texts on the subject.[26] In his book, which is an invaluable source of indirect information about the Sator Square, Congar calls the "nucleus" of divine tradition "Tradition" with a capital T, to differentiate it in literary terms from other Catholic traditions that were in circulation. He wants to go back to the source of Tradition, to study it anew and to revitalize it for the modern world.[27] Removing errors and novelties is part of this purification process. Congar's demand that the Church return Tradition to its pure state in accordance with divine Revelation and remove errors was not innovative; it was an integral part of the mandate of the Council of Trent.[28] Even Cyprian of Carthage, a Church Father, writes around the year 250:

> For if we return to the head and source of divine tradition, human error ceases; and having seen the reasons of the heavenly sacraments, whatever lay hid in obscurity under the gloom and cloud of darkness, is opened into the light of the truth.[29]

This process of purification and return to the primary divine source of Tradition and the Scriptures would allow the Church to come back to its foundations, reinvigorate its living tradition, update it, and ensure its development through progress so that it remains in step with the future.

Today many people believe that it is impossible to find that Tradition because it has been lost over the past 2,000 years in a mishmash of several elements. This opinion is echoed by some scholars, who doubt the veracity of the current Scriptures and believe that it is impossible to return to the original ones. If Congar, the Council of Trent, Cyprian and many others, including Pope Francis in his March 13, 2013 Apostolic Exhortation *Evangelii Gaudium* (10), all wanted to return to the original divine sources, clearly it is because they knew that the project was feasible. As I see it, these specific requests concern not only the content of Sacred Scripture, but especially the fixed content of Tradition, which I believe is the content of the Sator Square. Indeed, the artifact is structured to allow for multiple interpretations; it is extraordinary that its message can evolve over time with the use of only 25 letters. At the opening of Vatican II, Pope John XXIII issues a famous message: "We are not on earth as museum keepers, but to cultivate a flourishing garden of life and to prepare a glorious future." [30] Although this message was very clear to the conservatives at the Council, it was not fully understood by the public, since it appeared to refer to the Sator Square. If this is the case, then in his message, the Pope is asking the Council's participants to go back to the initial content of the Sator Square and revitalize it. Although Vatican II offers a compelling recognition of the existence of a sacred tradition, the fact remains that the Council is careful not to draw up a list of items included in this Tradition to differentiate it from other traditions. There has been a great deal of research, particularly by historians, to try to enumerate the traditions, but no formal list has been formulated to date. In 1963, in the midst of Vatican II, the Fourth Conference on Faith and Order—organized by the World Council of Churches and held in Montreal, Canada—asked where one could find the authentic Tradition (with a capital "T") and its undisclosed content.[31] Meanwhile, Vatican II saw fit to clarify that the Magisterium was subject to the Revelation it had received.[32] Why did the Council bother adding this specification? Vatican II seemed to want to issue a warning by stating that the Church can only teach what is included in the content of the deposit of faith and nothing else. Now that my analysis has suggested that the Sator Square is the fixed content of the sacred tradition, the next question that immediately comes to mind is: how is it possible that the apostolic Tradition is the Sator Square when it is stated in several places that the Christian tradition is only an oral one? Many researchers are convinced that the Christian tradition is solely oral. Is this really the case? Is the Church trying to steer us in this direction? Is this a tactic that the Church has used since the beginning of Christianity to hide the Sator Square? In the next chapter, my analysis proposes that the Church must have a law of silence and secret rules.

6

THE SECRET RULES,

DISCIPLINA ARCANI

My research suggests that the Church uses an array of tactics to protect the true identity of the Sator Square. Among other things, the institution seems to use a secret or esoteric language and most importantly, it appears to maintain the rule of silence. If this is indeed the case, it is astonishing to discover that these Church stratagems go back to the early days of Christianity. In fact, at the turn of the third century, Clement of Alexandria, the Greek Father of the Church, hinted at this secret language in *The Stromata*:

But since this tradition is not published alone for him who perceives the magnificence of the word; it is requisite, therefore, to hide in a mystery the wisdom spoken, which the Son of God taught.[1]

In this excerpt, Clement talks about a "tradition" that is hidden "in a mystery." We cannot help but think of the Sator Square, which possesses this feature.

In the mid-third century, Greek philosopher Celsius directly accuses Christians of hiding secret doctrines.[2] In response, Origen of Alexandria—Clement's successor and the father of biblical exegesis—does not refute the accusations, but he confirms that certain doctrines are secret.[3]

More than a century after Origen, Ambrose, Bishop of Milan, also states in *On the Mysteries*:

By which He signifies that the mystery ought to remain sealed up with you,... that it be not made known to thou, for whom it is not fitting, nor by garrulous talkativeness it be spread abroad among unbelievers. Your guardianship of the faith ought therefore to be good, that integrity of life and silence may endure unblemished.[4]

In the two previous excerpts, the Fathers of the Church do not speak of secrets but of mysteries. Some Christian writings state that the Christian religion has no secrets. Instead, it conceals mysteries because the divine Revelation cannot be fully understood; its comprehension is acquired progressively over time. The Apostle Paul clearly portrays this necessary spiritual journey and progression when he says metaphorically that the Corinthians only receive milk instead of solid food, since from the spiritual point of view, they are not ready to receive in-depth knowledge (1 Cor. 3:2).

Even Jesus Christ attests to this when he says:

> To you has been given the mystery of the kingdom of God, but those who are outside get everything in parables (Mk. 4:11 and Lk. 8:10).

> Do not give what is holy to dogs, and do not throw your pearls before swine, or they will trample them under their feet, and turn to tear you to pieces (Mt. 7:6).

While the Sator Square may be considered a mystery, it also remains a secret. The word "secret" is defined as something that is known to one person, but unknown to another. Christianity has never directly unveiled the message of the artifact, even though it preaches the underlying concepts.

The artifact is neither known to the vast majority of Christians, nor connected in any way to Christianity. Therefore, I believe that the secret kept by the Church is very real. It even has a name: *Disciplina arcani* in Latin, or the "Discipline of the Secret," "the Law of Secrecy," or "the Rule of the Secret." This discipline exists; it began a long time ago, even though the expression "Discipline of the Secret" comes from the 17th century.[5]

In the first few centuries after the death of Jesus Christ, this secret discipline protected the received deposit of faith against heretics. After that it seemed to vanish, only to suddenly come back in full force at the Council of Trent in the 16th century.

The Law of Silence still exists within the Church; my research indicates that it has been kept by and even shared among high-level Church leaders for almost two thousand years.

THE SECRET RULES

When my analysis led me to understand that the Sator Square was the apostolic Tradition, I observed that some undisclosed strategies seems to have been used to protect the artifact. Here are some of the strategies that I believe I have detected:

SECRET RULE No. 1: Combine the Content of the Sator Square with Several Other Elements under the Term "Tradition"

I believe that to protect the Sator Square for more than 2,000 years, the Church combined the divine content with an assortment of other elements, like the rites and customs of the ecclesiastical traditions, under the term "tradition." From my perspective, grouping the content encoded in the artifact with several other elements was a strategic move to reduce the risk of its discovery.

SECRET RULE No. 2: Use Several Pseudonyms to Represent the Content of the Sator Square

To preserve the anonymity of the Sator Square, several terms or periphrases, which I shall refer to as pseudonyms in this book, must have been used to designate the artifact. The word "tradition" in the singular was broadly used to represent the divine content. However, some Christian writers did not distinguish between "tradition" in the singular and "traditions" in the plural.[6] There are also expressions like "unwritten tradition," "sacred tradition" or "Tradition" with a capital T to refer, in my view, to the content of the Sator Square.

Throughout Christian history, sacred tradition (the information from the artifact) has also been known by several other pseudonyms, such as "Faith," "Truth," "Rule of Faith," "Rule of Truth,"[7] and "Christian Mystery, each of which has enormous significance for the Christian religion. Another important pseudonym will be revealed in Chapter 9. To further complicate matters, several of the pseudonyms, which initially represented only the content of sacred tradition, were also used to refer to Sacred Scripture,[8] or to both.

As we can see, the Sator Square must have been venerated and hidden under different names since its origins.

SECRET RULE No. 3: Use Both Meanings of the Word "Tradition"

The word "tradition," derived from *traditio* in Latin or *paradosis* (παράδοις) in Greek, has a double meaning and Christian writers have used both meanings for a very long time with the aim of disorienting others.

In the 1950s, experts began noticing that ancient Christian writers employed the dual use of the word "tradition."[9] The difference between the two meanings is critically important for understanding the next three secret rules, which are derived from this main principle. The two generally accepted meanings of tradition are the following:

---

1. The passive/objective form:

—Tradition is associated with the *content* that is transmitted.

2. The active form:

—Tradition is associated with the *act* of transmitting, or teaching, content.

These two meanings correspond precisely with the fixed Tradition and the living tradition outlined in the previous chapter.

Having read a number of Christian texts and given my familiarity with the content of the Sator Square, I believe that the Church uses a broader meaning of the word "tradition." For the Church, the tradition does not seem to be limited to these two meanings, which allows the Church to engage in wordplay and to obscure the text.

I am suggesting that the Catholic Church still uses both the active and passive meanings of tradition, but that the two meanings fall into two categories of transmission: esoteric (secret) and exoteric (public). Therefore, when the Church talks about "tradition," it seems to differentiate not only the active and passive aspects of tradition, but also its mode of transmission, which is secret or not, depending on the following structure:

A. <u>Esoteric Nature (Hidden)</u>

1. The passive/objective form:

—Tradition is associated with the *content* that is transmitted **secretly.**

2. The active form:

—Tradition is associated with the *act* of **secretly** transmitting, or teaching, this content **within** the restricted group of bishops.

B. <u>Exoteric Nature (Public)</u>

1. The passive/objective form:

—Tradition is associated with the *content* that is transmitted **publicly**[10].

2. The active form:

—Tradition is associated with the *act* of **publicly** transmitting, or teaching, this content **outside** of the restricted group of bishops.

The Church appears to differentiate between the content and the transmission that is offered to everyone, and the content and transmission that is only offered to the group of bishops within the Church. According to my research, the esoteric content—which I believe is the content of the Sator Square—comes from Christ, who handed it down to the apostles. From there, it was transmitted, in theory,[11] only among bishops from one generation to the next. Even though the esoteric content of the tradition, which I believe to be the Sator Square is crucial, the transmission of this content to the public by the Church is also extremely important. Without this teaching by the Church, any Christian message, secret or not, simply could not be fully disseminated.

The reality is that the meaning of the word "tradition" coincides exactly with the two most important responsibilities given to the Church by God with respect to sacred tradition: *the act of protecting* its source *within* the Church and *the act of transmitting* this divine Revelation *outside,* meaning to the world.[12]

My research shows that to fully understand the subtle language used by the Church, informed readers would simply have to consider the context in which the word "tradition" is used by a given author (one who knows the secret, of course). Readers would have to study the text to determine whether it deals with content that is secret and whether the content and the transmission of "tradition" (or one of its pseudonyms) occur within or outside the circle of bishops. If the Church really does differentiate between public and secret information when talking about tradition, we can discern in the following three rules some of the literary subtleties it uses to deflect readers.

SECRET RULE No. 4: Persuade Others that the Content of the Tradition and Its Transmission Are Solely in Oral Form

If I were to ask what is the opposite of a written communication, the response would almost always be oral communication. For instance, in the field of religion, Judaism and Islam each have their written works and their oral tradition, so you would expect that Christianity would also have written works as well as an oral tradition. However, the assumption that any form that is not written must automatically be oral is actually wrong. This automatic assumption leads people to incorrectly believe that the divine content of sacred tradition is in oral form, while the message of this tradition, which I consider to be the Sator Square is quite tangible and real.

The Use of the Term "Oral Tradition"

Based on my observations, when Christian writers[13] specifically state that tradition is "oral," they are *precisely* addressing the transmission of exoteric teaching to the faithful, meaning to those who are *outside* the privileged group. The stratagem consists of persuading people that the tradition received by the apostles and then by the bishops was handed down orally, thereby enabling the Church to protect the Sator Square.

The Second Epistle of Paul to the Thessalonians

I was bowled over when I realized that this ploy was used by none other than the first Christian writer, the Apostle Paul. He is very specific about the way the tradition is generally taught:

> So then, brethren, stand firm and hold to the traditions which you were taught, whether by word of mouth or by letter from us (2 Thess. 2:15).

In this excerpt, Paul states that these traditions come from his own oral teaching and letters to

Christians in general. However, the Apostle Paul is much less precise about the way he received the teaching when he says: "For I received from the Lord that which I also delivered to you" (1 Cor. 11:23). Paul structured this text very cleverly by not mentioning how he received his teaching and in what form. It is clear that the tradition that Paul received was already well established.

Dei Verbum, 8 and Catechism of the Catholic Church,
76

These two passages are constructed a bit differently, but they seem to use the same ruse as the Apostle Paul. The texts state that transmission, which *"comes from* the apostles," or is made *"by* the apostles," occurs orally and in written form. In my view, the two passages lead the reader to wrongly conclude that the transmission *received by* the apostles from Jesus Christ occurred in the same way. Also, Irenaeus, the staunch defender of the Catholic faith in the second century, specifies how apostolic transmission occurs:

> Clement [of Rome, who died in A.D. 99] was allotted the bishopric. This man, as he had seen the blessed apostles and had been conversant with them, might be said to have the preaching of

the apostles still echoing [in his ears], and their *traditions before their eyes.*[14]

As we can see in this excerpt, Clement of Rome, the fourth Pope of the Catholic Church, received two separate elements from the apostles: first, an oral teaching and second, an apostolic Tradition that was clearly visual and not oral.

The use of the word "transmission" in association with the Tradition

As a second ruse, some Christian texts pair the adjective "transmitted" with sacred tradition to persuade people that this Tradition is oral.[15]

Basil, Bishop of Caesarea (Treatise on the Holy Spirit)

The following passage from a treatise by Basil of Caesarea, a fourth-century bishop, unequivocally shows the secret transmission of an esoteric tradition:

> Some we possess derived from written teaching; others we have received delivered to us "in a mystery" by the tradition of the apostles.[16]

As you read this, I suspect you automatically assumed the following:

Some we possess derived from written teaching; others we have received delivered [*orally*] to us "in a mystery" by the tradition of the apostles.

In the original passage, Basil clearly wants readers to believe that the secret apostolic tradition is oral.

To achieve this, Basil first states that the divine information comes from both written documents and the apostolic tradition. We recognize these elements as the two sources of the deposit of faith, as discussed in the previous chapter. In this excerpt, Basil deliberately separates the two elements.

Then, to ascribe an oral connotation to the tradition, Basil uses the word "delivered" or "transmitted" and links these words to the tradition. He specifically uses the word "delivered" to emphasize the pairing "Tradition-oral."

Therefore, people who read this excerpt quickly may erroneously conclude that there are two pairs of two words: "Scripture-written" and "Tradition-oral." In fact, Basil intentionally omits the adjective "oral," since this secret transmission of the content of the tradition (which I believe to be the content of the Sator Square) among bishops from generation to generation is very tangible.

Titles of Chapters 2 to 5 in *Dei Verbum*

The Second Vatican Council appears to use the same stratagem in its document Dei Verbum, not in the body of the text as Basil did, but instead in the document's chapter titles. None of the six chapters in this document is dedicated to tradition. However, the word "tradition" appears 16 times, including 13 times in Chapter 2 alone, which is entitled "The Transmission of Divine Revelation." So, one might think that tradition and transmission are linked. The chapters that follow (3 to 5) deal only with the Scriptures and not with transmission. This leads the reader to believe that the sacred tradition is "transmitted" orally. Therefore, the Dei Verbum document reinforces the notion that there are two transmission pairs: "Scripture-written transmission" and "Tradition-oral transmission."

The Use of the Term "Unwritten"

The third ruse in rule number 4 seems to be to use the term "unwritten"[17] for the secret content of the Sator Square and its transmission by apostolic succession *within* the circle of elites. It is incorrect to think that the term "unwritten" in Christian texts is used as a synonym for the adjective "oral." The term was carefully and wisely chosen. Yves Congar, the Dominican religious expert, admits that "unwritten" means "by some means other than writing."[18]

Absence of Literality

Although the content of the Sator Square is not in oral form, some might conclude that it is in written form, while others might also conclude the opposite.

John E. Thiel, a brilliant professor of Religious Studies, obviously understands the meaning of the word "unwritten" when he specifies that an unwritten tradition has an "absence of literality."[19] This absence is not a disadvantage. On the contrary, it offers the benefit of being able to interpret text beyond the purely literal meaning of the words.

The information extracted from the Sator Square indubitably has this absence of literality. Someone who interprets the five words of the Magic Square in a literal way would not understand—or would barely understand—the message. Yet the wall of incomprehension breaks down for those who grasp the profound messages and concepts that emerge from the artifact.

The cross symbol formed with the two words *tenet* in the Magic Square also demonstrates an absence of literality. Taken together, the two words are completely meaningless, unless someone knows the profound meaning of the cross symbol.

In summary, using the different meanings of the word "tradition" and the term "unwritten" leads people to believe that the content and the transmission of the divine Tradition are oral. If the Tradition had been presented as a written document or as something tangible, it would have attracted the public's attention. Its protector would have experienced constant pressure from the public to reveal the secret they possessed.

Council of Trent—Fourth Session

In the 16th century, the Council of Trent specified that the words of Christ "are contained in the written books, and in the unwritten traditions."[20] In this passage, the Council seemed to be using Basil's text, which we discussed earlier. As with Basil's text, the Council document only referred to the *secret* content of the tradition transmitted within the circle of privileged members of the Church.[21] Therefore, the Council therefore appeared to have added what was missing in the passage from Basil. I believe that the text did not mention the word "oral," which would be deceptive. Instead, the

Council strategically selected the adjective "unwritten." I believe we can now discern the ruse.

The eminent theologian Yves Congar indirectly confirms secret rule number 4 by saying that Protestants—and most people who are unaware of the secret—wrongly believe that unwritten tradition means an oral tradition.[22] He also confirms the meaning of the term "unwritten" as something "which surpasses any written statement,"[23] meaning beyond the literal meaning.

SECRET RULE No. 5: Deify Things Other than the Content of the Sator Square

Before Vatican II, all the components that were grouped under the term "tradition," such as ecclesiastical traditions, were deified. Is the Church statement at Vatican II, that sacred tradition (or Tradition with a capital T) is the only tradition of divine origin, a way of ensuring that this tradition is purified of any other traditions that are not divine? Is the sacred tradition truly the equivalent of the content of the Sator Square? As previously discussed, the sacred tradition is apparently composed of the following three elements:

1. The sacred tradition has a fixed content given by Jesus Christ, which I believe is the content of the Sator Square.
2. From this fixed content, the Church inserted all the variable content that it considers to be progress in the sacred tradition.[24] As indicated in Chapter 5, this progress advances the divine fixed content of the sacred tradition. Since this variable content becomes part of the sacred tradition, the Church considers it to be divine, as it was established with the help of the Holy Spirit.[25]
3. The Church also includes the teaching of both the fixed and variable content in the sacred tradition.

Did Vatican II really purify the sacred tradition of all other traditional local, liturgical content, and even of things like monuments, artworks and churches? Does the sacred tradition only include divine elements? The fact that the Second Vatican Council acknowledges that there is a sacred tradition does not necessarily purify it. Vatican II provides no list of the elements that constitute the sacred tradition, casting doubt on its composition.

Therefore, from my perspective, it would be incorrect to think that the current sacred tradition contains only the fixed content of the Sator Square. In fact, nothing seems to have changed: the divine content of the sacred tradition remains hidden among many components under the term "sacred tradition," as stated in secret rule number 1.

SECRET RULE No. 6: Hide the Content of the Sator Square and Sometimes the Rites

As mentioned at the beginning of this chapter, the *Disciplina arcani* concept appears in the New Testament.[26] The discipline of the secret was practiced by the Church to protect the Christian doctrines. Between the late second century and the middle of the fifth century,[27] the Church extended its discipline of the secret not only to doctrines, but also to rites and sacramental practices such as baptism and the Eucharist. However, the third-century theologian Origen of Alexandria and the fourth-century bishop Basil of Caesarea maintained that only the doctrines needed to be kept secret.[28] Guy G. Stroumsa, Professor Emeritus of Comparative Religion at Hebrew University in Jerusalem, arrives at the same conclusion, that the discipline of the secret was initially limited to the doctrines.[29] Therefore, according to my research, the discipline has been implemented since the beginning of Christianity, primarily to hide the content and the source of the Sator Square.

One might think that the *Disciplina arcani* was no longer necessary in A.D. 313 when Emperor Constantine put an end to the persecution of Christians. Yet the discipline of the secret did not waver in the slightest; instead, it intensified over subsequent decades, because the Symbols of Faith (creeds), made official during this period, contain Christian doctrines that also had to be kept secret from all non-Christians. The instruction to all the faithful to keep the content of the Symbols of Faith secret was more or less obeyed, and around the end of the fifth century, the discipline disappeared.[30]

Then came the Reformation in the 15th century, with doctrines, such as justification by faith alone, that its adherents claimed were endorsed in the Scriptures. Of course, the Sator Square contains striking clarifications on these theological disputes. Therefore, the Church may have dusted it off to explain its position during the Council of Trent. To do so, the Church appears to have repeated its technique of "professional secrecy," which it used in the first five centuries A.D. to avoid revealing the source of the secret content of the sacred tradition (or Tradition with a capital T).

Consequently, it appears that the use of Sator Square content and the imposition of the *Disciplina arcani* fluctuated in the *same way* and during the *same periods*: both fell into obscurity in the fifth century and re-emerged in the fifteenth century.

SECRET RULE No. 7: The Content of the Sator Square Cannot Be Mentioned or Written; Rather It Must Be Memorized

While some Magic Squares have been discovered in Christian churches, the total number of these artifacts seems low given their apparent importance to the Church. No artifacts have been exposed to public view in the Vatican City State. To my knowledge, the true content of the Sator Square has never been mentioned word for word in any Christian writings.

Memorization (Learning by Heart)

The second-century bishop Irenaeus of Lyon states that tradition is "written in their hearts."[31] What does this expression mean? For many believers today, writing Jesus Christ's message in your heart means preserving it with utmost devotion and tenderness. For example, the Sacred Heart represents the heart of Jesus Christ and eternal divine love for humanity. This love deeply affects believers and calls on them to show him their love in return. While this is one of the figurative meanings of the word "heart," the New Testament frequently uses the word in another way.

In the New Testament, the word "heart," *lêb* [*H3820*] in Hebrew or *kardia* [*G2588*] in Greek, has a much broader meaning.[32] It means the center of a person's inner thoughts, knowledge and understanding. The heart is the seat of the intellect. Thus, the expression "keep it in your heart" is similar to the current expression "keep it in mind," meaning that people must fully assimilate the information at the intellectual level and in the depths of their being. Some traces of the old, broader meaning still persist in present-day speech. For example, the common expression "to learn by heart" involves not the emotions, but the intellect. It means to memorize information and integrate it into memory, to be able to recall it later.

The Two Meanings of the Word Rotas

Researchers used one of the two meanings of the Latin word *rotas* to support their theories about the secret of the artifact. One of the meanings is "you turn" (second person singular present active indicative of the verb *roto).* The other meaning is "wheels" (accusative plural of the noun *rota).*

Interestingly, the expression "learning by heart" is often related to the terms *"rote learning"* and *"by rote."* These two English terms are in fact a memorization method that uses repetition. Mary J. Carruthers, Professor of Literature and of English, Emerita, at New York University, highlights that there is an etymological link between the two English terms and the Latin word *rota,*[33] which means "wheel." The word *rotas* is the plural form of *rota*.

Thus, memorization through multiple repetitions can figuratively be represented by the continuous rotation of a wheel. Ultimately, the word *Rotas* in the Square is a request not to put the words in writing, but instead to memorize it by means of repetition.

Another memorization method can be found in the Eastern World. Many words that relate to the Magic Squares have been discovered in different locations. For example, Jesuit archeologist Jerphanion highlights a painting in an underground church in the city of Göreme, Cappadocia, that illustrates three shepherds in the Nativity story bearing the names Sator, Arepo and Teneton.[34] I strongly suspect that these names are actually used as reminders of the five words of the Magic Square, especially in countries where Latin was an infrequently used language. It is similar to the modern custom of hiding a note with hints to help someone remember a password.

Whatever the memorization method used, at the turn of the third century, Clement of Alexandria, the Greek Church Father, reaffirms the secret rule not to write down the mystery, but rather to memorize it.[35]

Birger Gerhardsson

Contemporary biblical scholar Birger Gerhardsson[36] and some other researchers rely on rabbinical practices to support their statement that Jesus of Nazareth used mnemonic exercises by means of repetition to ensure that his disciples would remember his teachings exactly. Many other researchers did not readily accept Gerhardsson's statement, citing a lack of persuasive evidence. His statement was also criticized for relying on the teaching methods of rabbinic Judaism that were established starting in the second century A.D.

However, let us not forget that rabbinic Judaism emerged from the Pharisaic Judaism of the second Temple of Jerusalem, and that at that time, Jesus of Nazareth was a first-century Jewish teacher.

Both positions are correct and are based on different types of "traditions." Most research on oral traditions uses "form criticism," which was employed by German Protestant theologians including Karl Ludwig Schmidt, Martin Dibelius and Rudolf Bultmann. Supporters of form criticism believe that the New Testament Gospels were written based on a set of small units of text that for the most part derived from *oral* traditions. If we look at this specific type of tradition, Gerhardsson does not seem to have enough evidence to prove that these units of information from the New Testament Gospels are constructed to facilitate mnemonic teaching by repetition.[37]

However, this book does not focus on this type of tradition, which relates to New Testament gospels. Rather, it is focused on the sacred *unwritten* tradition, which believe to be the Sator Square. This sacred tradition is a distinct entity—different from Scriptures—that comes directly from Jesus Christ. Consequently, by looking at the definition of the word *rotas*, which is a request to memorize by means of repetition, Gerhardsson's position seems coherent when it comes to the sacred tradition. In addition, the two sentences in the artifact have an aphoristic form that is appropriate for mnemonic learning,[38] as we will explore in Chapter 8.

Questioning the Reliability of the Deposit of Faith

At the Second Vatican Council, the Roman Catholic Church states that the deposit of faith is composed of two elements: the Sacred Scripture and the sacred tradition. The content of Sacred Scripture in written form is commonly perceived to be highly stable and reliable. However, in reality, it mainly comes from snippets of oral information that are often considered unreliable.

Furthermore, the content of sacred tradition is generally perceived as being in oral form and therefore unstable and easy to manipulate, while, in reality, it is fixed, authentic and reliable, if the content of the sacred tradition is in fact the content of the Sator Square. What a remarkable reversal!

SECRET RULE No. 8: Use key words to refer to the Sator Square

When I started my career as a tax accountant, I realized that members of a specific group of "professionals" recognize each other through the jargon they use. Specialized terminology also helps them identify those who are not part of the group. The terminological nuances typically require a high level of knowledge of the field that can be perceived and understood by specialists in that field.

The Church seems to work in the same way; official Church declarations and explanations, even if they are understood by the general public, often remain much more nuanced for Christian leaders. They are often literary masterpieces of wordplay. The subtleties appear to be used in communication among the highly placed in the Catholic Church to allow those individuals to recognize each other and to confirm their solid adherence to the same faith. Christine Mohrmann, a specialist in early Christian Latin, points out that the first Latin Christian writings frequently employ wordplay, including the use of words with more than one meaning.[39]

Numerous Christian texts contain coded language that I believe implies the existence of the Sator Square. These subtleties go undetected by most readers. As we have seen, many Christian texts use double and even multiple meanings of words like "tradition" and "unwritten." Furthermore, these texts frequently use agricultural terms found in the Sator Square, such as "turn" and "return."[40]

Christian authors who know the secret of the Sator Square appear to use distinct terminology in their writing to reassure the ecclesiastical elite that they are aware of the secret and that their message is in accordance with the meaning of the sacred tradition—the Sator Square.

Benedict XVI—General Audience on Wednesday of 3 May, 2006

Pope Benedict XVI states during this General Audience that the tradition that comes from the apostles must not be seen as "a collection of things or words, like a box of dead things."[41] This "collection of words" is not the group of sentences that formed the Creed. Rather, it seems to represent the sacred tradition with the five words of the Sator Square. Benedict XVI figuratively uses the word "box", which appears to depict the square shape of the artifact.[42] Finally, when Benedict XVI says that the content should not be considered as dead things, he appears to indirectly state that the content of the sacred tradition (i.e., the Sator Square in my view) already has an internal revitalization mechanism called the "living tradition." As such, the Pope's message is focused on preserving the content of the sacred tradition and on letting the tradition progress on its own.

Fifty years before Benedict XVI, rather than focusing directly on the artifact, the progressive Pope John XXIII advocates for a more active and dynamic Church when he states that the Church is not a museum keeper, but a gardener who cultivates flowers that bloom. John XXIII uses the metaphor to specify that the sacred tradition does not only grow by itself, it also needs the active intervention of the Church to progress. This is just one of the many subtleties that are only partially understood by believers, yet clearly grasped by the elite.

SECRET RULE No. 9: Hide the Identity of the Creator of the Sator Square

As established by my analysis in the previous chapter, the Sator Square must have originated from the teachings of Jesus. But who exactly is the creator of this marvel? Was it Peter, James or Paul, another apostle or someone like Mark, who was close to the apostles? Could it have been Jesus himself? One thing is certain, the identity of the creator of the artifact has not been revealed. We will delve more deeply into this in Chapter 13.

SECRET RULE No. 10: Hide the fact that the Sator Square May Be the Legacy of Jesus Christ

This rule will be covered in Chapter 9, which is dedicated to Jesus' secret legacy; it is a truly revolutionary statement.

My research indicates that the Church is carefully and brilliantly concealing the Sator Square using various ploys, much as Jesus did with his parables.

Let me be clear: The primary intention of this book is neither to discuss the Church's authority in the matter of interpretation, nor assess whether its interpretations or teachings are valid, nor to decide whether certain elements of sacred tradition should be included or not—far from it.

The book focuses on the heart of the Divine Revelation, which I believe to be the Sator Square, without detracting from the significance or legitimacy of other elements of the sacred tradition, or of any other Christian organizations.

My research suggests that the Catholic Church received this sacred tradition and has it in its possession. This does not prevent some people from believing that on countless occasions, the Church has moved away from sacred tradition and that Church reform is often required to correct the sacred tradition or move it forward. Others might wonder whether the divine gift was exclusively given to the Catholic Church, to the universal Church made up of certain denominations, to all Christian groups, or to everyone who believes in Christ.

BARRIERS TO ENTRY

The Sacred Scriptures and the sacred tradition encompass the entire foundation of Christianity. Both are hidden behind a veil that deliberately conceals the fundamental divine message. Indeed, in Sacred Scripture, the heart of the divine message is shrouded by a multitude of words in such a way that only a practiced eye can discern it.

My analysis leads me to believe that the heart of the divine message of the sacred tradition (i.e., the Sator Square in my view), is veiled by the difficulty of deciphering the artifact.

Once the artifact is deciphered, the essential divine message reveals itself in a concise and understandable way.

To close this part, I would like to present an excerpt from Yves Congar's book on the apostolic tradition:

> But again, one must avoid picturing the thing under the (imaginary) form of a sort of whispered communication from generation to generation, whose substance would at some future date be made publicly available.[43]

Congar skillfully attempts to persuade readers that there is no apostolic tradition that circulates secretly between successive generations by employing the word "whispering." Actually, Congar is saying the "thing" is not transmitted *orally* between generations; indeed, it is a very tangible item. Furthermore, one has to wonder if today is the "future day" that Congar refers to.

The next several chapters will show that here is much more to learn and admire about the Sator Square.

PART III

THE IMPRINT OF

JESUS OF NAZARETH

7

THE CRUCIFIED MAN

The Sator Square shows the presence of an authority that asks the reader to sow and to turn, or to stand up and to follow. To respond to this call, the reader must believe in this authority.

The need to believe is the focal point of Jesus' teaching. Believing is the foundation of hope, because *"All things are possible to him who believes"* (Mk. 9:23).

Who does Jesus actually want us to believe in? God? Jesus of Nazareth (a mere human who was born in Nazareth)? Jesus Christ, the Son of God? Both God and Jesus Christ? Or the Trinity, with the Holy Spirit included?

In the gospel of John, Jesus says:

> Truly, truly, I say to you, he who believes has eternal life (Jn. 6:47).

In the New Testament, it is clear that Jesus wants people to believe in him. But this is not sufficient; Jesus also poses a fundamental question, not only to his disciples, but also directly to each and every one of us: "But who do you say that I am?" (Mt. 16:15). A person's perspective on the identity of Jesus determines Jesus' impact on that individual's life.

REASON AND FAITH

For Christians, becoming aware of Jesus' identity involves both reason and faith.

Reason: Believing in Jesus of Nazareth

Those who believe in Jesus of Nazareth (the human being) believe that he existed. This belief requires only rationality; faith is not involved. They accept some of his human characteristics as true, as they would do for any other well-known figure from the past. Jesus' life and message are reconstructed based on historical data drawn from ancient writings, archeological finds, etc. For example, Jesus of Nazareth is commonly considered to be a wise man who was crucified.

Faith: Believing in Jesus Christ, the Son of God

For Christians, reasoning is necessary but incomplete. Christian faith begins with reason and then leads the human mind well beyond the rational. Christians who have faith in Jesus Christ fully subscribe, in their will and their heart, to the Divine Revelation, and above all in Jesus Christ as the Son of God. Basically, they are actively and confidently engaged in a relationship with God through Jesus Christ that brings them to salvation.

Faith Is Inseparable From Reason

Christians typically believe that faith directs reason. The elements are inseparable. [1] Thus a person who has faith in Jesus Christ as the Son of God must also believe, *a priori*, in a purely rational and logical way, that Jesus of Nazareth walked among us. For example, some doctrines of the Christian faith, such as the Incarnation and the Resurrection, rely first and foremost on Jesus' human nature.

So far we have established that the Sator Square comes from the teachings of Jesus. However, is there any other evidence in the artifact that could support this assertion? In this part of the book, we will focus on Jesus of Nazareth from a rational perspective, to see whether we can discern his human presence in the Sator Square. While there are many characteristics that are associated with Jesus of Nazareth, we will review the three main ones: he was crucified, he spoke in parables and he revealed the way of life.

This chapter covers Jesus' crucifixion and the next two explore his other human characteristics. The faith aspect will be discussed in Part IV.

THREE DEBATES RELATED TO THE CRUCIFIXION

Believing that Jesus of Nazareth was crucified seems to be an undeniable fact for most Christians and non-Christians alike. In truth, this seemingly simple statement has generated serious rifts over the years, some of which persist to this day.

Was Jesus Really Crucified?

Ever since the early centuries of our era, some people have maintained that Jesus of Nazareth was never crucified. This claim probably arises from Basilides, a second-century Gnostic teacher. He alleges that Simon of Cyrene, the man who helped Jesus Christ carry his cross (Mt. 27:32; Mk. 15:21-22; Lk. 23:26), took Jesus's place and that it was actually Simon who was crucified. As per Basilides, those who were present during the crucifixion wrongly and ignorantly believed that Jesus was the one who was crucified.[2] Where did this idea come from?

Gnosticism is a set of religious beliefs and practices that were advocated by some second-century Christian sects.[3] Gnosticism distinguishes the Supreme God who represents goodness and the intangible from the subordinate Demiurge god who is wicked and flawed. The latter is often identified as the Old Testament god who supposedly created the physical universe. This idea purports to explain the existence of evil and imperfection in the world.

Gnostics venerate Jesus as an *Aeon,* an emanation of the Supreme God who came to save humanity from the clutches of the flawed Demiurge and the material world by revealing the truth and the precepts of wisdom.

Some Gnostic ideas intersect with the doctrine of Docetism, which considers Jesus Christ to be an illusion or phantom, even if he appears to be made of flesh and blood.[4] These heretic groups do not accept Christ's suffering and shameful death by crucifixion, because he was the divine emanation of the Supreme God.

Despite these ancient rifts, the crucifixion of Jesus of Nazareth is now considered historical fact.

Was Jesus Really Crucified on a Cross?

Some disagree that Jesus of Nazareth was crucified on a traditional cross with a cross beam. In the Greek version of the Bible, the word *stauros (G716)* means cross, the instrument of the execution of Jesus of Nazareth, and it is the source of the debate. Some feel that the word *stauros* means a pointed pole or post, not a cross. In his 1896 book *The Non-Christian Cross*, John Denham Parsons supports this definition of the word *stauros* by demonstrating that the word was in fact used to mean pole in Ancient Greek literature, as seen in Homer's *Iliad* and *Odyssey*.[5] Anglican theologian Ethelbert W. Bullinger supports the same definition of the word *stauros* in his book *The Companion Bible.*

However, many references state that Jesus of Nazareth did indeed die on a cross with a cross beam and not on a post.[6] For example, Christian apologist Justin Martyr metaphorically describes the form of the cross of Jesus Christ:

> For the lamb, which is roasted, is roasted and dressed up in the form of the cross. For one spit is transfixed right through from the lower parts up to the head, and one across the back, to which are attached the legs of the lamb.[7]

Crucifixion was a punishment used particularly by the Romans at the turn of the Christian era. The condemned person was forced to carry the horizontal part of the cross, called the *patibulum,* to the location of the crucifixion.[8] Evidently, it was easier to carry the *patibulum* than the entire cross. Normally, a vertical post called a *stipes* had already been driven into the ground at the execution site. The *patibulum,* with the condemned person affixed to it, was probably placed into a groove and, using a pulley system, lifted up to the top of the *stipes,*[9] thus forming a "Tau cross"[10] (in the form of a capital T).

For those who were present, the moment when the body of Jesus was slowly lifted up to the top of the vertical post must have been intensely emotional. For many Christians today, this painful image prefigures Jesus' Resurrection.

According to French writer Frédérick Tristan, the charge against Jesus of Nazareth, which was inscribed above his head (Mt. 27:37), shows that the end of the cross exceeded the height of Jesus' arms. From that, Tristan deduced that the cross was not in the shape of a capital T, but a lower-case t, that is, in the shape of the Latin cross, in which the vertical part continues above the horizontal section.[11]

To summarize, most scholars agree that Jesus was crucified on a cross with a horizontal part—as opposed to a post—as represented in most cross symbols.[12]

Did Jesus Even Exist?

The divergence of views concerning the fact that Jesus was crucified is often associated with another profound debate, this one over his very existence. Did Jesus actually walk this earth?

When I was 10, my Grade 4 religion teacher began a lesson by saying, "One thing is certain: Jesus did exist! It's been proven!" I thought, "What? Do people believe otherwise?" The idea that people could doubt the existence of Jesus of Nazareth was inconceivable to me. I had been steeped in the Catholic religion since birth, so I never believed that proof was necessary.

In fact, some people maintain that Jesus of Nazareth never existed, that he is a myth. Although the statement has been made throughout the history of Christianity, a modern mythicist movement resurfaced in the late 18th century.[13]

The adherents of this movement advanced several theories to explain the mythic figure of Jesus. Some of them believed that Jesus was modeled on one or more pagan gods, like Osiris, Dionysus, Horus or Mithra.

Some believe that Jesus is a pure fabrication based on a variety of ideas and concepts, such as the old Jewish or pagan traditions or on traits taken from prominent Old Testament figures like Joshua and Moses. Others believe that Jesus' character is based on that of well-known figures like the Egyptian Pharaoh Tutankhamun,[14] the prescient Jesus, son of Ananias,[15] the philosopher Apollonius of Tyana[16] or the revolutionary Judas of Galilee.[17] Some even believe that the history of Jesus was constructed from moments in the lives of several real people who lived during the same period.

THE CRUCIFIED MAN | 143

American freethinker Kersey Graves was one of these individuals. In a book published in 1875, he boldly drew up a list of some thirty-five divinities with the following characteristics:

> These have all received divine honors, have nearly all been worshiped as Gods, or sons of Gods; were mostly incarnated as Christs, Saviors, Messiahs, or Mediators; not a few of them were reputedly born of virgins; some of them filling a character almost identical with that ascribed by the Christian's Bible to Jesus Christ; many of them, like him, are reported to have been crucified; and all of them, taken together, furnish a prototype and parallel for nearly every important incident and wonder-inciting miracle, doctrine, and precept recorded in the New Testament, of the Christian's savior.[18]

Nevertheless, many researchers dispute all studies that come from mythicism and similar beliefs. They cite the lack of references and suitable proof, along with the shameless use of improper extrapolation.[19] For these researchers, the characteristics that mythicism has paralleled with those of the life of Jesus of Nazareth are deemed to be unfounded.

One particular study in *Background of Early Christianity*, by renowned American author Everett

Ferguson, shows the many differences that exist between Jesus and the dead and resurrected gods, and lists the specific characteristics of Jesus.[20]

Being human, Jesus of Nazareth inevitably shared traits with the people of his time, without taking away his uniqueness. Ultimately, if Jesus were simply a myth, there would be no Incarnation, no Crucifixion, no Resurrection, and therefore no Christianity.

Although it is always latent, the debate over the existence of Jesus seems to have faded. A great deal of historical research now focuses on the "true" history of this incomparable figure. Who was in Jesus of Nazareth's inner circle? Did he have brothers and sisters, a wife, progeny? There are also discussions concerning his convictions and his message: was he a virtuous Essene monk, a member of the Pharisee religious sect or a revolutionary nationalist zealot?

THE OLDEST DOCUMENT

By exploring the two main mythicist arguments that refute the existence of Jesus of Nazareth, we will uncover some major findings about the illustrious Sator Square. The first argument is that there is insufficient ancient documentation attesting to the existence of Jesus. The second is that the few documents concerning Jesus that do exist are unreliable because they have undergone too many alterations.

Is There a Lack of Historical Evidence?

To support their position, adherents of mythicism frequently ask: if Jesus of Nazareth is such a notable historical figure, then why is there such a glaring lack of ancient references to him?[21] Let us examine whether this is the case.

The Epistles

Many of the oldest Christian documents are epistles, from the Greek *epistolē (G1992)*, meaning "letter." These functional, short-form letters were one of the best tools for communicating, teaching and guiding people's faith. They were adapted for reading aloud. Paul expressly asks the person receiving the letter to communicate the content orally to the faithful (1 Thess. 5:27). All 21 epistles in the New Testament refer to Jesus.

According to some scholars, only seven of the thirteen epistles of Paul can be authenticated as his.[22] These seven epistles date from around A.D. 50, barely seventeen years after the death of Jesus.

It is recognized that all the epistles of Paul were written before the Canonical gospels, even though the placement of the gospels before Paul's epistles in the New Testament suggests the opposite. The first epistle to the Thessalonians (A.D. 49-51) is considered today to be not only the earliest of Paul's epistles, but also the earliest Christian document.

The Gospels

Other ancient Christian documents about Jesus include the New Testament gospels. Few scholars believe that the four authors of the Canonical gospels were direct eyewitnesses to Jesus, that is, his first apostles or members of his entourage. Thus, the gospels were almost certainly written by later authors based on some Christian documents and various oral traditions. For example, the gospels of Matthew and Luke share some material that may originate from the undiscovered ancient document referred to as "the Q source."[23] Also, the gospels of Mark, Matthew and Luke all have a significant amount of material in common that stems from another source.[24]

In chronological order, the gospel of Mark, written between A.D. 65 and 70, comes first, followed by those of Matthew and Luke around the year 83, and John around the year 93.

There are also many other ancient Christian documents about Jesus that do not appear in the New Testament, such as the gospel of Thomas, the Didache (Doctrine of the Apostles), and the epistle of Barnabas.

Ancient Non-Christian Documents:

In addition to the Christian epistles and gospels, four ancient non-Christian documents, three Roman and one Jewish, refer to the existence of Jesus.

The first document consists of two passages written by the Roman historian and biographer Suetonius in A.D. 121. The first passage[25] mentions the persecution of Christians in the time of Nero. The second[26] states that Emperor Claudius expelled the people who had caused great turmoil in relation to *Chrestus*, or the Christ. This passage proves that there were Christians in Rome during Emperor Claudius's reign (A.D. 41 to 54).

The second Roman document, written in the *Annals* in 115, comes from Tacitus, the Roman historian and senator. Tacitus specifies that Christ was executed by Pontius Pilate. He also accuses

Emperor Nero of deliberately causing the great fire of A.D. 64 in Rome and blaming the Christians.[27] This proves the presence of a Christian community in Rome that was large enough that the emperor was able to refer to it. Did Christians leave the city of Rome and take refuge in Pompeii, only 155 miles (250 kilometers) south of Rome, during Claudius' reign? Or did they leave Rome during the persecution by Emperor Nero after July 64?

The third and oldest Roman document is from Pliny the Younger, the Imperial Roman Governor of the province of Bithynia and Pontus. He wrote a letter in 112 to Emperor Trajan, requesting information on the identification of Christians and the administration of their punishment. He also described Christian gatherings where people worshiped Christ as God.[28]

Last but not least, another non-Christian document that refers to the existence of Jesus comes from the renowned Jewish historian Flavius Josephus. Some see Josephus as a traitor, since he switched allegiance when he was caught for participating in the Jewish resistance against the Romans. Following his capture, he predicted that Vespasian would become Emperor of Rome. Josephus built a solid relationship with Emperor

Vespasian and his son Titus. He wrote two important literary works: *War of the Jews* in A.D. 75 and *Antiquities of the Jews* in 94. He provided key information on Jerusalem, the destruction of the second temple, the siege of Masada and the beginning of Christianity. Josephus mentions Jesus in two passages of *Antiquities of the Jews*. The first states that James is the brother of Jesus, who is known as the Christ (Messiah).[29] The second passage,[30] called *Testimonium Flavianum*, is disputed. It points out that Jesus is a teacher who is the Christ crucified by Pontius Pilate and resurrected. Some people doubt the authenticity of this passage and believe that additions to the original version altered the passage.[31] Nevertheless, in *A Marginal Jew,* American author John P. Meier clearly shows that even after removing everything that could be debated by detractors, the "purified" version of the second passage of Josephus still illustrates the presence of Jesus of Nazareth on Earth.[32]

As we can see, there is a substantial amount of ancient testimony that supports the existence of Jesus. Thus, it is surprising to learn that to this day, some researchers maintain that Jesus of Nazareth is a mythical figure.

Nevertheless, the goal of this section is not to refute the mythicist argument, but to make the following statement:

> *The Rotas Square is most likely one of the earliest—perhaps the earliest—Christian documents ever discovered.*[33]

Methods for dating ancient documents and other objects often provide unreliable results based on estimates that vary depending on the characteristics of the object. This lack of precision can generate a great deal of discussion.

However, the eruption of Vesuvius proves that the two oldest Rotas Squares discovered in Pompeii were conceived before the month of August 79. To my knowledge, there is no other early Christian document that can meet this high degree of reliability.

It is likely that the two Rotas Squares were created several years, if not decades, before the year 79 A.D.—therefore at some point between Jesus' time and the year 79. There may also be other Rotas Squares that predate the ones in Pompeii. Even if we assume (although it is highly unlikely)[34] that the first two artifacts were conceived in A.D. 79, the creator would have lived at the same time as many of the close disciples of Jesus of Nazareth. It is therefore quite possible that the creator was *one of Jesus' apostles.*

In addition, the first Rotas Squares may have been created in another language before the year A.D. 79 and later translated into Latin. However, this seems difficult, if not impossible to envision, considering the extreme complexity of the artifact's configuration and the importance of the Latin version of the artifact to certain Eastern Christian communities.

THE MOST AUTHENTIC DOCUMENT

The second main argument advanced by the adherents of mythicism is that there have been so many alterations to the ancient documents concerning Jesus' existence that it is impossible to know about his real life and true message.

Were All the Documents Altered?

Mythicist scholars, relying on multiple sources of exegetical research, state that even if Jesus did exist, very few ancient documents paint a true portrait of him because they have been so greatly altered and saturated with falsehoods.[35] This opens the door to the possibility that these documents do not correspond to the life of Jesus of Nazareth and his teachings.

In the early centuries, publishing and distributing documents among Christian communities was important to maintaining a common understanding of the Christian faith. At that time, the only way to reproduce the documents was to rewrite the texts by hand. As a result, when scribes copied the documents, they may have unintentionally made mistakes in the reproduction, including spelling errors and omitting or inserting words. In addition, some scribes made deliberate changes—in good faith—to try to clarify texts that they felt were difficult to understand or to correct texts they assumed were incorrect.[36] It is also conceivable that changes were made to serve political and personal agendas or to reorient the Christian faith in a desired direction. Another very important factor that should not be overlooked is translation errors. During this period, Christianity already covered an immense geographical area, so documents had to be translated to convey the faith to believers who spoke different languages. The great complexity of translating theological and religious texts can be attributed to elaborate terminology and concepts that were often abstract, symbolic and spiritual, with several nuances and levels of comprehension.

In taking account of all the errors, whether deliberate or not, that were copied many times in successive reproductions over time, we have to wonder about the authenticity of all or part of the modern-day Christian documents.

Control Systems

The books of the Old Testament face the same suspicions about alterations. Many researchers believe that the first five books, called the Pentateuch, were not authored by Moses, but written and revised by many people during different periods.[37] However, the old versions of the book of the Prophet Isaiah of the Dead Sea Scrolls discovered in the 1950s were compared with the oldest version known to date. Despite an approximately 1,000-year difference in their dates, they are almost identical.[38] This demonstrates that the Jews were able to preserve the divine writings of the Old Testament for a millennium, no doubt because they implemented a strict control system to ensure the integrity of copies. One of the system's techniques is the counting method used by the scribes, who are called the *soferim*. For instance, to ensure the correctness and precision of texts, they calculate letters, words and verses from the Torah, thus reducing the risk of errors or omissions.

Do the Christian community and the Church have a similar system for protecting the authenticity of New Testament writings?

Many ancient Christian documents include handwritten corrections within the text or in the margins.[39] For example, one page of the *Codex Vaticanus*, written in the fourth century, contains an annotation in the margin instructing the scribes to keep the old version.[40] Thus, a re-reading of the document by another person seems to be another control technique. In the late fourth century, the historian Rufinus of Aquileia confirms this when he states that since the work of the copyists is crucial, it must adhere to certain standards and undergo significant verification.[41]

In the end, this mythicist argument is quite plausible. To this day, no one can categorically claim beyond any doubt that the ancient Christian documents that have been found to date are the original ones—or even identical copies of the original documents. For instance, all the original epistles of Paul are missing; therefore, the authenticity of the current epistles cannot be confirmed. However, I can certainly make the following assertion:

> *The message of the Magic Square has never been altered; it is identical to the one that was originally created.*

The specific arrangement of the letters that form the Magic Square can be neither changed nor moved, because its message would become incomprehensible. Changing just one letter would completely destroy the Magic Square, as it would lose its palindromic form. The message remains absolutely identical to the one originally intended by its creator.

To my knowledge, there is no other message that has this unique disposition and this technical characteristic that prevents any alteration. It is absolutely astonishing that Christian Tradition has within it a control system against any potential alterations.

The fact that the primary source is unaltered remains its most significant quality. Nevertheless, this distinctive attribute can also turn out to be a pitfall, since the message cannot be changed if needed. Even if some people think the message in the Sator Square is imprecise, incorrect or a source of embarrassment or contradiction, they cannot change the message, thus giving the Church a highly reliable source. The Magic Square remains, to this day, the most authentic message from Jesus.

AN ACCESSIBLE DOCUMENT

In addition to being very old and inalterable, the Sator Square also has a literacy-related characteristic. Like Judaism, Christianity became enriched by literature. However, that does not mean that Christians were more literate and better educated than their contemporaries; according to second-century philosopher Celsius, Christians were uneducated fools.[42]

If the hidden message is in fact Christian in nature, it must be comprehensible to the general population and especially to people from the lower classes.[43] Its broad outlines must be clear and easy to understand, despite its profound meaning.

Estimates of the literacy rate of the population in the early centuries A.D. spark frequent debates. In *Ancient Literacy*, historian William Harris assumes that literate individuals never made up more than ten percent of the population of the Roman Empire.[44] The literacy rate among Jews and Christians was approximately the same.[45]

Harry Y. Gamble, the professor who specializes in Christian literature, reminds us that the word "literacy" encompasses a broad range of reading and writing abilities. For example, a person who can recognize some words does not have the same level of literacy as someone who can write an entire document.[46]

There is a third category that slips in between literate and illiterate: semiliterate. Citing various references, British New Testament Professor Chris Keith shows that the latter category in fact covers many people who were able to recognize basic words and sentences that were neither too long nor too complex[47] and were even able to learn words by memorization. Therefore, when it comes to the Magic Square, I can make the following statement:

The creator of the Magic Square adapted
its message to the literacy level
of the majority of Christians
in the early centuries to ensure that the
message was fully accessible.

Orators from that period could have used the Magic Square as a visual aid at public gatherings. Most participants would have been able to read and memorize its message, which was expressed in short sentences at the literacy level of a considerable proportion of the population of the time.

The lack of education and the scarcity of written texts created an environment that was not conducive to literacy. Yet public readings, where presenters added their own commentary to texts, certainly contributed to the audience's education.[48] In addition, the subject of the recent arrival of Christ was certainly of great interest at these gatherings. Also, public presentations of the teachings of Jesus, with a 25-letter visual support, would have undoubtedly immersed the audience in a mystical atmosphere. When I gaze at the artifact, I sense the same atmosphere—it truly is a Magic Square.

The message of the artifact is accessible to all. While its profound divine message is formulated using simple and familiar language, this does not mean that it is easy for everyone to understand its full meaning. However, its comprehension is not restricted to those with superior intellect, eminent theologians or highly placed people in the Church; the message can also be understood by uneducated people like the Apostles Peter and John (Acts 4:13).

8

JESUS SAYS

Professor Arland J. Hultgren, an eminent New Testament specialist, believes that there are two historical certainties about Jesus of Nazareth: he was crucified and he spoke in parables.[1] So far we have discussed his crucifixion, and in this chapter we will cover his parables.

As we saw, the Catholic Church refers to the information in the sacred tradition—the Sator Square—to explain its doctrines on salvation. This demonstrates the Church's deep respect and devotion to the artifact. As such, does the Church preserve the artifact because Jesus said the two sentences of the Sator Square? This is a legitimate question, because the earliest Rotas Squares from Pompeii date back to the first century A.D.

In the New Testament, the words of Jesus of Nazareth are not exclusive to the canonical gospels. They can be found elsewhere in the New Testament, for example in the first epistle of Paul to the Corinthians (11:24-25) and in the Acts of the Apostles (20:35).

Other words of Jesus, which are called *agrapha* (*agraphon* in the singular), have been discovered outside of the New Testament. One of the most significant external sources is undoubtedly the gospel of Thomas, one of many books from the Nag Hammadi Library discovered in Egypt in 1945. This document, which has some Gnostic tendencies, contains more than a hundred words that were purportedly spoken by Jesus.

Other non-canonical texts also claim to contain authentic words of Jesus. These include the Acts of John, Philip and Peter, the Gnostic gospels, the correspondence of King Abgar, and even the Koran. According to renowned German theologian Joachim Jeremias, some of these texts fall into the category of "fables of an edifying nature."[2]

Many experts are convinced that among the messages Jesus of Nazareth left for his disciples, some have yet to be discovered or are lost forever.[3] The *agrapha* provide important additional details that help us better understand Jesus Christ, his message and his entourage.

However, many people are also convinced that it is impossible to authenticate a word of Jesus. If this is true, it would be impossible to know whether the Magic Square contains Jesus' words. Furthermore, the artifact is not directly mentioned in any Christian writings, it has no title or signature, and it does not even begin with the famous "Jesus says."[4]

Some new approaches have been developed to try to authenticate words supposedly spoken by Jesus. Even though the results of this type of research are inconclusive, the research still provides details on the form and characteristics that a word of Jesus should have. In this chapter, we will closely examine whether the two sentences: "God [the sower] holds the plow, but you turn the furrows," are *ipsissima verba*—the precise words—of Jesus. Do the sentences respect the form and characteristics of an original parable of Jesus? As we will see, this review is based entirely on research carried out by noted specialists in the field.

THE LITERARY FORM OF A PARABLE OF JESUS

The gospels specify how Jesus communicated his words. They state that Jesus only spoke to the crowd in parables (Mt. 13:34) and that he "explained everything privately to his own disciples" (Mk. 4:34).

Thus, it is generally accepted that authentic words of Jesus of Nazareth are presented in the form of a parable. The passages that contain parables are rich and powerful; reading them is like being at Jesus' side and hearing the words coming from his mouth. In addition, Jesus' parables contain deep truths that cannot be fully understood by all.

It is difficult to list with any accuracy the total number of parables that were spoken by Jesus (perhaps 30 or 40), given that there is no universal agreement on whether a particular excerpt is considered a parable.

Most of the parables come from the three synoptic gospels—i.e., those of Matthew, Mark and Luke—and the non-canonical gospel of Thomas. The gospel of John apparently contains none. Some parables are exclusive to one gospel, while others can be found in more than one gospel.

Apart from those in the New Testament, it may seem impossible to identify the parables of Jesus, given that this literary form was also used by Aristotle, Socrates, Aesop and others.[5]

Nevertheless, many people, like the theologian Jeremias, believe that the parables of Jesus are unique; they have individual traits that distinguish them from others.[6] Likewise, after eight years spent researching existing documents in Western literature from the Late Antiquity (300 B.C. to A.D. 300), Canadian professor and financier James Breech provided scientific evidence that the parables of Jesus of Nazareth are unlike any others.[7]

Rabbinical parables share many similarities with those of Jesus of Nazareth.[8] Rabbinical language and the language of Jesus stem from a pre-Christian Judaic tradition containing a collection of images and metaphors from the Ancient Near East.[9] The Bible reveals the strongly rooted presence of this Judaic tradition. The fact that Jesus borrowed from this rich store of Semitic images and metaphors to explain his teachings does not diminish the significance and originality of his words; on the contrary, it validates the Jewish environment in which he lived.

The parables of Jesus are distinct from rabbinical parables in many ways, particularly because the latter are presented in the form of supplementary information related to a specific prescriptive text that is often biblical in nature.[10] Knowing that the first rabbinical parables emerged after the first Rotas Squares, we can therefore eliminate the possibility that the Latin Magic Square originates directly from Rabbinic Judaism.[11]

The Seed of Doubt Is Sown

German Protestant theologian Karl Ludwig Schmidt states in 1919 that each gospel is made up of a set of units that come mostly from oral traditions. The units were preserved and later consolidated by the gospel publisher.[12]

Were the words—and parables—of Jesus altered between the time that Jesus spoke them and when they were recorded decades later? The fact that some parables appear in several gospels with variances and different meanings raises doubts about the authenticity of these texts.[13]

Some scholars, including Schmidt, believe that a substantial portion of the authentic words of Jesus was altered. C. H. Dodd suspects that the changes were made by the evangelist, alone or in concert with his community.[14] Joachim Jeremias thinks that the changes are "updates" that were used in the early centuries A.D. to adapt the initial divine message to the intended audience, who finally realized that Christ would not be returning in the short term.[15] Jeremias states that the alterations stemmed from translating and adapting the texts to a Hellenic audience.[16] So how can we determine the authenticity of a word or parable of Jesus?

Based on the studies conducted by Schmidt and Martin Dibelius, Rudolf Bultmann, a German researcher and one of the most important biblical scholars of the early 20th century, concludes that a critical analysis of forms is required for studying not just the whole of a synoptic gospel, but its constituent components.

> The aim of form criticism is to determine the original form of a piece of narrative, a dominical saying or a parable. In the process we learn to distinguish secondary additions and forms, and these in turn lead to important results for the history of the tradition.[17]

The idea is to analyze small units of text individually to validate their authenticity. So to find the original message of Jesus, we have to go back and cleanse a piece of original text of all subsequent changes and additions.[18]

Studies on the Word "Parable"

There has also been etymological research on the word "parable," or *parabolē (G3850)* in Greek. *Masal (H4912)*, the equivalent Hebrew word, has a very broad definition and encompasses all sorts of figurative forms,[19] including parables, fables, allegories, proverbs and comparisons.

Many authors try to group these stylistic forms into categories to determine those that represent a valid parable. Even though no precise line can be drawn to delineate the categories, classifying the forms may help to authenticate a parable spoken by Jesus.[20] Bultmann proposes the following classification of stylistic forms:[21]

- A metaphor is the simplest form of figurative language. It compares two distinct elements by directly transferring the designation of one to the other. For example, the Sator Square uses the *Sator* or "sower" as a metaphor for God.

- A similitude provides more details than a comparison. It contains elements that are commonly found in real life and that are generally known to all, like the similitude of the growing seed (Mk. 4:26-29).

- A parable is a comparison that is developed in narrative form; it is a short story with comparisons, like the one about the lost sheep (Lk. 15:3-7) or the lost coin (Lk. 15:8-10).

- An exemplary story is a tale, in narrative form, that describes the appropriate behavior to be adopted. It is a concrete example and a direct message, as in the story of the rich man (Lk. 12:16-21). There are no comparisons in an exemplary story.

Two Literary Forms: Aphorisms and Parables

Bultmann's form criticism was revived in the early 1970s by John D. Crossan, the renowned Irish theologian and historian who strengthened the research on form criticism and the authenticity of the words of Jesus. In his book *In Parables*, he links Jesus' life with his parables, giving particular consideration to eschatology and the Kingdom of God.[22] In another book, *In Fragments*, he focuses on the aphorisms of Jesus. Aphorisms are short, forceful and incisive statements and are often confused with proverbs.[23]

Biblical expert Robert W. Funk supports Crossan's research. Funk argues that the heart of the authentic message of Jesus comes in only two literary forms: aphorisms and parables.[24] In 1985, Funk founds the *Jesus Seminar,* a group of biblical and lay experts seeking to determine the authenticity of the texts being studied as a word or parable of Jesus. They use an unusual process of authentication based on voting by experts. The group concludes that only about 18% of the parables and aphorisms presented are authentic.[25]

The Aphorism of the Sator Square

Let us focus on the aphorism which, as we saw earlier, is one of the generally accepted literary forms for a Jesus saying.

Although it is a brief, complete and independent statement containing a general truth, an aphorism is often attached to fragments of text.[26] It may be a small separate segment included within a sentence. While John T. Cullen considers that the Sator Square has a non-Christian origin, he identifies the form of the two sentences inscribed on the artifact as an aphorism.[27]

An aphorism is reduced to its minimum; it has no introduction or conclusion. It is a message in its most original, pure form. John D. Crossan cites other characteristics of an aphorism that are strikingly similar to those of the Sator Square. For example, an aphorism has missing information that prompts the reader to actively seek to gain a better understanding of its message.[28] Also, an aphorism is often formulated as a doublet, precisely like the two sentences of the Sator Square.[29] Crossan specifies that the two parts of an aphorism are closely intertwined and together form a provocative force.[30]

We can then conclude that the most authentic words of Jesus of Nazareth are often found as aphorisms, just like the form of the Sator Square.

THE CHARACTERISTICS OF A PARABLE OF JESUS

Form criticism is not enough to fully authenticate the words of Jesus. The original words of Jesus must also exhibit certain specific characteristics. Let's review whether the characteristics identified by experts are present in the two sentences of the Sator Square.

1. A Parable of Jesus Occurs in a Real Setting

In his parables, Jesus uses real-life situations from daily life in first-century Palestine,[31] such as the fisher in the Parable of the Net (Mt. 13:47-52) and the merchant in the Parable of the Pearl (Mt. 13:45-46). The parables are grounded in the real world.

Many of the parables evoke agricultural life. Examples include the Parable of the Sower (Mt.13:1-23; Mk. 4:1-20; Lk. 8:1-5 and Thomas 9), the Parable of the Budding Fig Tree (Mt. 24:32-35; Mk. 13:28-31 and Lk. 21:29-31), and the Parable of the Workers in the Vineyard (Mt. 20:1-16). His parables reflect daily life, thus facilitating audience comprehension. This characteristic is found in the two sentences of the Sator Square, as it is also set in an agricultural environment.

2. A Parable of Jesus Provides a Message that is Accessible to Everyone

The words used in the Sator Square are easy to grasp, but this does not mean that the deeper significance of Jesus' message will be fully understood by everyone. Jesus' message often contained several layers of understanding. For example, in the New Testament, Jesus related the Parable of the Sower to his entourage, knowing that it would not be fully understood by everyone in the group.[32] Jesus knew that his disciples would accept his message, and privately gave them additional explanations so they could better understand the parable and the mystery as a whole (Mk. 4:10).

3. A Parable of Jesus Does Not Provide Clarification

The authentic messages of Jesus are considered to be generally concise and straight to the point, with no lengthy explanations, thus leaving room for various interpretations.

The message in the artifact does not explain how to turn nor how to take the good or bad furrow. It also does not warn us of the consequences of following or not following instructions, nor does it provide the end result. The two sentences end abruptly. The aphoristic text of the Sator Square, put in its simplest and most concise form, is the very core of the divine message.

4. A Parable of Jesus Contains an Engaging Message

A parable of Jesus prompts the person to answer his call, to become involved and to take a position.[33] When people acknowledge the divine call and its instructions, it undoubtedly heightens their commitment to take action and follow him. This characteristic is found in the second sentence of the Sator Square with the pronoun "you," which is a call to action, and the phrase "you turn," which requires the participation of the individual.[34]

5. A Parable of Jesus Refers to Eschatology (The End of the World and the Beginning of the New World)

Most scholars believe that the eschatological element in the message of Jesus is a crucial feature.[35]

In the figurative sense, the harvest is often defined as the consequence or final result of all the efforts of the laborer. The New Testament mentions that few workers will benefit from a plentiful harvest (Lk. 10:2, Mt. 9:37) and that the weeds will be burned and the wheat will be saved at harvest time (Mt. 13:30). Thus, the harvest is not only associated with the advent of the Kingdom of God, but also with Judgment Day;[36] the two notions are combined in Christian eschatology.[37]

The harvest symbolizes the end of a world, meaning the end of the current journey. Its meaning does not stop there; it also evokes rehearsal and renewal. The hope of a future harvest leads Christians who have faith in Jesus Christ to look further, beyond the horizon, in search of a new path in the new world. Harvest is clearly implied in the two sentences of the artifact. Therefore, this parable meets this eschatological characteristic.

6. A Parable of Jesus Refers to the Kingdom of God

Experts agree that the Kingdom of God is an essential theme in Jesus' parables.[38]

In *The Mystery of the Kingdom of God* (1914), theologian and philosopher Albert Schweitzer says that Jesus Christ foreshadowed an imminent apocalyptic catastrophe, after which the Kingdom of God would emerge in a foreseeable future.

A few decades later, C. H. Dodd states instead that the Kingdom of God that Jesus Christ preached about has already been achieved or already exists.[39] In his view, the Kingdom of God is a current reality.

Today, many scholars agree with Schweitzer and Dodd that the Kingdom of God exists both in the present and in the future. The Kingdom of God arrived on Earth with Jesus Christ and is present every day for the faithful.

Once again, the Sator Square contains this characteristic. First, the integration of the person "in Christ" represented by the word *Sator* or "sower" demonstrates the currently existing Kingdom of God through the immediate submission and engagement of the person. Second, the harvest represents the future aspect of the Kingdom of God. Jesus Christ and the Church bring the faithful to the future.[40]

7. A Parable of Jesus Illustrates a Wisdom Tradition

The words of Jesus are steeped in wisdom. In the Bible, wisdom goes beyond good judgment or experience gained. A wise person is often seen as someone who understands, or seeks to understand, the structure of the world initially established by God during its creation. A wise person observes various things in the world to try to determine their interrelationships and God's order of Creation. This approach brings the person closer to God.

An aphoristic text, such as the one inscribed on the Sator Square, is considered ideal for the teaching of wisdom.[41] For example, the wisdom of King Solomon shows the ability of a skilled orator

to utter *meshamil,* or short parables.[42] Jesus
demonstrates his wisdom by using agricultural
terms, just as the prophet and wise man Hosea did
in the Old Testament.[43] Finally, Jesus of Nazareth is
not only a wise man. Just like the artifact, Jesus
clearly encourages people to acquire the necessary
wisdom to achieve salvation.[44]

8. A Parable of Jesus Contains an Ethical Message

Ethics is an important element in the message of
Jesus and is one of its characteristics.[45] Through a
wisdom tradition, Jesus uses his knowledge of
agriculture to transmit his messages on ethics.[46]
The ethical aspect of the message is clearly present
in the sentences on the Square; a person has the
choice to turn and take the good or the bad furrow,
which is the choice to do right or wrong.

9. A Parable of Jesus Must Have a Jewish Setting

According to Bultmann, an authentic word of Jesus
must have "double dissimilarity." It must diverge
from both Jewish tradition and the teachings of the
early Church. Although correct, the criterion of
double dissimilarity greatly limits the number of

authentic messages that can be attributed to Jesus. As a result, it is strongly criticized.[47]

For their part, Gerd Theissen and Dagmar Winter propose a refreshing new criterion of authenticity: plausibility. This criterion emphasizes the Jewish context in which Jesus operated. Thus, an authentic passage of Jesus of Nazareth has a Jewish context and shows affinity with the teachings of the early Church.

The criterion of plausibility places Jesus of Nazareth in his social context. He was a man, and like all human beings, Jesus lived in a society. He was born Jewish and he lived in the Jewish community of Galilee with Jewish family members, friends and neighbors. He operated in the political, economic, social and religious environment of that time. His message was influenced by Jewish tradition, as illustrated by several passages of the gospels.

As mentioned earlier, the text of the Sator Square is a *masal* and respects the Jewish tradition. In addition, the artifact's text has two interconnected themes that are found in Judaism: wisdom and eschatology. And finally, as we have seen, Jesus uses metaphors and images from the Jewish tradition. Amazingly, three metaphors in the two short sentences of the Sator Square are known in the Old Testament:

- The word "sower" represents God. In the book of Hosea (2:23), God says, "I will sow." This metaphor is drawn from the traditional Hebraic imagery.

- In the Sator Square, the verb "turn" refers to the Hebrew word *sûb (H7725)*. This word, commonly used in the Old Testament, means to turn toward God, to return, to convert, to repent to God or to turn away from evil. Here are a few examples of biblical excerpts using this word:

  Take words with you and return to the Lord (Hos. 14:2).

  Turn from your evil ways and keep My commandments (2 Kgs. 17:13).

  Do not turn to the right nor to the left; Turn your foot from evil (Prov. 4:27).

  Repent and turn away from all your transgressions (Ezek. 18:30).

- The word "furrow" in the Old Testament represents the good or bad direction that a person takes. Human beings can sow a furrow with a view of righteousness (Hos. 10:12), with poisonous weeds (Hos. 10:4), or beside stone heaps (Hos. 12:11). God waters the furrows (Ps. 65:10, Jb. 31:38).

10. A Parable of Jesus Assigns No Attributes to God

Another characteristic of a parable of Jesus is the manner in which he describes God. Without a doubt, God behaves like a human being. [48] Also, Jesus' parables do not provide any description of God's physical attributes. Breech goes even further in noting that this not only applies to God; none of the people mentioned in the parables of Jesus have any physical attributes, even though their actions are referred to.[49] Here again, this applies to the two sentences of the Sator Square. The artifact has no reference to any physical attribute and God—as the sower—is behaving like a human being by holding the plow.

FINDINGS OF THE ANALYSIS

In summary, there are generally two methods used to determine the authenticity of a word of Jesus:

studying the literary form and analyzing the characteristics of Jesus' parables.

With respect to the literary form, according to the experts, the aphorism that comes from the two sentences of the Sator Square corresponds to one of the best forms (if not the best) that one would expect to find in an authentic saying of Jesus.

In terms of the characteristics of Jesus' parables, it is impressive to note that the two sentences of the Sator Square undeniably have all ten of the most important characteristics of an authentic parable of Jesus. And all of this is achieved with just 25 letters arranged in a palindrome. How incredible! Taking into account the number of characteristics that are present, the message embedded in the Sator Square appears to reveal that the passage is not simply a parable of Jesus of Nazareth, but that it is an ultimate or *megaparable*.

Unveiling Another Parable of the Sower

The Parable of the Sower in the Scripture[50] is considered the *capital parable.* This parable is the key to understanding all of the parables of Jesus; it contains his core teaching.[51] Pope Francis confirms its importance during the *Angelus* of 13 July 2014.

It is remarkable that another Parable of the Sower appears on the Sator Square.

My research suggests that these two parables originate from the *same source*, from Jesus himself and lead me to make the following statement:

Jesus Christ more than likely revealed his core teaching through a Parable of the Sower, which appears not only in the New Testament, but also in the sacred tradition (the Sator Square).

As mentioned in Chapter 5, it is important to recall that the Church states that it preserves the words of God in the deposit of faith, which comprises the sacred tradition, which for me is the Sator Square, and Sacred Scripture. Remarkably, therefore, both contain a Parable of the Sower. I was even more astonished when I found the following excerpt by Clement of Alexandria:

> The farming is of two kinds: one unwritten [*agraphos*], the other written [*engraphos*]. But whichever method the Lord's worker uses to sow the good grain, to help the stalks to grow, and to

reap the harvest, he will clearly be seen as God's true farmer.[52]

When I first read this passage, my jaw dropped. Clement of Alexandria duly attests that there is a Parable of the Sower in the "unwritten" sacred tradition and another one in the "written" Sacred Scripture and that they both guide the laborer on the right path.

As Clement seems to indicate, the Parable of the Sower in the New Testament and the one in the Sator Square focus on the conditions necessary for a successful harvest rather than on the harvest as such.

The culmination of this review far exceeded my expectations. The words of the two sentences— thoroughly imbued with the message and presence of Jesus—probably came from his mouth! There is no doubt in my mind that the Sator Square unequivocally reveals the distinctive and eminent imprint of Jesus of Nazareth.

9

THE SECRET GOSPEL
OF JESUS

In the study of Jesus of Nazareth, we covered his two distinctive characteristics: he was crucified and he spoke in parables. The third characteristic, which we will explore in this chapter, is that Jesus revealed the way of life.

When reading the four gospels of the New Testament, we can easily fall under the spell of Jesus Christ's charisma. We soon notice that Jesus is not just addressing his disciples; in fact, he is speaking to each one of us. Sometimes it can feel as though we are living in Jesus' time and that we are part of his first-century audience or his inner circle of disciples. Jesus clearly invites each of us to set out on the path with him and to make the leap from being lost in the crowd to being one of his disciples.

In the New Testament, Jesus was sometimes called "rabbi,"[1] which means "master." As such, he was seen as a teacher. His disciples voluntarily chose to accompany him on his many travels. They walked and ate by his side. The disciples were fascinated, and above all, they wanted to be taught and to hear his words, as they were full of wisdom.

Jesus had a secret message that he unveiled through his parables. His disciples received in-depth explanations of this secret through his teachings. But what exactly did he teach that was so fascinating and so important? Before this question can be answered, two significant Judaic concepts need to be grasped: the Coming of the Messiah and the Resurrection.

THE COMING OF THE MESSIAH

The Coming of the Messiah may be the paramount theme in the Old Testament. A host of references in the Bible state that God will send the people of Israel a Messiah (Christ), an anointed person, a great priest and king from the line of David, to fight and defeat the enemy and to reign. The Messiah would lead Israel to a new world—the salvation of the New Israel.

Israel was controlled by many non-Jewish foreigners throughout most of its history. In 63 B.C., Consul Pompey the Great conquered Judea and it felt under the Roman yoke. Subsequently, heavy taxation during the reign of Emperor Tiberius[2] and outrages inflicted on the Jews,[3] including the trampling of their traditions, aggravated relations between the Jews and the Romans.

The tension was palpable. Jewish revolts against the Romans, including one shortly before the birth of Jesus, proved unsuccessful. The Roman noose continued to tighten in the face of the real risk of rebellion by the Jewish population. The Jews lived in constant fear of being crushed by Rome. The fear was justified, as the Roman emperor Titus destroyed the second Temple of Jerusalem in A.D. 70.

Still, many Jews believed that they possessed a secret weapon, an asset. They had the support of God and God's promise of a Messiah who would come to save them and end their despair. The Messiah would defeat the enemy's hold on them and lead Israel to a new age of divine justice.

The Hebrew Bible also nurtured the idea of the imminent arrival of this new era. In Chapter 9 of his book, the Prophet Daniel claims that the Angel Gabriel told him that there were 70 weeks left before the advent of eternal justice. This certainly fanned the flames and raised the hopes of the Jewish people, as that 70-week period, though it could be interpreted in several different ways, represented a foreseeable future.

The Jewish nationalist movement's struggle to throw off the Roman yoke was at its peak. In the midst of this turmoil, several people identified themselves as messiahs. Expectations concerning the imminent coming of a Messiah soared during the Second Temple period.

THE RESURRECTION

The Resurrection is the second key concept that helps us understand the teachings of Jesus. In the Hebrew Bible, God gives human beings a choice between two paths: the way of light and life or the way of darkness and death (Dt. 30:19, Prov. 12:28, Jer. 21:8). Ancient Hebrews believed that this choice could only have direct consequences for their life on earth, because for them, there was no possibility of survival after death.

In the Old Testament, the dead "go down to the pit" (Ps. 30:3; Jb. 33:24; Prov. 1:12), "into the lower parts of the earth" (Ezek. 26:20), to a place of darkness and silence (Ps. 94:17; 115:17), or to the kingdom of death known as *Sheol*. Once they are in that place, the dead remain in a permanent state of slumber with no possibility of escape (Jb. 3:17; 14:12-14). Consequently, the repercussions of a person's choice could be felt either by the person before death, later on by their descendants, or by the State of Israel. As one example, the ancient Hebrews considered leprosy to be God's earthly punishment for sins, as in the case of Moses's sister Miriam (Nb. 12:10).

However, much later, in the second century B.C., there is the astonishing revelation in the second book of the Maccabees that the Jews believed in the resurrection of the dead.[4] Later, Flavius Josephus, the first-century A.D. Jewish historiographer, confirmed that many Jewish groups at that time also believed in some form of resurrection. These groups included the Pharisees, experts in and protectors of Hebrew law and Jewish tradition, and the ascetics known as the Essenes.[5] However, again according to Josephus, the Sadducees, a very authoritarian faction whose powers included priestly authority over the Temple of Jerusalem, did not believe in resurrection. The Acts of the Apostles (23:8) in the New Testament repeat statements by Josephus according to which the Pharisees—as opposed to the Sadducees—believed in resurrection. Therefore, during the period around the life of Jesus, a considerable number of Jewish people believed that it was possible to wake up and leave *Sheol,* the kingdom of death.

The first five books of the Old Testament—called the Torah or the Pentateuch—contain no clear passages that might offer hope of resurrection, or a life after *Sheol.* However, the concept of resurrection was certainly debated by the Jews, since an excerpt from the Mishnah—the oral tradition of the Torah[6]—compiled at the end of the second century warns that those who do not believe that the resurrection of the dead was addressed in the Torah could not be part of the new world.

Subsequent writings in the Hebrew Bible support the possibility of awakening after death and having eternal life:

Many of those who sleep in the dust of the ground will awake, these to everlasting life, but the others to disgrace and everlasting contempt (Dn. 12:2).

Your dead will live; Their corpses will rise (Isa. 26:19).

Behold, I will open your graves and cause you to come up out of the graves, My people; and I will bring you into the land of Israel (Ezek. 37:12).

For You will not abandon my soul to Sheol; Nor will You allow Your Holy One to undergo decay. You will make known the path of life; Your presence is fullness of joy; In your right hand there are pleasures forever (Ps. 16:10-11).

And see if there be any hurtful way in me, And lead me in the everlasting way (Ps. 139:24).

The divine option of taking the way of life instead of the way of death now takes on greater significance. The repercussions of this choice of path are felt not only during the life that ends in death; they extend into eternal life, beyond death. Those who take the way of light "will shine brightly... like the stars forever and ever" (Dn. 12:3).

We cannot ignore how important the idea of the resurrection of the dead was in Jesus' time. The concepts of resurrection and eternal life were very popular, even before the birth of Jesus. The Jews extensively studied and debated the topic. The non-Christian Flavius Josephus and the Christian Acts of the Apostles explicitly refer to a divergence of opinion on resurrection among influential Jewish groups. Furthermore, the three synoptic gospels specify that the Sadducees did not believe in resurrection (Mk. 12:18; Mt. 22:23; Lk. 20:27). It is clear that this subject was immensely important in Jesus' time.[7]

Individual or communal salvation?

During the latter part of the Second Temple period, some apocalyptic texts reveal that there would soon be a significant disruption. The current world would be destroyed following the arrival of the Messiah, a new one would be established, and the dead would be resurrected. Here, we can clearly see that the Jewish population of this period considered the two fundamental concepts of the Coming of the Messiah and the Resurrection to be closely interrelated.

During that period, it was clear to the Jews that the new world would come soon after the long-awaited and impending arrival of the Messiah. The

Jewish people waiting for the Messiah experienced a mix of emotions—fear, joy and insecurity. The arrival of the Messiah was imminent, so adequate preparations for the new era had to be made.

In fact, the quoted excerpts from the book of Daniel and that of Mishnah Sanhedrin, among other passages, are problematic because they specify that not all Jews will follow the way of life. Many Jews knew that only the righteous ones—those who follow the path of life—will live happily in the new world and gain everlasting life.[8] The others will remain in *Sheol*, the kingdom of death, and suffer eternal punishment. Resurrection and the degree of elevation will therefore occur on *an individual basis.*[9]

There is no doubt that individual Jews at the time wondered: What do I personally have to do to be on the path of the righteous? Certain conditions have to be met to access the path of life being offered by God. This was no mean feat, as the Hebrew Bible provides few concise instructions on how to meet those conditions.

THE LEGACY OF JESUS OF NAZARETH

The prevailing climate on Jesus of Nazareth's arrival was one of insecurity, created by the increasing presence of the Roman military and the Jewish liberation movement, and by religious and existential questioning among the Jewish population. The new world was about to see the light of day.

When Jesus said, "You search the Scriptures because you think that in them you have eternal life" (Jn. 5:39), he was aware that many Jews scrutinized the Scriptures in an attempt to find the gateway to eternal life and understand how to get on the path of righteousness. For example, Old Testament texts on the apocalypse were highly prized by Jews in Jesus' time.[10]

Jesus knew that the secret of the way of life was not stated directly in the Scriptures, because it is the Lord who "knows the way of the righteous" (Ps. 1:6). In addition, according to two of Isaiah's messianic predictions that were echoed in the New Testament, the way could only be shown by the Messiah: "How lovely on the mountains Are the feet of him who brings good news, Who announces peace And brings good news of happiness, Who announces salvation, And says to Zion, Your God reigns!" (Isa. 52:7; cf. Rom. 10:15) or: "Because the Lord has anointed me To bring good news to the afflicted; He has sent me to bind up the brokenhearted" (Isa. 61:1; Lk. 4:18).[11]

The Samaritan woman in the gospel of John (4:25) who brought Jesus water to drink summed up the situation when she said: "I know that Messiah is coming (He who is called Christ); when that One comes, He will declare all things to us." Jesus Christ acknowledged that she did indeed understand.

In the Bible, Almighty God gave humanity a way of salvation, a path that leads to a new life. Thus, human beings are saved by God's grace and redemption.[12] This way of salvation is the Good News. The Apostle Paul is convinced that God gave knowledge of salvation through Jesus Christ (1 Thess. 5:9). In the book of Isaiah, the suffering servant, who many theologians associate with Jesus Christ, "will bring forth justice to the nations" (42:1) or he "will faithfully bring forth justice" (42:3) to bring people out of darkness.

In addition, the second-century Didache, one of the oldest non-canonical Christian documents, confirms that Jesus gave knowledge, life and immortality.[13] The document also mentions that each individual has the choice of following either the way of life or the way of death.[14]

Furthermore, in a New Testament passage, the young rich man believes that Jesus the Messiah knows this secret: "And someone came to Him and said, 'Teacher, what good thing shall I do so that I may obtain eternal life?'" (Mt. 19:16). In this quotation, the request for salvation made to Jesus is clearly expressed in individual rather than collective terms.

The people close to Jesus were convinced that he was the Messiah and that he knew the way to salvation. He had the key to saving Israel as well as each of them individually. Jesus provided the solution for attaining eternal life and for joining God in the Kingdom of Heaven.

Two of his apostles explicitly stated their desire to continue receiving teachings from Jesus, their rabbi-Messiah, about the path to be followed:

> Thomas said to Him, "Lord, we do not know where You are going, how do we know the way?" (Jn. 14:5).

> Simon Peter answered Him, "Lord, to whom shall we go? You have words of eternal life." (Jn. 6:68).

The people close to him (and eventually other Judeo-Christian groups) also recognized Jesus of

Nazareth as the prophet that God had announced to Moses:

> I will raise up a prophet from among their countrymen like you, and I will put My words in his mouth, and he shall speak to them all that I command him. It shall come about that whoever will not listen to My words which he shall speak in My name, I Myself will require it of him (Dt. 18:18-19).

Justin Martyr, one of the first Christian authors, said prior to his execution in the second century that Jesus was foretold as a teacher and a messenger of salvation.[15]

THE ONLY GOSPEL OF JESUS CHRIST

The word "gospel" comes from the Greek word *euangelion (G2098)*, which means "good news". Thus, the Good News is basically the way of the righteous, promised by God and revealed through Christ. Irenaeus of Lyon states that the Good News brings the plan of salvation to human beings.[16] Augustine goes further, by saying that the Gospel makes him hope for a blessing without end.[17] Thus, everything seems to point to the following statement:

The Sator Square must be the Gospel of Jesus Christ that preceded the New Testament gospels.

The Sator Square is apparently not one of the canonical or non-canonical gospels; it is the *only* Gospel—with a capital "G"—of Jesus handed down to the apostles; it is "the Gospel that preceded the gospels."[18] Therefore the date of the Gospel of Jesus Christ, which existed even before the New Testament gospels, perfectly coincides with the date of the first Magic Square.[19] As we have seen in Chapter 7, the Magic Square is one of the earliest Christian documents—perhaps the earliest.[20] The Gospel of Christ must be the most important pseudonym for the Sator Square. The Gospel of Christ and all of its pseudonyms, such as "faith" and "tradition," share another common feature with the Sator Square: they are all unalterable.

Here are some examples:

- The epistle of Jude mentions that: "the faith which was once for all handed down to the saints" (1:3).

- Irenaeus of Lyon maintains that there is "only one single tradition" for all Christians throughout the world and that nothing can be added or subtracted from it.[21]

- Yves Congar often stresses that the Gospel of Christ, also called the Tradition, was determined at one point and sealed for eternity without the possibility of making changes.[22] Congar is interested in the "form," whether that of the Gospel or of the Tradition; he specifies that both have "permanence of the form."[23] For him, tradition is "the communication of a *definite* object that retains the identity of its *inner nature* .... It affects the conservation, transmission and even the content of what is kept and passed on in a certain way that *does not destroy its identity.*"[24] The object that Congar is referring to must be the Sator Square.

If the Vatican is using the Sator Square as the Gospel of Christ, the unusual and unalterable structure of the Sator Square enables the Vatican to confidently assert that the Gospel is maintained in an intact or "pure" state."[25]

As in the case of Sacred Scripture, many believe that the content of the Gospel of Christ is mainly made up of a set of units that comes primarily from the oral and written traditions. Here, the Gospel of Christ is not directly linked to Sacred Scripture, but instead to the sacred tradition (in my view, to the Sator Square). This is supported by Congar when he mentions that the Council of Trent considers that "the content of the tradition is the Gospel."[26]

Based on my analysis, the core of the authentic message of the teaching of Jesus of Nazareth, concisely transmitted to the apostles, consists of just 25 letters. It is the secret divine recipe for salvation that was established by God through Jesus Christ. In the gospel of John (14:9), Jesus of Nazareth specifies that his teaching comes from God, who sent him to deliver the Good News. The two sentences indicate the way of life, or the way of the righteous, leading to the Kingdom of God.

Jesus of Nazareth taught the way of life while traveling throughout Palestine; he was thus showing that he knew "the Way." Jesus's way to salvation is often likened to the path traveled by Moses and the Jews to the Promised Land.

Like Jesus, the disciples who followed him were also traveling along "the way." The fact that they all walked together shows the crucial role of community in every Christian's path.

The teaching of the way of life, or the Good News, is so important that after Jesus's death,[27] the first group formed by those close to him called itself "the Way." They were "the disciples of the Way" or "the disciples of the Path" (Acts 9:2; 19:23; 22:4; 24:14).

After recounting his main parable of the sower, Jesus Christ was very clear when he said to the apostles:

> To you it has been granted to know the mysteries of the kingdom of heaven, but to them it has not been granted (Mt. 13:11).

The secret message of Jesus is very important and it was highly sought after. It represents the plan that one must follow in order to reconcile with God. For example, Bishop Eusebius of Caesaria[28] related the circumstances of the death of Jesus's brother, the Apostle James the Just. Almost thirty years after the death of Jesus, the apostle was asked to publicly repudiate Jesus as being the Christ and to answer the following question: What is the gate of Jesus? Here, the question relates to the passage in the gospel of Matthew (7:14): "For the gate is small and the way is narrow that leads to life, and few who find it." This divine gate is the one that leads to the way revealed by Jesus. Ultimately,

James maintained that his brother was the Messiah and did not answer the question about the gate of Jesus. For his stubbornness, he was thrown over a wall of the Temple and then stoned to death.

We have seen the importance of the need to believe and how it is ingrained in the Sator Square, which must be the Gospel of Christ. The Apostle Paul sums this up well when he says: "it [the Gospel] is the power of God for salvation to everyone who believes" (Rom. 1:16). This part of the book focused on the belief in Jesus of Nazareth, which considers only the rational aspect. We have determined that the Sator Square reveals valuable information on three distinctive human characteristics of Jesus of Nazareth: he was crucified, he taught through parables and he brought his Gospel or the Good News.[29]

Although these characteristics are extraordinary and striking in their own right, any other *human being* could have possessed them all. God could have chosen someone like a prophet or a teacher of great wisdom and endowed that person with the same exceptional characteristics. A Messiah with nothing but human characteristics—such as a terrestrial king from the line of David who was to bring the divine message and save the people from evil—would surely have met the messianic expectations of most Israelites.

After all, this part of the book indicates that Jesus of Nazareth, the human being, *carved his imprint on the Sator Square*. It would be quite reasonable to wonder if the artifact was intended to reveal that Jesus was a mere human with impressive characteristics.

In the next part of the book, we will further our exploration of Jesus's identity and message. As we will see, the Gospel of Christ (the Sator Square in this book) has always been acknowledged by Christians. However, the artifact has generated many different interpretations by various Christian groups; to this day, there is no consensus on the nature and the role of Jesus in salvation.

I would like to end this part with a pertinent excerpt from Psalms (16:8-11) that is repeated in the Acts of the Apostles (2:25-28):

> I have set the Lord continually before me;
>
> Because He is at my right hand, I will not be shaken.
>
> Therefore my heart is glad and my glory rejoices;
>
> My flesh also will dwell securely.
>
> For You will not abandon my soul to Sheol;

Nor will You allow Your Holy One to undergo decay.

You will make known to me the path of life;

In Your presence is fullness of joy;

In Your right hand there are pleasures forever.

PART IV

THE IMPRINT OF

JESUS, THE SON OF GOD

10

RECONSIDERING THE CHRISTIAN CROSS

As previously stated, anyone who recognizes the existence of Jesus of Nazareth believes in his human presence. This involves the recognition of some of his human characteristics. Since this recognition is determined through individual reasoning, the specific human characteristics of Jesus that are recognized may differ from person to person. However, many strongly believe that not only reason but faith is also required to answer Jesus's question, "who do you say that I am?"

A MATTER OF FAITH

In general, "having faith in God" means having complete trust in God and in his Revelation. Faith—considered a gift of God—prompts each individual to seek and accept the Truth, and encourages the person to be fully engaged.

Furthermore, "having faith in Christ" requires a faith centered on Christ, who is the Truth itself. This faith leads the individual to realize that Jesus Christ is the Son of God and encourages the person's desire to participate, to integrate into the mystical body of Jesus Christ, and to embark on the path to salvation.

In the third century, Clement of Alexandria said in *The Stromata*:

> And since choice is the beginning of action, faith is discovered to be the beginning of action .... Voluntarily to follow what is useful, is the first principle of understanding.[1]

FORMS OF THE CROSS SYMBOL

After the death of Jesus, his cross became a symbol that strengthened Christian faith. The Christian cross has carried a huge variety of symbolic meanings and taken on many forms since the beginning of Christianity. My goal here is simply to provide readers with an overview of the symbol and its connection to the artifact.

The Ânkh or Ansate Cross, the Crux Ansata: ♀

The shape of this cross corresponds to the letter "T" topped with a circle. Often considered an Egyptian hieroglyph, it was most often employed by the Coptic Christians of Egypt. One of the meanings of this particular cross symbol is "life."

The Latin Cross, the Crux Immissa: †

The Latin cross is very popular today, particularly in the Western World.[2] Its vertical axis is taller than its horizontal piece. Few Latin cross symbols have been discovered in Christian catacombs from the early centuries, but several have been dated to the fourth century. The crucifix—which is a Latin Christian cross with the body of Jesus—apparently only appeared in the fifth century.[3]

The Greek or Equilateral Cross, the Crux Quadrate: +

This cross, with its four equal branches, was also used in the world of Christianity. The two crossing lines represent the four cardinal points, among other things.

The Tau Cross: T

A cross in the shape of a capital "T" evokes the *tau*, the 19th letter of the Greek alphabet. The letter *tau* replaced the ancient Hebrew letter *thav* or *tav* following the translation of the Hebrew Bible into Greek (the Septuagint). In *An Answer to the Jews,* Tertullian specifies that in Ezekiel 9:4-6, the sign marked on the foreheads of people to save them from a massacre, was the symbol of the *tau*;[4] this sign was initially attributed to the Jewish *tav*.

Clearly, the interpretation of a symbol can change depending on time and location. For example, these days, the symbol "+" would generally be interpreted as the plus sign rather than the Greek Christian cross symbol.

It is important to note that the two words *tenet* in the Sator Square form a Greek or equilateral cross, which is a valid form of the Christian cross.

DID CHRISTIANS ONLY BEGIN USING THE CROSS SYMBOL AS OF THE FOURTH CENTURY?

Stating that the cross symbol became an important Christian symbol following the death of Jesus may seem obvious to most Christians and non-Christians alike. However, a great many contemporary scholars—I will refer to them in this chapter as the "majority bloc"—disagree with this statement. According to this majority bloc, Christians began using the symbol of the cross only as of the fourth century. The bloc relies on the following arguments to support their position.

First Argument: Reference to Marcus Minucius Felix

At the end of the 19th century, controversial British author John Denham Parsons wrote *The Non-Christian Cross*, in which he referred to Marcus Minucius Felix, a third-century Latin Christian apologist, who said that early Christians did not use the symbol of the cross.[5] According to Parsons, Minucius Felix believed that the cross was a pagan symbol. Building on that statement, some members of the majority bloc believe that Christians started to venerate the symbol of the cross only from the fourth century.

It seems that some majority bloc members are unaware of the existence of Christian texts that predate Minucius Felix's writing, which instead assert that the symbol of the cross was indeed used by Christians. For instance, in the mid-second century, Justin Martyr said in *First Apology*:

> But in no instance, not even in any of those called sons of Jupiter, did they imitate the being crucified; for it was not understood by them, all the things said of it having been put symbolically. And this, as the prophet foretold, is the greatest symbol of His power and rule.[6]

In addition, Tertullian specified at the turn of the third century that Christians were referred to as those who gave their "adoration to the cross."[7] During the same period, Clement of Alexandria said that the figure 300, equivalent to the Greek letter *Tau* (the symbol of the cross) in gematria,[8] was the "sign of the Lord."[9]

In the end, even Parsons admitted that Minucius Felix seemed to be the only Christian author who believed that the cross was a non-Christian symbol.[10] Some may see this line of argument as rather weak.

Second Argument: *The Negative Connotation of the Cross Symbol*

The majority bloc claims that the Christian cross symbol did not appear until the fourth century because the cross—which was associated with crucifixion—carried a negative connotation in the earlier centuries A.D. Crucifixion was considered one of the most abject punishments, reserved for the worst criminals and for rebels fighting against Roman power. It was also used to humiliate victims and to dissuade those who wanted to imitate the rebels. The majority bloc believes that the perception of crucifixion in the first centuries A.D. would have been similar to today's view of the electric chair. Thus, from their perspective, the idea that people in that early period venerated such a symbol is simply implausible.

They also believe that the negative connotation of the Christian cross symbol was based primarily on the following three factors:

To the Jews, the Cross Symbol is a Form of Idolatry

Jews consider veneration of any symbol, such as the cross, to be idolatry, which is the worship of something or someone other than God. It is a transgression of the biblical commandment against making a graven image or idol (Ex. 20:4). Among Jews, idolatry is strongly prohibited and strictly interpreted.[11] Therefore, the Jews accused early Christians of idolatry because of the symbol of the cross.

To the Jews, the Cross Symbol Is a Malediction (Scandal)

In addition to being condemned to a degrading punishment, the crucified person was labeled by Jews as having been rejected by God. To the Hebrews, crucifixion was the greatest misfortune that could strike a Jew; the condemned person was sentenced to be cursed by God. The book of Deuteronomy (21:23) contains this devastating sentence: "he who is hanged is accursed of God." It was unthinkable and even offensive for Jews to believe that their promised Messiah, who was supposed to triumph, could be crucified and thus damned. The Apostle Paul noted that the curse weighed not only on the crucified Christ, but also on every Christian (Gal. 3:13).

In *An Answer to the Jews*, Tertullian, like other Christian writers,[12] outlined the Jewish view of the crucifixion of Jesus. He confirmed that the Jews did not find it credible that God would expose his own son to a manner of death that he himself had cursed. However, Tertullian's reply to these accusations clarified that the book of Deuteronomy regarding the curse (Dt. 21:23) must be read in conjunction with the preceding verse (Dt. 21:22) which states, "If a man has committed a sin worthy of death and he is put to death, and you hang him on a tree... ." According to Tertullian, this made it possible to assert that Jesus, who had acted righteously all his life, was not subject to this curse.[13]

To the Gentiles, the Cross Symbol Is Foolishness

The Apostle Paul exposed the negative connotation of the cross when he said, "but we preach Christ crucified, to Jews a stumbling block [scandal] and to Gentiles foolishness" (1 Cor. 1:23). Christian writings from the latter half of the second century confirm that the Jews accused the Christians of idolatry and, being accursed, of being condemned by God.[14]

For their part, Gentiles (i.e., non-Jews) deemed the crucifixion of Jesus to be foolishness, since that method of punishment was fit for a criminal, but not for a god. To them, Jesus Christ was not a triumphant and all-powerful Savior, but simply an inferior being who succumbed to the forces of evil. Therefore, Christians were ridiculed. The *Alexamenos graffito* of the crucified man with the head of an ass is one example of this, as described in Chapter 7. Also, the second-century Roman historian Tacitus related that Christians endured jeering from the time of their arrest until their execution.[15]

In sum, according to the majority bloc, the three negative connotations associated with the cross prevented the Christian population from using the Christian cross symbol until the fourth century.[16]

Among Christians, the Cross Symbol Has a Positive Connotation

While the symbol of the cross was certainly a source of embarrassment for Christians in the early centuries A.D., I have some reservations about the impact of the three factors that triggered the negative connotation of the symbol. I believe that the impacts are grossly exaggerated and that they extend over too long a period. If the cross symbol had such serious and devastating significance, then how do we explain that the first Judeo-Christians were able to continue to follow the practices of

Judaism and attend the Temple of Jerusalem? And that James, the brother of Jesus, later became a dominant figure in the Jewish community of Jerusalem?[17]

Some Jews obviously erected barriers and sometimes used violence[18] to prevent conversion to Christianity, as the new sect with its Messiah did not conform to their expectations. In reality, I believe that these accusations were instead often relegated to the sort of open discussion and debate that rabbinical Jews still engage in today among themselves. For example, in the mid-second century, Justin Martyr quotes the Jew Trypho as saying: "we are in doubt," "I am exceedingly incredulous on this point" and asking for evidence: "prove to us."[19] This clearly demonstrates that he was not ready to accept Jesus as the Messiah and that the subject continued to spark discussion.

In fact, all these negative comments and condemnations come solely from those outside of the Christian world, and do not take account of the Apostle Paul's clear statements that the cross and the crucifixion of Christ were indisputable signs of victory and the central point of his teaching. Paul proudly declared: "but we preach Christ crucified" (1 Cor. 1:23). Paul's words are supported by many other Christian texts dating back to the first century, which show not embarrassment, but pure admiration for the Christian cross as the symbol of mercy, forgiveness, glory and salvation. The cross represents the power of Christ. Well before the fourth century, the Acts of the Martyrs described the joy that the tortured ones felt before their execution in being able to "carry the cross like Jesus."[20] In addition, the Apostle Peter asked the Romans to be crucified upside down,[21] thus showing deep respect for the crucifixion of Jesus Christ. Shortly after the death of Jesus, his closest followers surely understood that even crucified, Jesus was their Messiah, even before the conversion of the Apostle Paul. They continued their journey and spoke "in the name of Jesus" (Acts 5:40).

Clearly, the second argument of the majority bloc, that Christians did not use the symbol of the cross because it had a negative connotation, is in fact a counter-argument. The fact that Christians in the early centuries A.D. faced allegations of scandal and that they were accused of idolatry actually demonstrates that they *used* the cross, not the opposite. I see no disgrace in these faithful followers; quite the contrary. Christians by definition understood early on the deep and monumental meaning of the symbol of the cross, which far outweighed all of these accusations. The first Christians quickly realized that the cross of Jesus Christ is part of a divine design—a divine plan.

Third Argument: Lack of Archaeological Evidence

The principal argument of the majority bloc is that no *Christian* cross symbols from the early centuries A.D. have ever been found. However, the following examples of cross symbols from that period that are most likely Christian contradict this argument.

- French writer Frédérick Tristan estimates that there are about thirty crosses in the Christian catacombs of Rome.[22]

- An object in the shape of the Latin cross was embedded in the plaster above a wooden altar on the upper floor of the Bicentenary house in Herculaneum, which was destroyed by Vesuvius in 79.

- Several equilateral cross symbols were found in Pompeii.[23] In addition, a Latin cross was displayed in full view of the public in a bakery in that city.

- Six drawings of crosses were discovered in the cave of St. John the Baptist in Suba, west of Jerusalem.[24]

- Crosses inscribed on ossuaries were found near Jerusalem, including the one that renowned Israeli archaeologist Eliezer Sukenik discovered at Talpiot. It had crosses drawn in charcoal on each of its four sides and the Greek inscription *Iesous Iou*, a lament meaning "Jesus, woe" or "the misfortune of Jesus."[25]

The majority bloc has often provided the following explanations to deny the Christian nature of any cross symbols that date back to the early centuries:

- These cross drawings are not cross symbols, but rather masonry marks to facilitate adjustments to the ossuary lid.

- The cross symbol is of pagan origin. It is perhaps the oldest symbol in human history. The mark has multiple meanings: it is a solar symbol, a phallic emblem[26] or a Sun God.[27] An undeniable fact remains: cross symbols are used almost all over the world. However, this argument must take into account that the frequent use of the cross symbol before the coming of Jesus does not preclude that Christians could also have used the symbol. That being said, obviously not every cross that is discovered is necessarily Christian either.

- Some cross symbols are indeed Christian, but they were engraved after the death of Emperor Constantine I in the fourth century.

The bloc's explanations—often presented as the ultimate truth—resulted in several other cross symbol discoveries not being properly recorded[28] and simply being ignored.[29] Their vision, often considered limited, is not universally shared; many people have reservations about the veracity of their stances.

THE HIDDEN CROSS

In fact, early Christians worshipped the cross and have always venerated it. The reason few crosses were found is because Christians simply wanted to *hide* them.

Persecution of the Christians

Christians probably concealed their cross symbols for fear of provoking a scandal or being accused of idolatry; however, the fear of persecution seems to be the main reason.

In fact, the first persecution of early Christians was not unleashed by the Romans, but instead by a Jewish group that the Apostle Paul belonged to. That's right, the Apostle Paul! At the time he was called Saul of Tarsus (Tarsus is now a city in Turkey). Saul participated in the persecution and was a witness to the death of Stephen, the first Christian martyr (Acts 7:58-60). After Jesus appeared to him on the road from Jerusalem to Damascus, Saul converted to Christianity and took the name Paul.

Roman persecution began when Emperor Nero blamed the Christians for the Great Fire of Rome in July 64, and ended during the reign of Constantine I in 313. Persecutions occurred at differing levels of intensity, depending on the time and place. One of the most severe episodes is the Great Persecution (303-313), which took place during the reign of emperors Diocletian and Galerius, just before Emperor Constantine I came to power.

The Romans were aware of Christians' reverence for the cross. Recall the *Alexamenos graffito* and the mockery mentioned previously. Also, Justin Martyr did not hide the fact that the cross was a Christian symbol, as demonstrated in his *First Apology*, which was addressed to several Romans, including Emperor Antoninus Pius.[30] The writing of Roman magistrate Pliny the Younger depicts the danger faced by the Christian faithful when he describes the steps of the expedited method for exterminating Christians: arrest the suspects, question them and execute those who avow their allegiance to Christianity.

Concealing the Secret Meaning of the Cross Symbol

Another motive for not displaying the cross was to keep its symbolic meaning a secret. Above all, the cross is the sacred sign of a people who were protected and baptized by God, who leads Christian followers to their salvation. The cross is a unifying symbol that even today inspires a feeling of belonging among the members of the Christian community.

FINDINGS OF THE STUDY

Therefore, contrary to the three arguments brought forward by the majority bloc, my research allows me to make the following statement:

Christians have most likely used the cross symbol since the first century A.D.

I base this statement on the facts I have already presented, which demonstrate the Christian origin of the artifact, and on the oldest Rotas Squares found in Pompeii, which date back to before 79.[31]

Finally, my assertion is supported by the method used to conceal the cross. Numerous Christian drawings from the early centuries, like the anchor, the boat mast and the plow, concealed a cross within the symbol.[32] The epistle to the Hebrews (6:19) in the New Testament associates the anchor with hope. The symbol of the fish, which represents Jesus Christ, is sometimes combined with the symbol of the anchor; together they form the cross of Christ. We can also add a drawing of the mast of a boat that conceals a cross symbol, discovered in the Christian catacombs, as well as a drawing of Christian origin containing a set of letters in the form of a cross, found in the Baths of Neptune at Ostia Antica.[33] In addition, 20th-century French Cardinal Jean Daniélou reveals that when Bishop Irenaeus of Lyon and the apologist Justin Martyr saw a plow in the second century, they did in fact discern the cross.[34]

The key point here is that the earliest Christian communities used the same method of concealing the cross in their drawings as the creator of the Magic Square who hid the symbol of the cross in the two words *tenet.*

Supported by Cardinal Jean Daniélou

Cardinal Jean Daniélou specifies that the central cross of the Sator Square, formed with the two words *tenet,* represents a plow, as does the shape of Jesus Christ's cross. He believes that the combination of the two materials used in the plow, iron and wood, referred to by Irenaeus in *Against Heresies,*[35] corresponds to the complete integration of the human and the divine in the body of Jesus Christ.[36] All of the cardinal's concepts are present in the Sator Square.

Cardinal Daniélou explicitly names the Sator Square in his book. He agrees with French historian Jérôme Carcopino that second-century Bishop

Irenaeus of Lyon was very familiar with the Sator Square.[37] The cardinal also supports Carcopino's statement that each T at the beginning and end of the two words *tenet*, forms the extremities of an equilateral cross and represent a *tau* cross flanked by the letters "A" and "O." According to them, each of these *tau* crosses is located between Alpha and Omega;[38] it represents verse 22:13 of the book of Revelation: "I am the Alpha and the Omega, the first and the last, the beginning and the end."

Photo 4: A Sator Square engraved on the side of a barn portal near a castle that is now almost completely in ruins. The castle belonged to an old Templar commandery in Jarnac (Charente-Maritime). *Photo credit: Speraro.*

224 | THE IMPRINT OF JESUS, THE SON OF GOD

Thus, the eminent Cardinal firmly believes that Christians were using the symbol of the cross in the early centuries A.D. His explanations also support my previous findings that the Sator Square is of Christian origin.

In conclusion, even though the cross symbol was concealed, it seems clear that it has been highly venerated by Christians since the very beginning of Christianity. In *The Sign of the Cross*, Rancour-Laferriere says that the scandal of the cross forms part of the *Gospel* of Jesus Christ.[39] Indeed, the creator of the Sator Square included a cross symbol that went from being an offensive to a victorious one in the early centuries A.D. I hope that the majority bloc position will be reconsidered and even abandoned. For me, this current position is a major obstacle to an appropriate study of the cradle of Christianity.

11

THE SINGLE PATH

It is said that God is the architect and builder of the foundations of His city (Heb. 11:10). Irenaeus, bishop of Lyon adds:

> He, Himself, indeed, having need of nothing, but granting communion with Himself to those who stood in need of it, and sketching out, like an architect, the plan of salvation to those that pleased Him.[1]

God has set out an architectural plan of His city. An architectural plan, commonly known as a "blueprint," is usually a graphic and technical representation of a building provided by an architect, which guides its construction and related activities. The plan includes instructions that must be carefully executed to reflect the architect's requirements.

As seen in Chapter 9, the Gospel of Christ contains God's great plan of salvation. Through his Son Jesus Christ, God—the architect—gave the apostles the divine blueprint that must be followed to build the divine temple that is required for eternal salvation.

THE BASIC COMPONENTS OF THE DIVINE BLUEPRINT

This book's claim that the Sator Square is the Gospel of Christ means that the artifact is engraved with God's technical instructions, which must be meticulously followed in the construction of the divine building.

As we saw in Chapter 2, the seven key themes related to the grace of God, human free will and their interaction are technical instructions that were extracted from the two sentences of the Magic Square with the aim of uncovering the artifact's origin. Now let us look more closely at the technical instructions found in the Sator Square, concentrating on four basic components that are present in the artifact. These components focus on what humans must do to be saved, what can be expected by following the path, and the role of the cross symbol in the salvation process. These components are immensely important, because they establish the framework of the divine dwelling and are used to obtain salvation. Each of the four basic components of the Sator Square, together with a brief explanation, is indicated in Figure 11.1.

The first two components deal with the two fundamental freedoms that are given to human beings, that is, the freedom to believe and the freedom to work in synergy or through integration with the divine. How should human beings exercise those freedoms to reach their salvation? The third component concerns the destination, "the harvest." What are the expected outcomes when human beings arrive at their destination? The final component concerns the cross symbol in the center of the artifact. But what exactly does this symbol mean and where is it on the salvation path?

In Figure 11.1, I have provided an illustration to help us visualize where each of these components is found on the path to salvation.

Figure 11.1 The Components of the Magic Square

chuckstock/SunshineVector/Shutterstocks.com

1. To believe: Believing is implied in the artifact and occurs at the moment when someone agrees to follow the path of the divine power who holds the plow. In the illustration, this freedom is exercised at the intersection of the two ways. Believing means agreeing to embark on the path of life with the divine power, after receiving grace.

2. To work: This means agreeing to cooperate by working (or turning) with the divine power. Both wills—divine and human—are necessary to reach salvation. In the artifact, this occurs when the Christian obeys by turning with the divine power. This liberty can be exercised at any time along the path.

3. The Harvest: The concept of harvest is strongly implied in the artifact. However, the outcome of the harvest, located at the end of the path, is unclear.

4. The Cross Symbol: Although the cross symbol is present in the Sator Square, its meaning and exact role are not yet clearly identified.

Although these components are paramount, they are not detailed, so they leave room for interpretation; they are not all understood in the same way by Christians. This chapter will show that two influential Christian groups that were deemed heretical or unorthodox in the first four centuries A.D. followed the four components of the Magic Square. Figures for both groups will illustrate their understanding of the components and where they are located on the salvation path.

THE DIVINE BLUEPRINT ACCORDING TO ADOPTIONISM

During the early centuries of the Christian era, several Christian groups emerged with varied perceptions of the identity and message of Jesus.

Ebionites and the Jerusalem Church

One of these Judeo-Christian groups, known as "Ebionites," a word derived from the Hebrew, meaning "poor," believed that Jesus of Nazareth was only a prophet; he was merely a human being.[2] This group was considered heretical by some Church Fathers.[3] Studying the Ebionites is particularly important to understanding the earliest Judeo-Christians, because the group might be closely linked to, or even the successor to, the group called "the Disciples of the Way," "the Way," and later "the Jerusalem Church." The Disciples of the Way represented the first Judeo-Christian movement that brought together the close followers of Jesus of Nazareth. Apostles Peter and John were part of the group, which formed the Jerusalem Church led by James, the brother of Jesus. Indeed, Ebionism and the Jerusalem Church share two important concepts.

The first commonality is the belief that Jesus disclosed the path to salvation. The Ebionites considered Jesus to be the second messianic prophet announced to Moses by God, who was to bring the words of God.[4]

I will raise up a prophet from among their countrymen like you [Moses], and I will put My words in his mouth, and he shall speak to them all that I command him. (Deut. 18:18).

Likewise, the fact that the Jerusalem Church was called "The Way" shows that its members learned how to follow the path of life offered by God through Jesus of Nazareth, the prophet. Some of the early Judeo-Christian groups therefore identified Christ as a prophet[5]—at least for a while. However, the extreme devotion and total commitment to Jesus Christ by the Disciples of the Way—they were even willing to die for him—demonstrate that he was much more than one prophet among many, contrary to what the general Jewish population believed about Jesus.[6] The second commonality between Ebionism and the Jerusalem Church is their strong emphasis on righteousness. In the Ebionites' view, Jesus of Nazareth fulfilled the righteousness of God through his obedience. Thus, humans need to follow his path of righteousness. The Jerusalem Church also demonstrated the importance of righteousness by calling their leader James the Just. This showed that he was renowned as someone who manifested exemplary justice. James certainly wanted to imitate Jesus of Nazareth and show the path of righteousness leading to salvation for others to follow. Also, in his New Testament letter, James highlighted the importance of labor (good deeds) in the process of salvation.

Finally, both Judeo-Christian groups unquestionably recognized Jesus as a prophet of the Word of God and as a teacher. They also tried to imitate Jesus's exemplary life. To them, Jesus was an exceptional human being endowed with utmost wisdom.[7] The key point for now is that the two commonalities of the Ebionites and the Jerusalem Church are clearly present in the Sator Square. The artifact is the path of righteousness that comes from the teaching of Jesus.

Adoptionism

The Ebionites believed that Jesus' path was perfect, which allowed him to become the Son of God after his baptism by John the Baptist. This conviction is known as Adoptionism or "Low Christology.

Low Christology

The doctrine begins with the principle that Jesus is fundamentally a mere human. After having led an exemplary life, he was exalted and divine power dwelt in him. Low Christology, also known as "**Adoptionist Christology,**" holds that God the Father chose and adopted Jesus of Nazareth as a divine Son at a specific point in his life (whether during his baptism or Resurrection). Thus, Christ ascended from a mere human being to a divine one.

High Christology

The doctrine of High Christology, which we will cover in greater depth in the next chapter, states that Christ is eternal; he pre-existed as a divine being. Known as the Word or the Wisdom, he was present during the creation of the world. When Jesus Christ was born, the divine Word was incarnated among humans. Thus, this doctrine is often connected to "**Incarnational Christology**," in which Christ the divine descended by coming to Earth.

The first adherents of Adoptionism, generally Judeo-Christian groups such as the Ebionites, claimed that Jesus of Nazareth's particular human characteristics allowed him to be adopted by God and make the path known to humanity. They recognized Jesus as a prophet, a teacher, and the most righteous of all human beings. These Judeo-Christian groups mainly promoted "jesuism," an ideology focused on the life of Jesus of Nazareth.

Thus, Jesus basically fulfills the fundamental expectation of the Jewish people about the coming of a fully human messiah who would save them and establish the new world. Furthermore, these groups did not recognize the high Christology belief that before his birth, Jesus Christ pre-existed as a divine being called the Word and the Wisdom. Did the Adoptionist groups follow the Gospel of Christ (the Sator Square)? To answer this question, we need to pay attention to Apollos.

Apollos, the Alexandrian Jew

Biblical passages about Apollos truly enlighten our understanding of the early Judeo-Christian groups. The Apostle Paul came up against the preacher Apollos on a few occasions during his travels. The latter was undoubtedly a Christian, as he preached to the Jews that Jesus was the Messiah (Acts 18:28).

Baptism by Apollos Without Jesus Christ

The Apostle Paul criticized Apollos, saying that his baptisms, conducted based on John the Baptist's method, were inappropriate or incomplete (Acts 18:25; 19:3). According to Paul, Apollos was not baptizing in the name of Jesus Christ (Acts 19:5), therefore he was not giving the Holy

THE SINGLE PATH | 235

Spirit to the people he was baptizing, as Apollos was unaware of the correct way to administer a baptism (Acts 19:2-5).

The fact that Jesus Christ was not recognized in Apollos' baptisms undoubtedly means that he was not directly required to achieve human salvation, meaning that Apollos did *not* consider Jesus Christ to be God, who saves humans.

Apollos Followed the Way

Even if Apollos considered that Jesus was not directly required to obtain eternal salvation, Paul nonetheless recognized that Apollos was following the same path, meaning that they both used the same divine blueprint. This is demonstrated in the following New Testament passages:

- Apollos "has been instructed in the way of the Lord" (Acts 18:24).

- Apollos is like a "brother" (1 Cor. 16:12).[8] Specifically, Christians who refer to "brothers" and "sisters" consider them to be individuals who follow the same path of life, even if they have a different interpretation of the instructions on how to follow the path.[9] As we saw previously, Augustine of Hippo used the same figure of speech by referring to John

Cassian as a "brother." This is the recognition of Christian unity in plurality within one and the same truth.

- "I planted, Apollos watered, but God was causing the growth .... Now he who plants and he who waters are one; but each will receive his own reward according to his own labor" (1 Cor. 3:6, 3:8). Once again, Paul shows that they are both following the divine path, and that they are of equal importance. Like the Magic Square, this excerpt takes place in an agricultural setting. Paul indicates that his primary mission is to plant, meaning to pave the way by preaching the Gospel of Christ "so that the cross of Christ would not be made void" (1 Cor. 1:17). To Paul, planting means laying the foundation of the divine temple, while watering—that is, baptizing, as Apollos has been doing—means building on that foundation. Paul was careful to inform the Corinthians that a person can only build on Jesus Christ, who is both the foundation and the temple of God (1 Cor. 3:11-15).

To sum up, according to Paul, a person is a Christian if he or she follows the divine blueprint and believes that Jesus, whether human or divine, is Christ. This means that Apollos was a Christian, even though he did not baptize people in the name of Jesus and did not, at least for a while, think that Jesus was necessary during a baptism.

Was the Jerusalem Church an Adoptionist Group?

The Jerusalem Church was comprised of people who lived with Jesus, such as his apostles. It is very likely that the members of this group were adherents of Adoptionism at some point, considering the two commonalities that they shared with the Ebionites. In addition, Apollos, who as we will see was an Adoptionist, was probably also a member of the Jerusalem Church and sent on a mission by the apostle James. However, there is no incontrovertible proof that the doctrine of Adoptionism was embraced by the Jerusalem Church. Paul suggested that there were up to four possible *interpretations* of the divine message: those of Paul, Apollos, Peter and perhaps even Jesus.[10] Did the Apostle James, the head of the Jerusalem Church, have the same interpretation as Peter[11] or Apollos? In fact, it may be that there were only two interpretations: that of Paul, who preached High Christology, which we will examine in the next chapter, and that of others, such as the Ebionites, Apollos and probably for a while the apostle James, who preached the doctrine of Adoptionism, or Low Christology. The New Testament shows that Peter's position changed from Low to High Christology. Peter acquired a more universal view of salvation,[12] similar to that of Paul. In many instances, Peter, occasionally accompanied by John, baptized people in the name of Jesus Christ.[13] It is quite plausible that the members of the Jerusalem Church changed their interpretation of the message of salvation and the identity of Jesus. The evangelist John specifies that after the Resurrection of Christ, Jesus' disciples suddenly believed and understood Jesus' words (Jn. 2:21-22). As mentioned in Chapter 5, the ongoing process of understanding by the apostles concurs with the principle that the Divine Revelation transmitted by Jesus Christ evolves over time until the Parousia (his return).

The Same Path to Be Followed by All, According to Adoptionism

If, as I claim, Adoptionist groups like the Ebionites did in fact follow the Magic Square, figure 11.2 shows how they interpret it.

Figure 11.2 Adoptionist Understanding of the Magic Square

chuckstock/SunshineVector/Shutterstocks.com

1. <u>To believe:</u> This means to believe in the one God, after receiving grace.

2. <u>To work:</u> It requires both wills.

A. <u>Divine Will:</u>

It originates *solely from God*.

B. <u>Human Will:</u>

This means Jesus of Nazareth, as a human being, remained in a close covenant relationship with God to walk his own way, as others must do for their own path of salvation.

3. <u>Harvest:</u> The Christian who follows the path of righteousness is bound to God and will be resurrected (the harvest). The exaltation of Jesus of Nazareth, at his baptism or at his Resurrection, demonstrates that he was totally bound to God due to his exemplary life.

4. Cross symbol: The meaning and the location of the cross on the path of life are explained below.

In their view, there is only one path for all human beings to follow. It is identical to the one that Jesus, a mere human, took; however, he followed it to perfection, which is what makes him the Son of God. Therefore, the primary focus of Adoptionism is on Jesus' human characteristics, which ultimately led to his exaltation.

Finally, according to Adoptionism, throughout their journey, human beings can *only* rely on synergy with God, *not* with Jesus Christ.

The Cross Symbol and Adoptionism?

To complete Figure 11.2, we need to understand what the cross symbol in the center of the Sator Square might mean to Adoptionists. But first, we have to examine another pseudonym of the Tradition (i.e., the Sator Square, according to my research): the "rule of faith," which we briefly mentioned in Chapter 5.

The Rule of Faith

The "rule of faith," *regula fidei* in Latin, or the "rule of truth" is linked with the Gospel[14] and with the Tradition.[15]

The rule of faith was used in the time of the Apostle Paul; he referred to it in the following passage: "And those who will walk by this rule, peace and mercy be upon them, and upon the Israel of God" (Gal. 6:16). This rule, although cited, was not defined. The first Apostolic Father, Clement of Rome, confirmed that this rule did exist at the end of the first century.[16]

A century later, Bishop Irenaeus of Lyon specified that the rule of faith had been used during baptism since the beginning of Christianity.[17] Furthermore, the Gospel of Christ has also been related to baptism.[18] As such, my study raises the question of how the Sator Square—a pseudonym of the rule of faith and of the Gospel of Christ—was used during baptism.

Indeed, the rite of baptism has many elements that can also be found in the artifact.

- Rite of initiation: Without a doubt, experts agree that the baptism of Jesus of Nazareth did in fact take place.[19] The four gospels recount the event in their opening pages. According to

Christianity, baptism is an extremely important rite of initiation; it is the first sacrament, the first step on the path to salvation. In the Sator Square, the rite of initiation occurs when a person believes in the divine call and wishes to remain with the divine power—by figuratively embarking on the plow.

- Profession of Faith and Incorporation into the Body of Christ: During baptism, a Christian becomes united with the body of Christ. As explained in Chapter 2, the notion "to be in Christ" is figuratively represented by the sower in the Sator Square. The sower portrays both the divine part and the human part that walk together on the path.

- Covenant with a Seal: Baptism reflects the covenant between the human being and the divine. This relationship is contractual and requires a sign or seal.[20] Receiving the divine seal confirms entry to and membership in the Christian community. The cross symbol is considered to be the Christian seal of the covenant, which is displayed in the center of the Sator Square.

- Repentance and Conversion: To be baptized, the individual must believe and repent.[21] "Repent, and each of you be baptized in the name of Jesus Christ for the forgiveness of your sins; and you will receive the gift of the Holy Spirit (Acts 2:38)." The individual must have a conversion of the heart. As seen in Chapter 8, the verbs "to repent" and "to convert" are reflected in the Sator Square by the verb "to turn," or *sûb* in Hebrew.

Ultimately, all the elements of baptism are found in the Sator Square, as in the rule of faith. Thus the Sator Square seems to have been used to administer baptisms in the early centuries A.D.

Baptism by John the Baptist

With the exception of Paul, Christ's apostles had one thing in common: they were baptized by John the Baptist.[22] This apostolic criterion was paramount. In fact, after the death of Jesus, the twelfth apostle chosen to replace Judas had to be baptized by John the Baptist (Acts 1:22). In addition, Jesus was baptized by John the Baptist and supported his mission on numerous occasions.[23]

Baptism administered by John the Baptist occurred when an individual became a member of a messianic group. The person being baptized understood that he or she was entering into a covenant with the divine and undoubtedly saw the rite of baptism as a new starting point and a restoration. In preaching *the Gospel of God,* John the Baptist demanded that people believe and repent (Mk. 1:14-15). As we have seen, these are the same requests that appear in the Magic Square, as the two sentences ask people to answer the divine call by figuratively embarking on the plow (to believe) and turning (to repent). Therefore, the baptisms performed using John the Baptist's method share similarities with the artifact.

A Fundamental Question

To determine what the cross symbol meant to Adoptionists, let us consider that:

- Jesus Christ gave the Magic Square to his apostles for the purpose of baptizing the faithful,

- all the apostles who were baptized by John the Baptist administered the rite of baptism of repentance according to John the Baptist's method to others, such as Apollos, and

- this type of baptism did not specify Christ's name, at least for a period of time following the death of Christ.

If we accept these points, then how might the apostles have interpreted the cross symbol in the Magic Square used for baptisms, if not as a symbol of the death and Resurrection of Jesus Christ?

My answer to this question is the following:

> ***To the apostles of Jesus Christ, the cross symbol in the Sator Square originally represented the Hebrew letter tav.***

The statement in the previous chapter was that the symbol of the cross had been used by early Christians since the first century; however, it was not specified what the cross *represented* to them before and shortly after the crucifixion of Christ.

The Semitic Letter Tav or Taw: + or X

The *tav* is the twenty-second and final letter of the Semitic alphabet and is in the form of the letter "x" or the Greek cross "+." This letter is a rich Hebrew symbol that encompasses a variety of meanings in the Old Testament. In the book of Job (31:35) the *tav* is a signature. The *tav* is also the signature with God's name, and probably the name of the divine Messiah.[24] While the *tav* bears the name of God, his name is unknown. To Jewish people, the name of God is extremely important and sacred, since it represents the divine power needed for salvation;[25] the *name of God* is nothing less than *God Himself*. As per the Hebrew tradition, the sign (or seal) is applied to people's foreheads, indicating that they now belong exclusively to God; they "bear the *tav*" or "bear the name." In the book of Ezekiel (9:4-6), the prophet reveals that the faithful who have this sign on their forehead will be saved by the divine power. Those who receive this sign are now among God's chosen people, or part of the covenant with God. Therefore, the sign takes on an eschatological aspect, given that the people who "bear the name" will be saved.[26]

The first Judeo-Christian groups were familiar with the *tav* symbol. Apollos and other Christians baptized the first Christians according to John the Baptist's method. For them, the cross symbol in the middle of the artifact shows the *tav*, the name of God, or God Himself, and not the death and Resurrection of Jesus Christ. They join a group whose members God alone will protect.

This observation confirms what many writers, such as Cardinal Jean Daniélou, believe:

> Nowadays the sign of the cross normally calls to mind the gibbet to which Christ was nailed. But we have to ask ourselves whether this was the primary origin of the sign on the forehead in the primitive Christine community. It seems indeed that it was not, that in the beginning it was a matter of a sign that had a different significance.[27]

As mentioned, Apollos did not baptize "in the name of the Lord Jesus" (Acts 19:5). Therefore, when administering baptism, he did not perceive the direct salvation power of Christ in the symbol of the cross (the *tav*). We can now complete the fourth component of the cross symbol from Figure 11.2 for Adoptionism:

4. Cross Symbol: The symbol of the cross, formed with the words *tenet,* indicates the name of God (*tav*) among Adoptionist groups. In the illustration, the cross is located at the intersection of the paths, since it is required at the beginning of a process in baptism; it represents a rite of passage into a messianic group supported by God.

Therefore, to Adoptionists, the symbol of the cross or *tav* was not associated with the Crucifixion, death or Resurrection of Jesus Christ—it represented the symbol and the name of the One God.

Some writers try to show that the baptisms of repentance advocated by John the Baptist are completely different from those advocated by Jesus. However, some New Testament passages (Acts 1:5; 11:16; 13:24) state that the baptisms performed by John the Baptist were not inaccurate or ineffective, but instead incomplete, until the coming of Jesus Christ.

Evangelists proclaimed that John the Baptist paved the way for Jesus Christ. Therefore, the baptisms advocated by Christ were also baptisms of repentance, like those of John the Baptist, but Christ completed them through his arrival, death and Resurrection.

In summary, Adoptionism advocated that Jesus was a mere human who became divine, and that every human being (including Jesus) must follow the same path. Neither of these notions contradict in any way the four components of the divine plan in the Sator Square—they actually support them, as illustrated in Figure 11.2.

THE DIVINE BLUEPRINT ACCORDING TO THE ARIANS

A few centuries later, Arius, a monk from Alexandria who became a presbyter, professed a doctrine called "Arianism", which was not universally endorsed. In fact, the Arians became one of the fiercest heretical groups that the Church has faced over the course of its history. Particularly in the fourth century, Arianism shook the Catholic institution and its existing internal structure.

Arius's ideas and his degree of political influence remain highly polemic subjects, because few of his documents have survived. His ideas have often been restated in the subjective writing of his adversaries.

Looking at the divine blueprint, one might believe that Arianism did not follow Tradition. But is that really the case?

A Created God, but Not God

The central point of Arius's doctrine clearly hinges on the desire to maintain the transcendence and distance of a single God, who is not created and who is eternal, absolute, and completely separate from everything.[28] To Arius, Jesus Christ, the Son of

God, can only be a creature; he was created by God the Father. What is the opinion of the Arians on the nature of this creature? Alexander of Alexandria, the anti-Arian patriarch, stated that the Arians considered Jesus to be a simple human being[29] like other humans. According to Alexander, Arius's doctrine was similar to that of the Ebionites.[30]

Although the Son of God (the Word) was a creature in Arius's view, Jesus' status was higher than that of a common mortal or a mere human. In fact, Arius proclaimed Jesus Christ to be the Son of God the divine, the first begotten by God the Father, and present during the creation of the universe.

Although he declared that "the Word is God" (Jn. 1:1), Arius did not consider that god as eternal or as God the Father, but simply *a created god*. He believed that the Son of God is not of the same substance as God the Father, since the latter is completely separate from everything. Subordinate to the Supreme God, this god named "the Word" was able to become flesh and suffer to save humanity, because he was inferior to the Supreme God. This contradicts the orthodox Catholic position, which considers that the Son of God was not created; he has always existed and is of the same substance as God the Father.

Figure 11.3 Arian Understanding of the Magic Square

chuckstock/SunshineVector/Shutterstocks.com

1. To believe: This means to believe in the one God the Father.

2. To work: It requires both wills.
A. Divine Will:
It originates *solely from God the Father*.
Being unique in nature, God the Father is the only one who has the grace that is necessary for salvation.
B. The Will of a Creature:
Each creature needs to maintain its participation with God. Since Christ was made, like humans, of a substance that is foreign to God the Father, Christ had to participate with God, as other human beings subsequently had to do.

3. Harvest: The harvest means to reach sanctification by participating with God the Father.

4. Cross Symbol: To Arians, the cross symbol primarily represents God the Father or "the name of God." It represents neither the death nor the resurrection of Christ, but his Passion expiated the sins of the world.

Arius believed that Christ calls himself "god" only because he participated (in synergy) with the Supreme God.[31] If, as I claim, Arius used the Sator Square, then figure 11.3 illustrates how he interpreted it. To the Arians, there is only one way to follow.

The path taken by the Son of God as a creature, even if he is divine, is the *same* path as that of every other human creature and only differs by time.[32] The path of the Son of God that was followed in close synergy with God the Father made him divine.[33]

This principle of the *single path* resembles that of the Ebionites. According to the Arians, all human beings must have an exclusive synergistic participation with God the Father and *not* with the Son of God, because God the Father and the Son of God do not have the same substance. Arians believe that all the grace of Christ was given to him by God the Father; it did not emanate from him.

To the Arians, the Son of God, being an inferior god, was able to become flesh and ultimately suffer for the forgiveness of human sin. Therefore, there is some connection between the Passion of the Son of God and the salvation of the faithful given the importance that Arius placed on divine suffering for human salvation.[34]

The Trinitarian doctrine spoken during baptism, "in the name of the Father, the Son and the Holy Spirit," means that the baptized person recognizes that God is the one God in three persons who have one and the same substance. However, while Arius supported this Trinitarian statement, he assigned a very different meaning to the Trinity.[35] Likely influenced by Neoplatonic philosophy,[36] he saw this Trinitarian list as a hierarchical order based on importance. Consequently, the Father is much more important than the Son and both are more important than the Holy Spirit. They make up three distinct hypostases or substances. Thus, prior to the Nicene-Constantinopolitan Creed promulgated in A.D. 381, two baptized Christians who believed in the Trinity did not necessarily have the same understanding of the concept. The Arians provided a plausible but limited interpretation of the Trinity. The Arian position resembles the Ebionites'

Adoptionist position, which talks about a single path for everyone, but differs from the latter in the nature of Jesus, his pre-existence and his role during baptism.

The ideas of the Arians coincided in large part with the divine blueprint of the Sator Square. If the Sator Square truly is the secret deposit held by the Church, it is not surprising, that the Arians would be familiar with it, given that some Arians held office and were influential individuals within the Catholic Church itself, like bishops Eusebius of Nicomedia and Theognis of Nicaea.

By relying on certain Biblical passages and proposing a plausible interpretation of the divine blueprint, the Arian doctrine became a great threat to the Christian orthodoxy of the period. An array of major defenders of orthodoxy, including Alexander of Alexandria, Athanasius of Alexandria and the Cappadocians, were deployed in an attempt to eradicate the spread of Arianism and its heretic theories.

To summarize, the members of two influential heretical groups—Adoptionism and Arianism— believed that humans, like Jesus, must follow one single path. This path must be made in synergy with God alone, since to them, the symbol of the cross, *tav,* is limited to the name of God the Father.

Even if these two groups conformed to the divine blueprint of the Magic Square to some degree—contrary to the Pelagians—they were still considered heretical because both of their interpretations of the divine blueprint were deemed rudimentary, as we will observe in the next chapter.

12

THE TWO PATHS

oes the Sator Square merely show that the Prophet Jesus of Nazareth became divine by leading an exemplary life?

Two ardent defenders of Catholic orthodoxy, the Apostle Paul and Bishop Athanasius of Alexandria, challenged the heretic groups' interpretations, deeming them false and incomplete.

In this chapter, we will first look at Paul's take on the divine blueprint, which opposed that of the first-century Adoptionist groups. Then we will examine Athanasius's interpretation, which contested the Arian doctrines of the fourth century. Both Paul's and Athanasius' perspectives are consistent with the one the Catholic Church promotes.

THE DIVINE BLUEPRINT ACCORDING TO THE APOSTLE PAUL

Unlike the Adoptionist groups, the Pauline position understands the essential role of Jesus Christ during baptism and in the salvation of human beings.

Believing in Jesus Christ

In the New Testament, believing in Jesus Christ is a mandatory condition of salvation:

> Therefore I said to you that you will die in your sins; for unless you believe that I am He, you will die in your sins (Jn. 8:24).

> Believe in the Lord Jesus, and you will be saved, you and your household (Acts 16:31).

Believing is paramount for Paul as well. Not just believing in God, as the vast majority of Jews believe, but believing in God the Father *through* the Son of God, since it is through God's Son that salvation is possible.

For Paul, using the cross symbol during baptism represents the need to believe in Jesus Christ in order to walk with him and in him on the path to salvation. The evangelist Mark supports Paul when he says:

> The one who has believed and has been baptized will be saved; but the one who has not believed will be condemned (16:16).

Death and Rebirth

Baptism is a very important step in salvation. It is often perceived as the beginning of a new life; however, for Paul, the rite signifies much more than the beginning of a new life or a rebirth.

Paul goes further when he clarifies the importance of Christ in baptism:

> Or do you not know that all of us who have been baptized into Christ Jesus have been baptized into His death? Therefore, we have been buried with Him through baptism into death, so that as Christ was raised from the dead through the glory of the Father, so we too might walk in the newness of life... Now if we have died with Christ, we believe that we shall also live with Him, knowing that Christ, having been raised from the dead, is never to die again (Rom. 6:3-4 and 8).

During baptism, every individual must first die to sin with Christ who was raised, so that he or she can then be reborn to life with and in him. In essence, baptism is an imitation of the death and rebirth of Christ.[1]

Baptism and Death/Resurrection According to John

The third chapter of the gospel of John also establishes the connection between baptism and the death and Resurrection of Christ.

- Baptism: When Jesus meets his disciple Nicodemus, a high-ranking Pharisee, he says to him: "Truly, truly, I say to you, unless one is born of water and the Spirit he cannot enter into the kingdom of God." (Jn. 3:3). Being born again involves a baptism of water and the Holy Spirit (Jn. 3:5).

- Death and Resurrection: In his discussion with Nicodemus, Jesus makes an unusual connection:

  As Moses lifted up the serpent in the wilderness, even so must the Son of Man be lifted up; so that whoever believes will in Him have eternal life (Jn. 3:14-15).

In this excerpt, Jesus is referring to the Old Testament book of Numbers. A passage from this book recounts that the Hebrews committed the sin of speaking against God and Moses on several occasions while walking in the desert during their exodus from Egypt. To punish them, God sent venomous serpents, which killed many of them. Repenting their sin, those who remained then asked Moses to pray for them. Then at God's command:

Moses made a bronze serpent and set it on the standard; and it came about, that if a serpent bit any man, when he looked to the bronze serpent, he lived (Nb. 21:9).

The Hebrews had to look skyward at the serpent on the perch to be saved. Thus, when Jesus says to Nicodemus that the Son of man has to be lifted up like the serpent of Moses to have eternal life, he is inviting Nicodemus not only to be reborn through baptism, but also to lift his eyes to him who will be crucified. Jesus Christ is the solution and the sole intermediary who can save Nicodemus and humanity.[2] Thus, Christians must die and be reborn with Christ through baptism.

Paul emphasizes the importance of believing that Jesus Christ *died* for the sins of human beings and then was *raised* to free humans from their sins and for their resurrection. If those two assertions are not accepted as one statement, then Christ died in vain, and Paul concludes: "And if Christ has not been raised, your faith is worthless; you are still in your sins. Then also those who have fallen asleep in Christ have perished" (1 Cor. 15:17-18).

The Two Different Paths According to Paul

In the New Testament, Jesus often challenges his disciples to "follow" him (Mt. 16:24). He is not speaking solely to the disciples who accompanied him, but to every human being. What does it mean to follow Jesus? Should human beings follow exactly the same path as Jesus?

Contrary to Adoptionism and Arianism, who believe that the path traveled by Jesus and the path of humanity are identical, Paul states that they are two different paths. First, Jesus leads by embarking on his own path; then Christians make their own way with Jesus's help. If Paul used the Magic Square, figure 12.1 illustrates how he interpreted the components of the artifact for each of the two different paths.

Figure 12.1 Understanding of the Magic Square by Paul

i)　　**The Specific Path of Jesus Christ**

chuchstock/syncdesignsolutions/Shutterstock.com

1. To believe: Although Jesus believes in God the father, he has a fully divine nature in him. In the illustration, Jesus Christ is at the fork in the road, as he is both fully divine and fully human from birth.

2. To work: Requires both wills (divine and human). This will be explained when we look at Athanasius's position.

3. Harvest: Christ enables human beings to be freed from their sins through his Crucifixion and Resurrection, both of which are illustrated at the end of the path. Therefore, he clears the path that leads to the gate of the Kingdom of God.

4. Cross Symbol: The cross stands at the end of Christ's path. It represents his Passion, Crucifixion and Resurrection.

ii)   The Path of a Christian

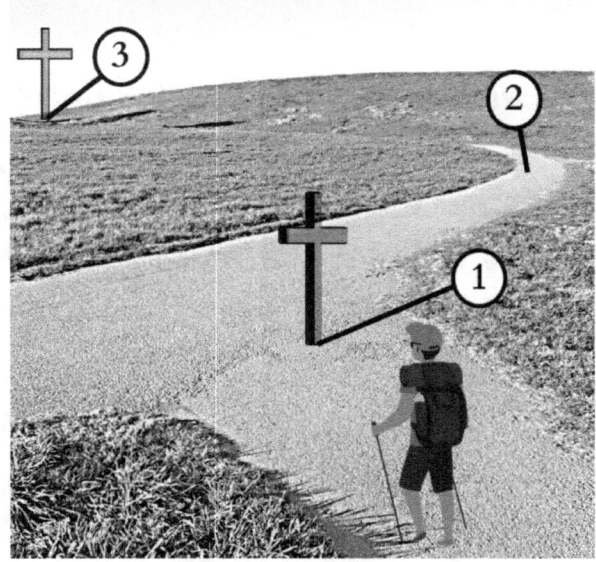

chuckstock/SunshineVector/Shutterstocks.com

1. To believe: After receiving grace, this means to believe in Christ.by agreeing to die and be reborn in him.

2. To work: Requires both wills.

A. Divine Will: Originates from God the Father *through His Son Jesus Christ.*

B. Human Will: This means that the Christian wants to cooperate (to turn) with Christ (the only intermediary) and to be part of his mystical resurrected body.

3. Harvest: In Christ, each human being created in the image and likeness of the Son of God can be sanctified and obtain eternal life at the end of the path.

4. Cross Symbol: The cross at the beginning of the path represents the willingness to die and be reborn in Christ. The cross at the end means "to be resurrected." In a sense, the cross is present

> throughout the life of a Christian, as it is in all the sacraments.

In other words, the *path of Jesus Christ* on Earth began when the Word (i.e., Jesus Christ) became flesh. He came to Earth to take the path that humans must take. At the end of his path, Christ died and rose again for the remission of human sins.[3] His Resurrection was a declaration, confirming that he was the Son of God and that he had come to save humanity.

In addition, the *path of a Christian* begins when a person answers the call and professes faith in Jesus Christ, the Son of God by agreeing to die and be reborn with him.

Through Christ, human beings can be reconciled with God and can follow the path of life. Like the first sentence of the Sator Square, it is an individual invitation. Jesus Christ visits each person separately: "Behold, I stand at the door and knock; if anyone hears My voice and opens the door, I will come in to him and will dine with him, and he with Me" (Rev. 3:20). Like the second sentence of the artifact, the Christian is called to turn toward Jesus Christ and to remain with him "always, to the end of the age" (Mt. 28:20). The gospel of John states:

Then Jesus again spoke to them, saying, "I am the Light of the world; he who follows Me will not walk in the darkness, but will have the Light of life" (8:12).

Therefore, according to Paul, a Christian needs to walk with Jesus Christ to obtain salvation. In his view, it does not matter if the grace required for salvation comes only from Christ,[4] or jointly with that of God;[5] in fact, Paul attaches great importance to Christ as the *only* intermediary or mediator of salvation.

The Central Link Between the Two Paths

Even though the path of Jesus Christ and a Christian's path are different, they are closely interlinked and contain several similarities.

In his writings, Paul often professes that the power exercised by Jesus Christ over human beings goes well beyond his earthly life, as opposed to the views of the two heretic groups from the previous chapter. As indicated in the idea of "death and rebirth," the death and Resurrection of Christ allow Christians to be freed from their sins so that they can follow their own path of salvation.

Thus, we must think about the two paths as being *linear and connected*—instead of in parallel, with no intersection as the two heretic groups believe. For Paul, the cross symbol, which signifies the death and Resurrection of Jesus Christ, is the essential link that unites the two paths. Indeed, Christ's death and Resurrection at the end of the path of Christ on Earth are necessary in order to begin the path of a Christian at baptism. The cross is positioned in the middle of the two paths, just as the cross symbol is located in the middle of the Sator Square. The following diagram illustrates this:

The Path of Christ → † → **The Path of a Christian**

For Paul, belief in Jesus Christ occurs when a Christian accepts that the path of Christ becomes an integral part of his or her own path. I can therefore make the following statement:

As with Paul's position, the Magic Square demonstrates that two paths are necessary for salvation: the path of Christ that a Christian must believe in, and the path that a Christian must follow.

This means that the four components of the divine blueprint are used *twice*, as indicated in Figure 12.1. As we will see, Athanasius uses the same interpretation of the artifact as Paul.

To Bear the Name

As noted in Chapter 11, *tav*, which stands for the name of God, has a cross shape. The Hebrew expression "to bear the *tav*" is also called "to bear the name." Thus, some Christian texts from the first two centuries A.D. specify that the faithful bore the name "of the Son of God," "of Christ," or "of Jesus Christ" during their baptism.

These three expressions can be found in various early Christian documents. For instance, the expression "to bear the name of the Son of God"[6] appears in *The Shepherd of Hermas*, a second-century Christian document. Also, in his first epistle, the Apostle Peter mentions "the name of Christ" (4:14). There are other examples in the Acts of the Apostles: "Peter said to them, Repent, and each of you be baptized in the name of Jesus Christ."[7] Furthermore, the Trinitarian formula "baptizing them in the name of the Father and the Son and the Holy Spirit" in the gospel of Matthew (28:19) is illustrated in the cross-shaped *tav*. It is therefore evident that these authors associate Jesus Christ with the *tav*; they establish a link between Christ and the unknown name of God in the Hebrew *tav* and reveal his divine filiation.

This name substitution—which discloses that Jesus Christ is the unknown name of God—seemed to have displeased most Jews. Around the third century, a controversial anti-Christian Jewish document entitled *Toledot Yeshou* accused Jesus of Nazareth of having stolen the name of God, that is, the name of the *tav.*[8]

To Bear the Cross

Many scholars believe that when Jesus asked the crowd to "bear the cross,"[9] the expression is equivalent to "bear the *tav*"[10] or "bear the name."[11]

Indeed, the term "bear the cross" is above all a request to believe in the symbol of the cross as being the name of the Son of God who, through his death and Resurrection, came to save humanity. In other words, it means agreeing to use the indispensable link to salvation that unites the path of Christ with the path of the faithful. It is also a request to bear the symbol of the cross that is not only marked on one's forehead, but also integrated in one's heart throughout the believer's life.

John the Baptist made the essential link between the baptism of a human being and the death of Christ when he said: "Behold, the Lamb of God who takes away the sin of the world!"[12] This statement recalls Chapter 12 of the book of Exodus, in which the Jewish people were protected from death following the spraying of the blood of the sacrificial lamb onto the lintel of their doors.[13] German theologian Erick Dinkler believes that this sign marked with blood was the *tav*.[14] Clearly, there is a connection between the *tav* sign inscribed with the blood of the sacrificial lamb that saved the people of God, and the cross symbolizing the death and Resurrection of Jesus Christ, which saves Christians.

Knowing the rich significance of the Hebrew *tav*, could the early Christians have associated the *tav*'s cross shape with the Crucifixion and Resurrection of Christ? As highlighted in Chapter 11, it is quite likely that the apostles established this link at some point in their lives. As for Paul, an educated Jew who was zealous for God (Acts 22:3), it is clear from his epistles that he did establish this link.

Other Jews were also familiar with the *tav* during the period surrounding the life of Jesus. Jack Finegan, Professor of Archaeology and New

Testament History, says that the *Damascus Document*[15] relates that people who were marked with the *tav* would be saved when the Messiah came. In addition to the *tav*, this Jewish religious manuscript outlines the two notions we saw in Chapter 9: the promised Messiah and the resurrection of those who would become part of the new world.

In short, by asking people to "carry the cross," Jesus Christ was inviting them to accept the *tav* with his name during baptism and to use his grace to obtain eternal salvation. Christ formally asked people to consider him to be divine and the only one who could lead them to salvation.

As mentioned in Chapter 10, Cardinal Jean Daniélou—who obviously knows the Sator Square—believes that Bishop Irenaeus of Lyon and apologist Justin Martyr understood the plow as a cross.[16] Thus, metaphorically speaking, the first sentence of the Sator Square, that the sower holds the plow, means that the sower bears the cross along the path of salvation.

Shortly after the death of Jesus, the cross symbol or *tav* used during baptism revealed not only the divine name of Jesus Christ, but also the presence of God on Earth, who came to save humanity. As mentioned, with his arrival, death and Resurrection, Christ fulfilled the baptisms of repentance preached by John the Baptist.

The essential interconnection between the death and Resurrection of Jesus with baptism is represented by the symbol of the cross in the center of the Sator Square, which has become the symbol of the Christian faith. To Paul, this link is essential "so that the cross of Christ would not be made void" (1 Cor. 1:17).

The Gesture of the Sign of the Cross

Christian tradition has been handing down this gesture since the birth of Christianity. The fourth-century Cappadocian Father, Basil of Caesarea, is perfectly clear about the origin of the sign of the cross when he says that the *unwritten* teachings [the Magic Square] have shown how to "sign with the sign of the cross those who have trusted in the name of our Lord Jesus Christ."[17]

Although this sign is particularly important during baptism, it is also built into all the sacraments. Furthermore, the sign of the cross can be made at any time in a Christian's life. Tertullian of Carthage illustrates this as follows:

At every forward step and movement, at every going in and out, when we put on our clothes and shoes, when we bathe, when we sit at a table, when we light the lamps, on couch, on seat, in all the ordinary actions of daily life, we trace upon the forehead the sign.[18]

This practice shows the divine omnipresence of Jesus Christ in the daily lives of Christians.

The Cross: At the Centre of the Magic Square

The epistles of Paul undeniably focus on Christ, his Crucifixion and his Resurrection. In relation to these specific events, terms such as "central" and "at the center" are repeatedly mentioned in Christian documents. The centrality of Christ is such a popular idea that it generated the word "Christocentrism."

I believe that several authors who know the esoteric content of the Sator Square often play with the double meaning of these terms. For example, some mention that "the cross is at the center of the Christian Faith." In this phrase, people typically understand that the cross is "fundamental" or "essential." However, those who are familiar with the secret Magic Square message understand that these terms indicate—first and foremost—*the central location* of the cross made with the two words *tenet.*

Instead of directly stating that the cross formed by the two words *tenet* is in the center of the Magic Square, many of these authors use similar standardized phrases, composed of the three following parts:

FIRST PART	SECOND PART	THIRD PART
Any word(s) that can be represented by the Symbol of the cross, such as:	Any term that indicates the central location, such as:	Any pseudonym for the Sator Square, such as:
- *Cross*	- *is at the center of*	- *Tradition*
- *Jesus Christ or Christ*	- *stands at the center of*	- *Plan of Salvation*
- *Lamb of God*	- *is the center of*	- *Faith*
- *Paschal Mystery*	- *is centered on*	- *Truth*
- *Crucifixion*	- *is central to*	- *Revelation*
- *Resurrection*		- *Good News*

For example, the *Catechism of the Catholic Church* says, "resurrection stands at the center of the Good News" (CCC 571). This sentence structure can also be found in numerous other Christian documents.[19]

It appears that by using this type of wordplay, the writers are discreetly informing the ecclesiastical elite that they know about the Magic Square and that their positions align with its message.

IMAGINE THIS SCENE

I could not contain my elation when I understood the Apostle Paul's explanations concerning the content of the Magic Square.

I envisioned a scene unfolding barely a few decades after the death of Jesus Christ.

A group of about a dozen Christians gathers at sunrise each morning in an open space, safe from prying eyes, as the town slowly awakes. They typically sing praises, collect testimonies about Jesus Christ and welcome new Christians.

However, today the people at the gathering are particularly eager, because they are waiting for a man who is coming from far away to bring them the Good News, which he supposedly received directly from Jesus Christ. This eagerly awaited man is the Apostle Paul.

Paul finally arrives, limping, at the meeting site. Though fatigued from his long journey, he nonetheless decides to remain standing before the audience and begins to recount the Good

News. Every person in the small group of Christians is watching his every move and drinking in his precious words.

Then suddenly, Paul turns to a 5-by-4 inch (12 cm × 10 cm) Rotas Square engraved on a stone pillar and says, "I have come a long way to explain to you the secret message given by our Lord Jesus Christ, which is written on this stone."

His crooked, trembling forefinger slowly indicates the five words of the Magic Square and he adds, "It is true, as you have heard from some of our brothers, that these five words written on this stone indicate the path of salvation of God." Paul is referring to Christians who preach Adoptionism and only see the plan of salvation of the Magic Square (i.e., the two sentences made with the five words) that was transmitted by the Prophet Jesus of Nazareth.

He continues in a firm, dry tone of voice, peering into the eyes of those who are gathered there, "But I say to you, the essential point of the Good News is not the path."

After a brief sigh, he continues, "Instead, it is the cross of Christ." With the same finger, he traces the cross inscribed with the two words *tenet*, moving his finger up and down, then left to right.

He adds, "This cross shows the death and Resurrection of Jesus Christ, who has saved us, those of us who want to be in him, from the power of evil and death."

"Look! Look closely, he is here!" Paul points at the letter "N" in the center of the cross of the Magic Square, then nods, inviting people to come closer.

When the astounded crowd approaches to get a better look at the stone, Paul concludes by saying, "Christ is here in the center of this cross. Yes, he is here for us. God revealed himself to us through His Son. Jesus Christ is the Sator, the sower, who came to bear the burden of our sins, as the sower bears the weight by holding the plow. Jesus Christ died for us. He is the only solution; he himself is the only path to our salvation."

In this imagined scene, Paul shows that with faith, the cross reveals the true God—Jesus Christ. Astonishingly, the Sator Square reveals the two most dominant Christian positions advocated not long after the death of Jesus Christ: the Low Christology of Adoptionism, which focuses on the path brought by Jesus of Nazareth, and the High Christology of Paul, which focuses on Jesus Christ, who is simultaneously the only mediator, the Son of God—*and the Sator* (the sower). The definitions of High and Low Christology can be found in Chapter 11.

In fact, considering that the Apostle Paul was near Pompeii when he landed at Puteoli (Acts 28:13), a scene like the one I visualized could very well have taken place in the outdoor courtyard in the Large Palestra of Pompeii. Indeed, a small Rotas Square is engraved about 5 feet (1.5 m) off the ground on a stucco-covered tufa column that is part of the colonnade supporting one of the Palestra's four porticoes.

The Birth of the Disciples of Christ

When we look at the New Testament, it is also possible that this scene took place in the city of Antioch. It is said in Acts 11:25-26 that the disciple Barnabas took the Apostle Paul to Antioch, where they taught gatherings of people. Verse 26 ends by saying that the numerous disciples in Antioch were called "Christians" for the first time.

This gives rise to the following questions: Did Paul make the faithful in Antioch aware, through a visual demonstration of the Magic Square, that the central point of the message is Jesus Christ (i.e., the cross) and not the Way of salvation described by the five words? If so, once the faithful understood Paul's perspective, did they then stop referring to themselves as "the disciples of the Way" and instead take on the name "the disciples of Christ?"

THE STUMBLING BLOCK

In the first epistle to the Corinthians, Paul says:

> we preach Christ crucified, to Jews a stumbling block and to Gentiles foolishness (1:23).

In this excerpt, the Apostle Paul evokes the Jewish reticence to associate the crucifixion of Christ with a divine messianic sign. To them, venerating the crucifixion of Christ is a scandal or idolatry. Furthermore, Paul uses the second sense of the Greek word *skandalon* (scandal) that means an obstacle or a stumbling block, which is defined as a stone in the road that one trips over. Given this, I can make the following statement:

*The creator of the artifact wishes to reveal
that the stumbling block for Jews
is the Magic Square.*

In the above excerpt, Paul implies that the Jewish people could not accept that the symbol of the cross represents the crucifixion of Christ. Anyone who believed that the cross-shaped *tav* represents the cross of Christ was simultaneously stating that the name of God *is* Jesus Christ—which to the Jews is truly a scandal.

As we know, numerous Magic Squares are engraved on *stones*. Since the stones have a cross-shaped *tav* in the center, they seemed to become a stumbling block for the Jews. As a result, the Magic Square became an obstacle, preventing the Jews from recognizing the divine Christ. Jesus himself announced that all his disciples will fall away [stumble][20] because of Him (Mt. 26:31).

A Sign and a Parable (Ezekiel 14:1-11)

When I read this passage in the Old Testament book of Ezekiel that mentions this stumbling block, I made another astonishing discovery.

This excerpt says that those among the people of Israel who keep idolatry in their hearts are placing a stumbling block in their own path. Thus, the Jews later relied on that passage to accuse early Christians of idolatry, because they were setting before them the divine symbol of the cross on the Magic Square, which represents the crucifixion of Jesus. Paul countered the Jews' position by saying that instead, they were the ones who had once committed idolatry.

In this passage from Ezekiel, the *word* of the Lord states that before removing a person from the group chosen by God, he will make a "*sign* [*oth (H226)* in Hebrew; the word is linked to the sign of the Covenant][21] *and a proverb* [*masal,* which includes the parable]" so that people will know that he is the Lord (14:8).

The Two Elements of the Stumbling Block

I was truly stunned when I read the passage from Ezekiel. Both elements of this passage appear in the Magic Square: a sign of the covenant, which is the cross, and a parable, which is the Parable of the Sower. Thus, this strongly supports my statement that for the creator of the artifact the Magic Square is the stumbling block.

The Word Is the Lord

A close connection can be made between the stumbling block that is the Magic Square, and the two elements *made by the word* of the Lord. At the end of verse 14:8, it is said that the word of the Lord made the two elements to show that He is the Lord. Consequently, it is obvious that the creator of the artifact is emphasizing that Jesus Christ (the Word) is the Lord. The artifact's existence reveals that the word of the Lord came to earth, and irrefutably illustrates High Christology and the Incarnation of the Word of God.

THE DIVINE BLUEPRINT ACCORDING TO ATHANASIUS

During the First Council of Nicaea in A.D. 325, the Arians came with an interpretation of the mysteries of Christology and the Trinity that sparked a lively debate. The Church was forced to define and deepen the interpretation of its dogma.

Athanasius, secretary to Bishop Alexander during the Council and then bishop of Alexandria beginning in 328, proved to be a skillful opponent of the Arian interpretations. He was among the most tenacious protectors of the Christian faith and one of the most respected and venerated Fathers of the Church. Athanasius of Alexandria bolstered his convictions about Christology and the Trinity with numerous Biblical references. As we will see in the following sections, Athanasius also referred to the Sator Square, considering that he attributed immense importance to respecting tradition.[22]

Christology

This was the first controversial theme at the Council. Christology deals with the nature of Christ and his relationship to God. Was Jesus Christ the Supreme God, an intermediary being, a subordinate god to God the Father, an angel, or in the end, a mere human? These fundamental questions were at the heart of fourth-century Christian discussions.

Jesus Christ Is the Word

Christ's nature is well stated at the beginning of the gospel of John. The passages "In the beginning was the Word, and the Word was with God, and the Word was God" (Jn. 1:1) and "the Word became flesh" (Jn. 1:14) confirm that the Son of God, being the divine Word, was present at the beginning of creation and then became flesh by incarnating as Jesus of Nazareth.

Although he was human by nature, Jesus Christ retained his fully divine, eternal and pre-existing nature. The High Christology position (see the definition in Chapter 11), considers that the divine Christ in the heavens descended with his Incarnation.

The Hypostatic Union of Christ and Incorporation Into Christ

The writings of Athanasius of Alexandria clearly describe hypostatic union (the union of the two natures, divine and human, of Jesus Christ). Thus, Jesus Christ is not considered to be two people, but one single person. Nor is that single person a mixture of two natures, half-human and half-divine, but a single person with both a fully divine and a fully human nature.

The proportion of each nature, divine and human, in the hypostatic union of Jesus Christ reminds us of the concepts of synergy and integration in Jesus Christ that we discussed in Chapter 2. To achieve salvation requires 100% from God and 100% from the person. The integration of these two parts is represented by the incorporation of a Christian into one of the members of the mystical body of Jesus Christ.

To facilitate our understanding, let us look at where the concepts of the hypostatic union of Christ and incorporation into Christ are found in the divine blueprint according to Athanasius.

The Integration Concept on the Path of Christ

The Incarnation, so dear to Athanasius, represents the beginning of the entire divine plan of salvation. He repeats an important passage that was written more than 160 years earlier by Clement of Alexandria:

> The Word of God became man, that you mayest learn from man how man may become God.[23]

He is the Incarnation of divine goodness. The gospel of John attests to the divine fullness of the Son of God when John says that "the Word was God" (1:1) and that "the Word became flesh, and dwelt among us ... full of grace and truth" (1:14). This passage reveals that Christ had his own divine grace at birth; he did not acquire it, as claimed by others, including the Adoptionists.

Hypostatic union began at the moment of the Incarnation of the Word. Jesus Christ has grace and free will in him, which attests to his full divinity and full humanity, respectively. Therefore, hypostatic union not only shows the human and divine natures of Jesus Christ; it also reveals that Christ has both the necessary human and divine wills within himself,[24] which allow him to follow his path *alone*. These two wills in Christ illustrate complete integration. Even though he does not walk the same path as human beings, his path demonstrates the proportions (100% each) that are needed for salvation. More than a unity of wills, Christ demonstrates a unity in nature with God the Father.

Three centuries after the Apostle Paul, Athanasius appears to support Paul's understanding of the Sator Square.

Therefore, the section "To Work" of Jesus Christ's specific path in Figure 12.1 can be completed as follows:

2. To work: Both wills (divine and human) are necessary.

A. Divine Will: Being 100 percent divine, Jesus Christ has the divine will required for salvation within himself.

B. Human Will: Being 100 percent human, Jesus Christ was able to follow his way perfectly, thus demonstrating the human will required for salvation.

The Integration Concept on a Christian's Path

As we have seen, in addition to revealing the divine nature of Jesus Christ, his hypostatic union indicates that to obtain salvation, a Christian must take the spiritual path that focuses on a close relationship with the divine will. This relationship begins at baptism.

In his *Discourse Against the Arians*, Athanasius says that human beings do not have within them the divine part that Jesus Christ possesses and so they cannot achieve their salvation on their own by themselves. Therefore, each human being needs the divine part, which consists of Christ's divine grace (Jn. 1:17).

However, Athanasius specified that the incorporation that makes a person "in God the Father and in the Son" is different from the relationship of the Father in the Son and the Son in the Father.[25] A person can only be in the Father *through his Son*.[26] Remaining incorporated in Christ allows the person to restore their previously broken connection with God.

The interpretation put forth by Athanasius accords with the message of the Sator Square. Like the Apostle Paul, Athanasius applies the divine blueprint of the Sator Square twice: once for the path of Christ, and then again for the path of the faithful. Though the two paths are similar, they are not identical.

The Trinity

In the fourth century, in addition to Christological questions, the Church was also challenged on the relationship between the Father, the Son and the Holy Spirit.

Homoousios

To explain the mystery of the Trinity, Athanasius uses the word *homoousios*,[27] meaning "consubstantiality" or "same substance." Therefore, Jesus the Son has the same substance as God the Father. This same substance is also found in the Holy Spirit, according to the doctrine of the Trinity.

The term *homoousios* shows that the divine nature of Jesus Christ that is necessary for the salvation of the faithful is identical to that of God the Father. In his book *Discourse Against the Arians*,[28] Athanasius supports the *homoousios* doctrine with these two biblical passages: "I and the Father are one" (Jn. 10:30) and "the Father is in Me, and I in the Father" (Jn. 10:38).

The symbol of the cross at the heart of the Sator Square represents the Trinity, which can be discerned when a Christian makes the sign of the cross with one hand, starting with the head and then moving to the chest and each shoulder, and says, "in the name of the Father and the Son and the Holy Spirit."

Interchangeability

To bolster his position that Jesus Christ the Son of God is made of the same substance as God the Father, Athanasius quotes the passage "for whatever the Father does, these things the Son also does in like manner"[29] (Jn. 5:19). He specifies that all actions and statements concerning the Father also concern the Son—except for the unique titles of Father, given to God, and Son, given to Jesus Christ. As an example, Bishop Athanasius underscores the similarity between the radiance of the Son and the light of the Father.[30] He even makes a comparison that evokes the sower in the Magic Square in the following quotation: "when the Son works, the Father is the Worker." [31]

This divine interchangeability between God and Christ, which is also mentioned by subsequent Fathers of the Church,[32] is present in the composition of the Sator Square. For example, the following questions can be answered by either God or Christ: who is the sower? Who initially calls us to hold the plow? Who offers His grace? Whom should we believe? With whom should we have a synergy? With whom should we follow the path? Who provides the light that leads to life? This divine interchangeability also occurs with the Holy Spirit. In the end, who saves us? Athanasius used this question to show that the Father, the Son and the Holy Spirit were all made of the same substance.

Athanasius and his orthodox contemporaries arranged the pieces of a jigsaw puzzle to describe the dogma that had existed since the beginning of the Christian era. To expand his reasoning on the doctrines of the Incarnation and the Trinity, Athanasius said that he was following Tradition and Scripture. In fact, both the Apostle Paul's and Athanasius's explanations are based on their interpretations of the Tradition (i.e., the Sator Square in my view) and the Scriptures. The Catholic Church deems their arguments supporting High Christology and Incarnation to be substantiated and appropriate.

JESUS CHRIST IS THE PLAN OF SALVATION

In addition to the above examination, we must refer to other passages in the New Testament to clarify these positions and better appreciate the richness of the Sator Square message.

According to the evangelist John, Jesus Christ reveals that he himself is: "the way, and the truth, and the life" (14:6), "the Light of the world" (8:12), "the door" required for salvation (10:9), "the good shepherd" (10:11), and "the resurrection and the life" (11:25). All these elements are present in the Sator Square. This leads me to make the following statement:

The creator of the Sator Square reveals that Jesus Christ is the plan of salvation.

Like the New Testament, the Sator Square demonstrates that Jesus Christ identifies himself not only as an example to follow, a prophet and a messenger who brings the path of life, but above all as the person who is an integral part of, and who fulfills, the divine blueprint.

The artifact reveals that Jesus Christ is the plan of salvation. All five words on the Sator Square (which reveals the path of salvation) touch the central cross (i.e., Jesus Christ) formed with the repeated word *tenet*. Jesus Christ not only brings the solution; he *is* the solution. Everyone must go through him, as he is the sole intermediary for obtaining salvation. As the evangelist Mark writes at the beginning of his gospel, the Good News is Jesus Christ (1:1). In addition, the Jew Simon the Just says that Jesus is the divine "salvation" (Lk. 2:30). Jesus Christ is God, who came to Earth to save humanity. Irenaeus of Lyon says: "For Christ is the treasure which was hid in the field."[33]

My research appears to show that the Sator Square is, among other things, the Good News, the Gospel of Christ, the sacred tradition and the divine blueprint. The artifact directs readers to its central element, which is the cross symbol. Like the Bible as a whole, all of the Sator Square's elements point to a single and sublime common denominator: Jesus Christ, the Son of God. In the Sator Square, someone is calling out to the reader: "Hello, I am here for you, you just have to believe in me and turn towards me." It is a personal call. The one who calls us stands in the middle of the Sator Square; he is the crucified and risen Son of God.

OPTIMAL VIEWING ANGLE

As we have seen, the cross symbol and the words on the Magic Square can be interpreted from different viewpoints. While the cross remains the central element of the Magic Square, the optimal viewing angle is at stake. As mentioned in the conclusion of Part I, changing the ancient Rotas Square to the more recent Sator Square is accomplished by simply rotating the artifact. The primary reason for the rotation is to emphasize the top horizontal word, either "Rotas" or "Sator," to differentiate the versions of the artifact. Thus, the following statement can be made:

In the early centuries A.D., Rotas Squares were replaced by Sator Squares to achieve the optimal viewing angle.

I realized that the ancient Rotas Squares focus on the human aspects of Jesus of Nazareth. The Latin word *rotas* has multiple meanings. One meaning is "you memorize" or "you repeat," which identifies Jesus of Nazareth as a teacher or a rabbi. Amazingly, the word *rotas* also has an etymological link with the French word *route*,[34] meaning "road" in English. This is further evidence of the Magic Square hiding a secret path that leads to a treasure, much like a treasure map. This also shows that Jesus of Nazareth is the long-awaited prophet who unveiled the path of life.

The Adoptionist groups seemed to interpret the cross symbol and the vertical word *sator* as representing God the Father; Jesus is not involved. Therefore, the Rotas Square is a reflection of the Christian perspective advocated by Low Christology, which focuses on the human characteristics specific to Jesus of Nazareth that were used to exalt him. However, the evolution from a Rotas to a Sator Square provides the optimal viewing angle, due to the greater focus on the word "sower." The cross symbol (the *tav*) now represents Jesus as God. The word Sator becomes a metaphor for both God and Jesus Christ. This permutation highlights that Jesus Christ is God who came to earth to save us. Therefore, the Sator Square's optimal viewing angle corresponds to the perspective advocated by High Christology.

The Unusual Rotas Squares

Rotas Squares usually date from the early centuries A.D. While the permutation of the Sator Square has generally been adopted, some Rotas Squares appear to have been inscribed much later than we might expect. The following are examples of these untypical Rotas Squares:[35]

1. The Rotas Square in Acquaviva Collecroce, Italy. The artifact is engraved on a movable piece of stone near the church of Santa Maria Ester. This ancient Church, rebuilt in 1715, is located in the small village of Acquaviva Collecroce in the Molise region of Southern Italy.

2. The Rotas Square in Capestrano, Italy. A stone with a Rotas Square inscription was installed upside down in the doorway of the church of San Pietro ad Oratorium near Capestrano, Italy. The church, founded around the year 750 with the help of Desiderius, the last Lombard king, was restored in the 17th century.

3. The Rotas Square in Valbonnais, France. Dating back to the 17th or 18th century, the Rotas Square from Valbonnais (photo 5), near the main road of the village, is engraved on a piece of gneiss that originally adorned the house of justice.

Photo 5: The Rotas Square in Valbonnais. *Photo credit:*
Speraro

Most Rotas Squares were inscribed in the early centuries A.D. and subsequently lost, due to the transition to the Sator Square, until the archaeological discoveries of the 19th century. But if they were lost prior to the 19th century, then how do we explain the dating of these unusual Rotas Squares? For example, why was the Rotas Square in Valbonnais written in the 17th or 18th century? There are only two possible reasons:

either because the original dating of these unusual Rotas Squares is inaccurate, or because these Rotas Squares were inscribed much later. In the latter case, it is clear that those who inscribed these Rotas Squares wished to secretly perpetuate the ancient Rotas Square Christian tradition (probably the Judeo-Christian tradition that advocated Adoptionism) over the centuries, or even the millennia.

WHAT DOES THE CROSS SYMBOL ULTIMATELY REPRESENT?

As we have seen in this part of the book, the artifact's components can be interpreted in different ways. The Magic Square illustrates the divine blueprint that apparently has not only been used by defenders of Christian orthodoxy like the Apostle Paul and Athanasius of Alexandria, but also by some important heretic groups.

The Magic Square has an extraordinary form and was brilliantly designed to contain two messages with the same arrangement of letters that can be viewed from two different angles. The Christians who advocated the older Rotas Square angle had an adequate but limited understanding of the artifact,

THE TWO PATHS | 297

compared to those who advocated for the Sator Square, which provides the optimal viewing angle. Yet, the Rotas Square is also significant.

In fact, the full understanding of the message must include both the Rotas Square (the human nature of Jesus) and the Sator Square (the divine nature of Christ). Together the two versions of the Square show the hypostatic union of Jesus Christ. Therefore, through the ingenious use of two viewing angles, the creator of the Magic Square sought to hide the divine nature of Jesus Christ from certain people.

Based on the canonical gospels, Jesus operated in the same way by providing clues, in word and deed, to his divine nature. Was it Jesus's ultimate aim to progressively reveal his divine nature to humanity? The cross symbol occupies the central position of both the Rotas and the Sator Squares. Thus, Lord Jesus Christ came among humans to deliver them from evil and from death. He set his cross as the centerpiece of his Gospel.[36] The symbol of the authentic apostolic faith has always been the symbol of the cross, from the birth of Christianity to the present day.

The key point undeniably lies in the meaning of the symbol of the cross and of the identity of Jesus.

Everything comes down to the following: What does Jesus represent for you? What does the cross in the Sator Square represent for you? Ultimately, it is a matter of faith as to which path you take and with whom.

For me, the artifact has lifted the veil, opened my eyes, and provided me with a clear and convincing answer: I take the path of salvation with Jesus Christ, the Son of God. I have seen, I believe, and I testify.

PART V

ANSWERING

THE FINAL QUESTIONS

13

WHO CREATED THE ARTIFACT?

Two crucial questions remain unanswered. Who created the first Magic Square? Why was it written in Latin? The next two chapters will answer these questions.

THE CREATOR OF THE MAGIC SQUARE IS JUDEO-CHRISTIAN

The Sator Square is unquestionably of Jewish origin. It unveils a unique God and has numerous explicit links with the Hebrew tradition. The artifact also exhibits biblical issues like morality and the path of life. This rules out Greek mythology as the origin of the artifact, since neither of these topics are part of their belief system.[1]

We have established that in addition to being of Jewish origin, the Magic Square is also Christian. Even today, a certain number of artifacts are affixed to Christian buildings. Let us recap some of the information that supports the Sator Square's Christian origin:

- The artifact contains the heart of Jesus' teaching: a Parable of the Sower, a path to follow and a cross symbol.

- It is perfectly consistent with the Scriptures, Christian literature and with what the Church has been preaching since the beginnings of Christianity.

- It follows the form and features that are unique to the parables of Jesus Christ.

- The oldest Magic Square dates back to around the time of Jesus. Indeed, the artifact suddenly emerged in the first century; this period coincides with the era of nascent Christianity.

The Magic Square's message comes from the teachings of Jesus, but that doesn't necessarily prove that he created the artifact. In any event, based on what we know so far, the creator is quite likely a first-century Judeo-Christian individual.

COULD IT BE ONE OF THE JUDEO-CHRISTIANS WHO CONVERTED TO CHRISTIANITY ON THE DAY OF PENTECOST?

Cardinal Jean Daniélou, who has a particular interest in the Sator Square, notes that a Judeo-Christian community that used Vulgar Latin was established very early in the city of Rome.[2] Therefore, considering that the artifact is in Latin, the creator may have been part of this community.

Could it be possible that the creator of the Magic Square is one of the Roman Jewish visitors (Acts 2:10) who gathered and converted to Christianity on the Day of Pentecost approximately seven weeks after the death of Christ? Indeed, Franz Cumont, a Belgian historian and archaeologist who has conducted extensive research on the cult of Mithra, proposed to the Roman Academy of Archaeology that the Magic Square was written by "a converted Jew."[3]

Nonetheless, based on my research, this theory can be ruled out, since none of the Roman visitors were apostles. The Church has clearly established that the sacred tradition (i.e., the Sator Square, in my view) that comes from the teaching of Jesus is of apostolic origin. As such, the creator must be Jesus or one of his apostles.

COULD IT BE THE EVANGELIST MARK?

Mark is another potential candidate. His gospel was written in Rome,[4] where Latin was the predominant language. Although his gospel was written in Greek, the text contains many Greek words that were derived from Latin words.[5] Thus, Mark had a certain knowledge of the Latin language.

In 1958, an American professor named Morton Smith discovered a letter from the early third century in the Mar Saba Monastery near Jerusalem. The letter, probably written by Clement of Alexandria, reveals that Mark wrote a second gospel, the *Secret Gospel of Mark*, containing a more profound teaching. Could this secret gospel be the Sator Square?

But that is not the case, since the *Secret Gospel of Mark* is a text and not a palindrome. In addition, some excerpts from this secret gospel do not directly relate to the Magic Square. Besides, although Mark was greatly influenced by the Apostle Peter, he was not one of the apostles of Jesus.

COULD IT BE THE APOSTLE PAUL?

Who better to create this artifact than Paul? After all, he is the Apostle to the Gentiles (Acts 9:15; Gal. 2:8).

Even though Paul's writings can be considered to be of apostolic origin, they bear further examination. Each of the following five questions presents an argument suggesting that Paul is the creator of the Magic Square, and is followed by a counter-argument. Taken together, the counter-arguments ultimately prove that Paul is *not* the creator of the artifact.

Is Paul the Founder of Christianity?

Argument No. 1

Some scholars believe that the founder of Christianity is the Apostle Paul and that he supposedly bypassed the authentic messages of Jesus Christ and his disciples.[6]

Earlier, I established the artifact's importance, as the sacred tradition, to Christianity; it is an integral part of the glorious deposit of faith. Thus, one could argue that by creating the artifact, Paul made a gospel for non-Jews that served as a tool to convert them and to keep them away from Judaizers.[7] In addition, all the concepts in the Magic Square can clearly be found in Paul's epistles.

Counter-Argument No. 1

In fact, Paul did not consider himself to be the originator of Christianity; he did not even imply that in his writings. Paul, who was known as an apostle, instead saw himself as an intermediary or messenger. He transmitted the apostolic tradition he received and preached it to others.[8] Paul was very clear that he had received divine information.[9] He was rigorously honest and specific about his sources. In his writings, he distinguished the information he received from the divine from his personal statements. His epistles are based largely on his understanding of the divine message, which was often strongly influenced by his cultural environment. Even though all the concepts in the Magic Square are found in Paul's epistles, they can also be found throughout other New Testament writings. A close look at the content of the Sator Square makes it obvious that the artifact was not designed to please Paul; it is definitely not a Pauline propaganda tool. If Paul had created the artifact, he would have mentioned elements that are specifically adapted for non-Jewish Christian readers, for example, that the Jewish ritual of circumcision was not required.

The reality is that the artifact reveals a universal message that is not addressed exclusively to the Jews or exclusively to non-Jews.

My research suggests that Paul was guided by the divine blueprint, as were the authors of all the other New Testament writings and most of the other early Christian writers.

The divine content was not created to meet the specific needs of a particular Christian subgroup, whether Jewish or non-Jewish. The Magic Square cannot be modified; it is undeniably neutral, pure and authentic.

Did Paul Have his Own Good News?

Argument No. 2

The second argument is closely linked to the first. By asserting that he had his own gospel, Paul seems to demonstrate that the Good News that he preached came from him alone. If this is true, it could mean that the Gospel of Christ (i.e., the Sator Square, in my view) was created by Paul.

Also, in his epistles, Paul showed a marked interest in the gospel. He cited the word "gospel" more frequently in his epistles than any other New Testament author.

Counter-Argument No. 2

When Paul specified that he had *"his gospel,"*[10] he was not claiming to have different content than that of the other apostles; instead, he meant that he had his own understanding of the divine content.

Paul expressly stated that he had received the Gospel of Christ (Gal. 1:11-12) and that he was teaching it (Rom. 15:19). He was very clear that there is only one Gospel of Christ (Gal. 1:17). Consequently, the gospel of Paul is not the Gospel of Christ, but rather his own interpretation of it. As highlighted in Chapter 11, Paul's epistles mention that other interpretations of the Gospel of Christ existed during that time.

We must not forget that Paul was brilliant. He was an expert on the Torah, the first five books of the Hebrew Bible, and had a deep knowledge of Judaism. Before his conversion, Paul was a Pharisee and a strict orthodox Jew. He used to say that he was "extremely zealous" about his ancestral traditions (Gal. 1:14). Not only did he preach the Torah, but he was even prepared to commit wrongdoing to ensure conformance with it. Throughout his life, Paul kept Judaism foremost in his mind. We see this clearly in the arguments stated in his epistles. One might ask whether Paul was behaving like a rabbi.[11]

It is common for Jews to have differing interpretations about the content of the Torah. Disagreements between the Sadducees and the Pharisees are an obvious example.[12] Even if Paul's biblical interpretations respected the analytical method of these Jewish groups, they were not accepted by many Jews, since they disrupted their existing paradigms.[13] In addition to the Jewish Bible, Paul probably perceived the Rotas Square in his possession as the basis for his interpretation of the divine message.

In the second century, Bishop Irenaeus of Lyon said that Paul's interpretation and that of Luke were consistent with the "rule of unaltered truth."[14] As we have seen, this rule could be one of the pseudonyms for the Magic Square.

In the epistles of Timothy, Paul entrusted not only the content of the divine deposit, the artifact, to Timothy, but also the method of teaching it.[15] Thus, it was important to Paul not only to transmit the content, but also to teach it.

Paul Must Have Received the Rotas Square

On the road to Damascus, Paul met Christ and lost his sight (Acts 9:3-8). Not long after, the disciple Ananias of Damascus had a vision in which he was ordered by Jesus Christ to go to Paul so the latter could regain his sight and be filled with the Holy Spirit (Acts 9:17).

I believe that Ananias must have revealed the Rotas Square and the apostles' interpretation of it to Paul while in Damascus. Ananias said that at that moment, Paul became a witness to what he *saw* and heard (Acts 22:15).

Indeed, Paul was entitled to receive the secret of the artifact from Ananias because Jesus Christ had previously confirmed to the disciple that Paul was an apostle (Acts 9:15). Christ also said to Ananias "for I will show him how much he must suffer *for My name*'s sake" (Acts 9:16); therefore, Christ showed Paul that the cross (*tav*) in the center of the Magic Square means the death and Resurrection of Christ.

Did Paul Speak and Write in Latin?

Argument No. 3

The Apostle Paul probably knew Latin.[16] He was born of a Roman father and he bore the name Paul, which is derived from the Latin name *Paulus*. Also, his epistles contain several Latinisms. Furthermore, considering the record of Paul travels,[17] and some of the people that he met, some scholars believe that Paul very likely spoke Latin. For example, theologian Paul Berry is convinced that the

Christians Paul met in Pozzuoli, near the city of Pompeii, spoke Latin.[18] Therefore, it could be argued that Paul created the Magic Square in Latin with the intention of preaching it in the Western Roman Empire.

Counter-Argument No. 3

Paul wrote his epistle to the Romans in Greek, not Latin. This seems to indicate that Latin was not his preferred language of communication in terms of reaching the people in the western part of the Roman Empire. Therefore, some might believe that Paul used a Latin artifact not by personal preference, but out of obligation.

En Route to Arabia (Epistle to the Galatians 1:14-17)

In verse 14, Paul displays his advanced knowledge of Judaism. Then he says:

> But when God, who had set me apart even from my mother's womb and called me through His grace, was pleased to reveal His Son in me so that I might preach Him among the Gentiles, I did not immediately consult with flesh and blood, nor did I go up to Jerusalem to those who were apostles

before me; but I went away to Arabia, and returned once more to Damascus. (Gal. 1:15-17).

When he received the divine revelation, Paul understood that God had prepared him by giving him two abilities. Along with the ability to understand the complex concepts of Judaism, Paul says in verse 15 that he received another skill from God in childhood. What was this other skill? I would suggest that it was early knowledge of the Latin language. Paul's father was Roman, and as we will see in the next chapter, Paul had Roman citizenship. Thus, based on my understanding, when Paul noticed that the Gospel of Christ that Ananias gave him was written in Latin, he realized that God had chosen him to decipher, interpret, and announce the Gospel to the Gentiles. Convinced that he had been called to this mission due to his knowledge of both Latin and Judaism, Paul felt the need to deepen his understanding of the Magic Square by traveling, not to meet certain people in Jerusalem, but God in Arabia.

Finally, Paul may have written this passage of the epistle to the Galatians not long after his conversion and acceptance of his divine mission. This pivotal moment in his life most likely led to deep introspection and surely caused him to ponder the following questions: Why me and not someone else? Am I the right person for this mission? Paul realized that despite the wrongdoing he had committed, God had chosen him and prepared him from a young age to fulfill the mission by placing him in an environment that was conducive to his developing the necessary abilities.

Did Paul feel compelled to create a Magic Square in Latin in accordance with previously written content in a Semitic language such as Aramaic or Hebrew? Although this is plausible, building such an artifact by reproducing exactly the same message in another language seems impossible, considering the artifact's complexity. However, when it comes to God, all things are possible.

Did Paul Receive Divine Revelations?

Argument No. 4

In addition to Christ appearing to him and his conversion, Paul claimed that he subsequently received some personal revelations. Mount Sinai in Arabia, where Paul stayed, was a sacred site and a suitable place to receive a revelation; it is the very place where Moses received the words of God. Therefore, it is possible that his divine revelations inspired him to create the Magic Square.

Counter-Argument No. 4

In my view, Paul received the Magic Square; he did not create it. Indeed, he developed his interpretation of the artifact with divine help. Unfortunately, Paul's revelations have frequently been discredited and considered fraudulent because their content can be perceived as very disturbing. Yet, this is not the only reference in the Bible to personal revelations from God. What would Paul have gained by declaring that he had received such revelations? Paul spoke and acted like someone who had received instructions through personal revelations. His deep devotion to his evangelist mission continued until the end of his life. He courageously set out on a burgeoning, yet dangerous, path filled with obstacles and suffering.

Did Paul Work Alone?

Argument No. 5

After his conversion, Paul preached in Damascus, Syria, and stayed in Arabia for a total of three years instead of meeting the apostles in Jerusalem. Without the knowledge of the other Judeo-Christian disciples, Paul taught his own interpretations, which probably contradicted those of his fellows. Some scholars[19] maintain that Paul accomplished a solo mission that was much more personal than communal, and that he did not accept any human authority. Once again, we could deduce with these allegations that Paul single-handedly created the Magic Square based on his own beliefs.

Counter-Argument No. 5

On the contrary, Paul was a team player, not a loner. In fact, Paul went to Jerusalem specifically to meet with the Apostle Peter and stayed with him for 15 days (Gal. 1:18). This noteworthy passage means that shortly after his stay in Arabia, Paul visited the apostle Peter to explain his new interpretation of the artifact. Paul remained a member of the Jerusalem Church, which did not reject him. During his two trips to Jerusalem, fourteen years apart, the churches of Judea glorified God because of him (Gal. 1:24). The most important apostles—James, Peter and John—recognized the divine gift received by Paul. In addition, they all agreed to share with Paul the mission that Christ had entrusted to them (Gal. 2:7-9). If Paul had delivered a message that was completely different from the Gospel of Christ, the result would have been disastrous. Of course, there were differences of opinion about conditions for membership, rituals and circumcision, but no divergence existed in relation to the very foundation of the divine Gospel. Despite differences between some of Paul's interpretations and those of the Jerusalem Church led by James the Just, the two apostles accepted each other, because each knew that the other was following the same blueprint of the Sator Square, as stated in Chapters 11 and 12. Two significant passages from early Christian texts show that the parties reached an agreement, even if their views diverged on some aspects. The first passage is found in a Christian document written around the year A.D. 60 by Justin Martyr.[20] The author clearly stresses that he cannot prove the pre-existence of Jesus Christ, nor his virgin birth. However, in his view, it was indisputable that all Christians were united under the same belief that Jesus was "the Christ of God," even though some Judeo-Christians considered him to be a mere human. Also, Justin Martyr's passage is aligned with Paul's passage, which says that those who lay their foundation in Jesus Christ are already on the right path (1 Cor. 3:11). The second passage, written towards the end of the second century by Tertullian, the promoter of Latin theology, is about the relationship between Peter and Paul; it also indirectly reveals Christian unity on the following three statements:

> For it does not appear from this, that any other God than the Creator or any other Christ than [the son] of Mary, or any other hope than the resurrection, was announced [by Peter].[21]

Tertullian's assertion indirectly exposes the existence of divergences, as well as a certain tolerance. For Paul, the new era began with the arrival of Christ, who came not only to save the Jews, but also non-Jews. Paul did not hide his epistles or his theological position. Peter was aware of the divine grace that Paul had received and accepted his epistles, even if he felt that some elements were difficult to understand (2 Pet. 3:15-16). In summary, I can conclude that Paul is *not* the creator of the Latin Magic Square. This outcome is the cause of my gray hairs. It would have been much simpler for me to advocate that the Apostle Paul is the creator of the artifact and that it was addressed to non-Jews; however, this is not the case.

COULD IT BE JESUS OF NAZARETH?

Considering that the first Rotas Squares dates from the first century, it would be difficult to claim that the creator is from the primitive Church, given that the latter was only in its infancy during that period.

Many are convinced that the content of the Tradition was not created after Jesus' death, but was instead created when Jesus taught his apostles.[22] For example, the four evangelists believed that the "mystery of the Kingdom of God"[23] was given to the disciples during the lifetime of Jesus. Multiple references indicate that the source of the divine message comes from the teaching of Jesus of Nazareth; the apostolic tradition is based on this. As previously demonstrated, if the Sator Square is indeed the Gospel *of Christ,* this could indicate that the artifact not only stemmed from the teachings of Jesus, but that it was also created by him. Furthermore,

Richard Pietschmann, a German archaeologist and Egyptologist, is of the opinion that the individual who wrote the inscription "these are the names of the verses of Christ"[24] beside a Latin Sator Square in a Faras chapel in Sudan, believed that the five words were directly from Jesus Christ.

While several Christian writings mention that Jesus of Nazareth never wrote anything down, it does not, however, eliminate the possibility that he is the creator of the artifact. As we saw, it is possible that this kind of statement is a trick—part of the *Disciplina arcani*—which considers the artifact as "unwritten" or another similar tactic.[25]

For example, while the author Yves Congar says that Jesus never wrote anything down, he adds that Jesus' method of teaching the tradition was in the form of a synthesis.[26] Indeed, the Sator Square has an absence of literality (unwritten), as explained in Chapter 6 (Secret rule No. 4); the artifact is presented in a synthesized way, comprising just five words. As we will see in the rest of this chapter, the creator of the Magic Square wished to reveal that he really is Jesus or falsely claims to be Jesus. He is the one who brings the plan of salvation that is indicated in the Magic Square. Whether these assertions are true or false, let us assume that Jesus inscribed the Magic Square; this will allow us to discover additional information on the artifact.

The Apostle Peter Received a Stone

After the apostle Peter confessed that Jesus is Christ and the Son of the living God, Jesus said to him, as quoted in this well-known and controversial verse of the gospel of Matthew:

> I also say to you that you are Peter, and upon this rock I will build My church; and the gates of Hades will not overpower it (16:18).

One point of controversy concerns the precise meaning of the rock. What is this rock? Did Jesus show Peter a rock? The book of Isaiah mentions something about a foundation stone:

> Behold, I am laying in Zion a stone, a tested stone, a costly cornerstone for the foundation, firmly placed. He who believes in it will not be disturbed (28:16).

Together, these two passages mean that the cornerstone given to Peter is the foundation stone of the church of Jesus Christ. The book of Psalms specifies that this cornerstone was previously rejected:

> The stone which the builders rejected Has become the chief corner stone. This is the Lord's doing (118:22-23).

The book of Psalms passage about the rejected stone that became precious is very prominent in the New Testament; it appears in all of the synoptic gospels and in the Acts of the Apostles.[27] Therefore, I can make the following bold assertion:

The creator of the Magic Square wishes to show that the rock that Peter received from Jesus is the Magic Square, the cornerstone for the foundation of the Church of Jesus Christ.

As explained in Chapter 12, the Magic Square is presented as the stumbling block. It is probably the stone that was rejected by the Jews,[28] because they did not accept that the cross symbol in the middle of the Magic Square represented Jesus Christ as divine. Although the stone was rejected, the Bible says that it was selected by God as the cornerstone for the foundation of His divine Temple. In fact, many Magic Squares have been found in the walls of churches, such as the one embedded in a stone on the external wall of the majestic cathedral in Siena, Tuscany that is also called the *Duomo di Siena.* Another is inscribed on the stone portal of the façade San Pietro ad Oratorium Church, in Capestrano in the Abruzzo region of Italy. Another example is the Basilica Santa Maria Maggiore in Rome, a property that was built on Roman ruins and belongs to the Vatican. In 1966, when the Church foundation was being repaired, a well-preserved Roman residence that probably dates back to a few centuries before Jesus Christ was discovered in the basement. In the residence, a fresco stretching across two walls shows a Roman calendar depicting agricultural activities like plowing and harvesting. A Rotas Square was found not far from this calendar, and the calendar recalls the Parable of the Sower on the Magic Square. Is it purely coincidental that a Rotas Square lay under this prestigious church? Could there be other Magic Squares hidden in other church basements?

Peter Received the Keys

In addition to the stone, Jesus Christ gave Peter the keys to the hidden gate that provides access to the Kingdom of God (Mt. 16:19). Therefore, this passage seems to demonstrate the following point:

Peter was given the master key
that unlocks the secret message
of the Magic Square, which leads
to the path of salvation.

Thus, not only did Jesus appear to hand Peter a Magic Square inscribed on a stone; he also provided him with secret instructions on how to decipher it. Surprisingly, even some heretics, such as the Jewish Christian Ebionites, supported the statement that Peter received such instructions.[29] By being in possession of the keys, Peter metaphorically gained access to the gate of salvation—he became the gatekeeper. Thus, one might believe that Peter alone decided who gained access to the secret message of the artifact.

Peter Went to Rome

If the apostle Peter received the Magic Square with its secret instructions, he most likely brought the "symbol" to Rome.[30] Although some scholars maintain that Peter neither went to Rome nor died in that city, others believe that he made a few trips to Rome. These scholars think that Peter's first trip to Rome occurred sometime between the year 40 and the Council of Jerusalem in 49.[31] Did he travel through Pompeii on his way to Rome during this period to establish Christian communities in both cities, long before the Apostle Paul's trip? Indeed, we can see in Paul's epistle to the Romans that a large Christian community had already been established in Rome well before Paul's arrival. Paul also met members of a small established community based in Pozzuoli, near Pompeii. Thus, it is possible that it was Peter and not Paul who inscribed the two oldest Rotas Squares that were found in Pompeii. Some writings mention that Peter did in fact go to Rome. For example, the first epistle of Peter contains a significant indication that Peter was actually in Rome when he says: "She who is in Babylon, chosen together with you, sends you greetings" (5:13). The word "Babylon" is a known metaphor for Rome. Some Church Fathers, such as Ignatius of Antioch, Irenaeus of Lyon, and Eusebius of Caesarea also support the fact that Peter went to Rome.[32] An unusual event is also reported in the text of Eusebius. Some Roman citizens, who had heard the apostle Peter and were eager to understand the divine message, were unsatisfied with Peter's *"unwritten"* [in Greek, ἀγράφῳ] teaching of the divine *"Gospel* [of Christ]." They pleaded with Mark, Peter's companion, to write his gospel.[33] It is quite possible that the root cause of the Latin audience's dissatisfaction was due to the difficulty that Peter, a Jewish apostle who spoke Aramaic, had in providing an effective explanation of the Magic Square's secret message in Latin.

Each Apostle Received a Stone

In the gospel of Matthew, Christ said:

> Go therefore and make disciples of all the nations, baptizing them in the name of the Father and the Son and the Holy Spirit, teaching them to observe all that I commanded you; and lo, I am with you always, even to the end of the age (28:19-20).

This passage mentions baptism and observance of Jesus Christ's commands, which are linked to the two concepts of the Magic Square "to believe" and "to turn." Could Christ have given each apostle a stone with the Rotas Square inscribed on it? This is a reasonable question, given that something similar is mentioned in the Old Testament book of Joshua, which recounts the conquest of the Land of Israel. Following a divine request, Joshua called together twelve men, one from each tribe:

> And Joshua said to them, "Cross again to the ark of the Lord your God into the middle of the Jordan, and each of you take a stone on his shoulder, according to the number of the tribes of the sons of Israel. Let this be a sign among you..." (Josh. 4:5-6).

The Jordan River mentioned in this passage is often linked to Christian baptism, referenced in the passage from Matthew above. The sign indicated in the passage from the book of Joshua might represent the *tav* letter on a stone, which later signified the cross of Christ on a stone (i.e., the Magic Square). Overall, Joshua's and Matthew's passages contain the same requests as the Magic

Square: to baptize and to *bear the cross* (as we saw in Chapter 11).

Further, a passage from the apocryphal gospel of Thomas shares some common features with the two previous passages when Jesus says:

> If you become my disciples and if you hear my words, these stones will serve you.[34]

This passage demonstrates that Jesus may have provided multiple stones. While one might expect that the stones were tangible objects, that is not necessarily the case. It is possible that the stones were not physically transported by the apostles to evangelize throughout the world, but rather kept in their heart through the memorization of the words on the Magic Square, as indicated by the Latin word *rotas*.

Note that Jesus gave Peter the mission and the stone *during his lifetime*; however, the mission assigned to the eleven apostles in the gospel of Matthew came from the *resurrected* Christ.

If Jesus did in fact give a Rotas Square to Peter and to all the other apostles, it represented a difficult and unexpected mission, as the content was written in Latin, which at that time was strongly associated with the Roman Empire. The fact that we were able to accept the artifact, which was burdensome at the very least, might indicate that the request could only have come from Jesus.

Over time, the apostle Peter seemed to gradually deepen his interpretation of the message on the Rotas Square. He apparently understood the universality of the divine message during the baptism of Cornelius the Roman Centurion (Acts 10:47). Since the message of the Magic Square was in Latin, Peter must have realized that Jesus wanted his establishment to be located in Rome and not in Jerusalem, which explains why Peter went to Rome. Let us not forget that the founder of the Church of Rome isn't the Apostle Paul, but Peter.

The Divine Stone

In the previous chapter, we concluded that the creator of the Sator Square reveals that Christ is the Son of God and that he himself is the plan of salvation. Like the Sator Square, Jesus Christ is "the cornerstone"[35] and "the rock of my salvation" mentioned in the book of Psalms.[36] He is the Good News and the solution to salvation. Jesus Christ is not only the cornerstone; he is also the Temple of God (Eph. 2:20-22.) This leads us to the following statement:

The creator of the Sator Square represents Jesus Christ as the Temple of God.

The artifact reveals that the body of Christ is the Temple of God. The first epistle of Peter says that the Lord is a living stone (2:4). This shows that since his Incarnation, Jesus Christ, just like the Sator Square, is still with us today. If we revisit the end of verse 118:23 of the Book of Psalms, Jesus Christ directly states that the stone from the *Lord*. In addition, the artifact once again shows the divine nature of Jesus Christ and that the divine blueprint is Christ himself.

Ultimately, I believe that the creator of the artifact was divinely inspired or was divine in nature. I am not the only one who believes this; the Catholic Church holds the same belief. In fact, the institution has expended tremendous effort over the past 2,000 years to protect the Square.

TWO-WAY MESSAGE

At this point, some might still conclude that the Apostle Paul created his own non-Jewish gospel in Latin, or declare that Jesus could not have created his Gospel in Latin, since he was only targeting Jewish Christians. However, in reality, the Latin Sator Square message does not discriminate, as attested by the following assertion:

The palindromic shape of the Sator Square facilitates understanding for Semitic readers.

It was important to Jesus to have a universal message that did not exclude the Jews. The inverted letter "N" in the center of many Squares, such as the ones in Jarnac, Oppède-le-Vieux and Valbonnais, indicates that the artifact can be read from left to right or from right to left. The Sator Square at Oppède-le-Vieux also has two inverted "S" letters.

When we look in a mirror, the inverted letters can be read from left to right. This example of mirror, or specular, writing is similar to the right-to-left script that Leonardo da Vinci, one of the greatest geniuses of all time, used in his notebooks.

Therefore, someone who understands Aramaic or Hebrew and reads a Sator Square *horizontally* (from right to left) would see a Rotas Square. Extraordinarily, someone who understands Aramaic or Hebrew and reads ta Sator Square *vertically* (from top to bottom) would also see a Rotas Square.[37]

Photo 6: The Sator Square of Oppède-le-Vieux written on the right side of a wooden front door; *Photo credit: Jean-Pierre Gerault*

The Sator Square seems to contain a universal message comprised of two versions: one addressed to the Jews and one to non-Jews. The Sator Square never ceases to amaze. As Jesus said about the rejected stone that became a cornerstone:

> The Lord has done this,
> and it is marvelous to our eyes.[38]

14

WHY LATIN?

Jesus understood Aramaic and Hebrew. Even though the New Testament contains a few instances of sentence structure and individual words from those languages, no texts of Jesus' teachings in either language have ever been found.

The New Testament texts were originally written in Greek, for several reasons.[1] During the early centuries of our era, the Jewish diaspora, including the Judeo-Christian population, spread around the Mediterranean. The Greek Christian texts reached a large Christian audience because Greek was the dominant and most influential language throughout this vast territory. In addition, Hellenic Christian authors had the Greek version of the Hebrew Bible (the Septuagint) at their disposal when they were writing the New Testament in Greek. Furthermore, the destruction of the Second Temple of Jerusalem in A.D. 70 severely damaged the initial control center of Christianity in Jerusalem, leading to its decentralization. Thus, this period favored the continued development of Christianity in the Greek language.

So, did Jesus of Nazareth speak Greek? It is quite likely that he did. Did he speak other languages of that time, such as Latin? It is unlikely, but according to some authors, it's possible. In *The Christian Inscription at Pompeii*, Paul Berry states that Jesus may have spoken Latin, for example when he met the centurion from Capernaum, and when he met Pontius Pilate.[2] However, to date, there is no convincing proof of this.[3]

Even if Jesus did speak a bit of Latin, why would he create the Magic Square in Latin? How could he promote a Latin artifact in a Jewish community? At that time, Romans were seen as evil, the Jews' worst enemy, who would be vanquished upon the arrival of the Jewish Messiah. Also, if Jesus wanted to spread the divine message to other nations, would he not use Greek instead of Latin?

Jesus often cited Old Testament passages to explain how he was fulfilling his mission. In this chapter, we will look at four biblical passages that provide a plausible explanation for why Jesus might have written his Gospel in Latin.

GENESIS 11:1

> Now the whole earth used the same language and the same words.

This verse is part of the story of the tower of Babel (Gn. 11:1-9). According to the book of Genesis, all human beings used the same language. They wanted to build a city with a tower to make a name for themselves and avoid being dispersed (Gn. 11:4). God destroyed the city and the tower and cursed the people by spreading the use of many languages among them to confuse and scatter them.[4] Hence, humanity was plunged into a confusion of languages.

The tower and the city, commonly identified with the ancient city of Babylon, were destroyed because they had been built out of arrogance and pride.⁵ In wanting to "bear the name"—a familiar expression—the people wanted to bear the name of the *tav,* to be designated as God.⁶

In the Bible, God continuously reveals that He is a God of justice. Some Bible passages state: "God is opposed to the proud, but gives grace to the humble."⁷ Therefore, God does not just destroy evil, God is good and does good.

Building a City with a Tower

The Bible shows that God wishes to establish a united Kingdom. The divine dwelling is chosen and built by God (2 Sam. 7:1-13), not by human beings, as in the tower of Babel. Unlike Babel, this construction will not be made by human hands (Acts 7:48). God is both the architect and the builder of the spiritual edifice called "The Temple of God."

Neither the new city and Tower that God wants will be built in Babylon, but in "New Jerusalem" or the "heavenly Jerusalem." The book of the Prophet Ezekiel and John's book of Revelation specifically mention the construction of this city and tower. Ezekiel and John agree on one important point, that this "New Jerusalem" has a *square shape*.[8] By designing an artifact with the same shape, the creator of the Sator Square intended to show that the artifact is the Temple of God, as revealed in the previous chapter.

Jesus Christ is represented in various ways In the New Testament. As previously mentioned, God chose a stone that had been rejected by human beings and used it as the cornerstone (i.e., Jesus Christ) for the foundation of His dwelling. In addition, according to the book of Revelation, the temple of the city mentioned by Ezekiel is the Lamb (Rev. 21:22), or Jesus Christ. Therefore, Christ presents himself both as the cornerstone needed for the foundation of the Temple, and as the Temple of God itself.

God established his dwelling through his Son, Jesus Christ, and built it for the *name* of God.[9] Therefore, Christ came to earth to establish this unified Kingdom of God; his body became the Temple of God.

In essence, Jesus Christ is the only mediator[10] leading to God and his Kingdom. The only tower (Temple) that can be erected to serve as a ladder to reach God is built with Christ, not with human arrogance.

Built on Square Stones

Christians are invited to take part in the construction of the spiritual Temple. According to a second-century text, *The Shepherd of Hermas,* the square-shaped Temple was built of square stones.[11] This statement figuratively demonstrates that each Christian must first carry their own square stone with a cross symbol—or in other words "carry the cross," which implies the recognition that Christ came, died and rose again for the remission of human sins. Then, each Christian must lay the stone down on the cornerstone (i.e., the Sator Square) that is Jesus Christ. Thus, each stone merges with the cornerstone to form the Temple, the mystical body of Christ. By being in Christ, each Christian becomes a member of his mystical body.

The relationship between humans and God, which was broken on many occasions by humans, is re-established by Jesus Christ, the Good News. Christ came to restore the divine order and reverse the curse of Babel, just as he reversed the curses of Adam and Eve and of the cross. In summary, the reversal of the curse of Babel brings us back to the conditions mentioned in verse 11:1 of Genesis. Therefore, all Christians in Christ join the Kingdom of God and are no longer dispersed. They are all now gathered and use "the same language [Latin] and the same words [the five words: SATOR, AREPO, TENET, OPERA and ROTAS]."

ISAIAH 28:11

While these explanations coincide with biblical passages and the information from the Magic Square, the Latin language is not specifically indicated in the book of Genesis. Let us examine a second passage from the Bible. Referring to verse 28:11 of the book of Isaiah in the Old Testament,[12] Paul announced that God wishes to speak in a foreign language other than the one spoken in Israel:

> In the Law it is written, "By men of strange tongues and by the lips of strangers I will speak to this people, and even so they will not listen to Me," says the Lord (1 Cor.14:21).

The other foreign tongue chosen by God is not specified.

DEUTERONOMY 28:49

A third Old Testament passage, Deuteronomy 28:49, indirectly reveals the other foreign tongue mentioned in Isaiah:

> The Lord will bring a nation against you from afar, from the end of the earth, as the eagle swoops down, a nation whose language you shall not understand.

The eagle, or *aquila* in Latin, is a military symbol representing a Roman legion.[13] This military representation was well known in the time of Jesus. For example, Flavius Josephus, the first-century historian, confirms this.[14]

Thus, in addition to predicting the Roman destruction of the second temple of Jerusalem, the verse reveals that the foreign language is actually Latin, the language of the Romans.

We know that educated people from the early centuries A.D., including high-ranking officials of the Roman Empire, knew Greek, since the language enjoyed a certain social prestige.[15] However,

Roman emperors from that period advocated the use of Latin in Roman territory. Romanization served to integrate and solidify the Empire's supremacy. In Rome, people spoke mainly Latin. While Greek remained the official language of Christian liturgy until the fourth century, in Rome, Christian liturgy was performed in Latin.[16] In addition, Roman soldiers spoke Latin; it was the official language of the Roman military.[17] Actually, the conquering Roman army promoted the Latin language throughout the vast Roman Empire.[18] Therefore, I can make the following statement:

Christian Roman soldiers spread the Latin Magic Square across the Roman Empire.

This could explain why so many Magic Squares were discovered where Roman soldiers had been posted. It is quite likely that Christianity quietly grew in the vast Roman Empire due to the propagation of the divine message by Christian soldiers, sometimes without the knowledge of the Roman authorities.

Speaking in Tongues

In Chapter 14 of the first epistle to the Corinthians, Paul mentions that some Christians received the special gift of "speaking in tongues" or "speaking a tongue."

This power, called "glossolalia," is specific to Christianity.[19] For example, some Christians, such as numerous Pentecostals, believe that people with this gift involuntarily utter words that are often incomprehensible, under the guidance of the Holy Spirit. However, I would like to suggest an alternative meaning of the term.

As it is in the same chapter of the aforementioned verse 1 Cor. 14:21, this gift of "speaking in a tongue" is closely linked to the "foreign language" that God wants to establish.

I would also suggest, considering verse 28:49 of Deuteronomy, that the term "speaking in a tongue" means "speaking in the foreign tongue" or simply put, "speaking Latin."

Therefore, if we replace "in a tongue" or "in tongues" with the word "Latin" in Chapter 14 of the first epistle to the Corinthians,[20] we get the following modified biblical passage:

14(2) For one who speaks in <u>Latin</u> does not speak to men but to God; for no one understands, but in his spirit he speaks mysteries .... (4) One who speaks in <u>Latin</u> edifies himself; but one who prophesies edifies the church. (5) Now, I wish that you all spoke in <u>Latin</u>, but even more that you would prophesy; and greater is one who prophesies than one who speaks <u>Latin</u>.... (6) But now, brethren, if I come to you speaking in <u>Latin</u> what will I profit you unless I speak to you either by way of revelation .... (13) Therefore let one who speaks in <u>Latin</u> pray that he may interpret. (14) For if I pray in <u>Latin</u>, my spirit prays, but my mind is unfruitful .... (18) I thank God, I speak in <u>Latin</u> more than you all.[21]

Then, he ends with this striking verse:

14(19) ... however, in the church, I desire to speak five words with my mind so that I may instruct others also, rather than ten thousand words in <u>Latin</u>.

In other words, Paul prefers speaking five words in Latin with his mind rather than speaking ten thousand words in Latin. These five words have got to be the five words of the Magic Square. Here, the mind or intellect, *noûs (G3563)* in Greek, is spiritual; it represents the part of the human being that perceives and accepts the words of God through faith.[22] Therefore, the substitution of the word "Latin" is fully justified on the grounds that the foreign language in 1 Cor. 14:21 is in the same chapter as the modified passage, and on Paul's statement regarding the five words.

Let us go back to the modified biblical passage. Although speaking in Latin is an asset, Paul considers this ability nonessential. He values the power, provided by the Holy Spirit, to understand, to interpret and to preach the divine message that was designed in Latin. Biblical scholar Émile Lombard could not have expressed it any better: "Quand l'interprétation n'accompagne pas la glossolalie, celle-ci se réduit pour les assistants à un mystérieux exercice spirituel dont ils ne retirent aucune édification."[23] ["For listeners, glossolalia unaccompanied by interpretation is reduced to a mysterious spiritual exercise from which they derive no edification."]

Indeed, those who consider that the Sator Square to be a simple palindromic word game gain no spiritual elevation from it.

Finally, in the Acts of the Apostles, receiving the gift of "speaking in tongues" is associated with receiving the Holy Spirit at baptism.[24] This association supports my assertion in Chapter 11 that the Latin Sator Square is the rule of faith, which was used during baptisms in the early centuries A.D.

All in all, armed with this new knowledge, we can better understand why the Catholic Church so carefully preserves Latin as the universal Christian language.[25] To the Church, it is the unified foreign language foretold by the Prophet Isaiah. Even today, Latin remains the official language of the Roman Catholic Church.

EPHESIANS 3:3

In Paul's epistle to the Ephesians, the apostle writes:

> (3:3) that by revelation there was made known to me the mystery, as I wrote before in brief [in few words].

The terms "in brief" or "in few words" take on their full meaning when applied to the Sator

Square. In this passage, the revelation has made him understand the mystery. Paul says that he wrote the mystery; it does not say that he conceived it. A few verses later, he states:

> (3:6) to be specific that the Gentiles are fellow heirs and fellow members of the body, and fellow partakers of the promise in Christ Jesus through the gospel.

The Apostle Paul indirectly notes that the universality of the message of the mystery (i.e., the Sator Square in my view) can be seen simply by looking at the five words of the Sator Square written *in the Latin language*. Thus, the message is not intended solely for Jewish people.

CHAPTER 7 OF THE BOOK OF DANIEL

In the highly apocalyptic book of Daniel, the Babylonian Jewish prophet relates various stories and describes his visions. This Old Testament document dating to the second century B.C. was taken seriously because it announced that God would soon come to save the oppressed and punish their oppressors.

The book of Daniel contains details of the divine arrival. In Chapter 7, Daniel describes a strange dream in which four great beasts arise from the sea (Dn. 7:3). He then specifies that "these ... are four kings who will arise from the earth" (Dn. 7:17). Many texts have established that these four great beasts represent the Babylonian, Medo-Persian, Greek and Roman empires.

The Fourth Great Beast

Daniel takes a great interest in and attributes significant status to the fourth great beast—the Roman Empire. Among other things, he states that during the reign of this beast, the saints will be persecuted (Dn. 7:25) and the Son of Man will have everlasting dominion over all (Dn. 7:13-14). Daniel's vision is very revealing to a follower of the Christian religion. Indeed, Daniel writes that this new *eternal* reign will be established during the reign of the fourth great beast. Therefore, the eternal reign does not refer to the Roman Empire as such, but to a power that will emerge from Roman domination.[26] The Prophet Daniel says that

God chose to build his building in Rome, not in Jerusalem. Daniel also indicates:

> In the days of those kings the God of Heaven will set up a kingdom which will never be destroyed, and that kingdom will not be left for another people... Inasmuch as you saw that a stone was cut out of the mountain without hands and that it crushed the iron, the bronze, the clay, the silver and the gold, the great God has made known to the king what will take place in the future; so the dream is true and its interpretation is trustworthy (2:44-45).

For the creator of the artifact, the stone mentioned by Daniel can only be the Sator Square. During the reign of the fourth great beast, the cut stone indicated a new kingdom and originated from the Messianic period. The stone cut "without hands" means that the stone was extracted by God.[27] The French Jesuit archeologist Guillaume de Jerphanion confirms this assertion when he specifies that many Magic Squares were discovered in close proximity to words, often in the Coptic language, linked to the four beasts,[28] as if to justify the legitimacy of the Latin Magic Square and the foundation of Christianity in Rome.

THE WORD "ROMAN" SOMETIMES MEANS "LATIN"

In the early centuries of our era, the Latin language was closely linked with the city of Rome. When texts mention "Roman language" they mean the "Latin language." For example, in the year A.D. 248, Origen of Alexandria declared that any word could be translated in the "Roman language."[29] He clearly specified that the Roman language is different from the Greek language. He also pointed out the importance of the Latin language in Rome.

In the early second millennium, Christianity's strong advocate, Gregory Pakourianos, took care to specify in his *Typikon* that there is *one Roman gospel* [singular] in addition to the gospels [plural] written in Greek.[30] He could not be clearer when he made a distinction between the Latin Gospel of Christ (i.e., the Sator Square in my view) and the other four Greek canonical gospels.

Also, recall that the monk John Cassian was nicknamed "Cassian the Roman." As I suggested in Chapter 2, the word "Roman" could mean that

Cassian spoke Latin or that he understood the secret of the Latin Sator Square.

We can also look at the example of Paul, who claimed to be a Roman citizen. Having Roman citizenship was extremely advantageous, as it provided the bearer with a set of rights and freedoms that included access to a structured education and the ability to move about freely in Roman territory. Today, researchers have various theories as to the basis of his citizenship. Many believe that it was granted to him because he was born in Tarsus, a free city in the Roman Empire. Others argue that his citizenship comes from his family's military background. Still others believe that Paul simply resorted to the subterfuge of Roman citizenship to save his life.

A mere 150 years after the Apostle Paul's death, a Roman historian named Cassius Dio reported that a person who did not speak Latin could not obtain Roman citizenship or benefit from certain privileges.[31] Consequently, Paul would have to have spoken Latin, given that he had Roman citizenship. Furthermore, to avoid trouble with Roman authorities, Paul must have strategically used Latin to prove his Roman citizenship.

Also, the New Testament notes that Paul was "speaking out boldly in the name of the Lord" (Acts 9:28) even before his first visit to Jerusalem. It is quite possible that is confidence resulted not only from feeling guided by a divine force, but also from his ability to speak Latin and understand the Sator Square.

TOWARDS ROME

Even today, some people believe that Jesus of Nazareth was a radical revolutionary accompanied by zealots who wanted to remove impure strangers from among the people of Israel. Others see Jesus as a revolutionary, yes, but also as someone who wished to transmit and promote a universal message focused on his divinity and on love for one's neighbor.

A passage in the gospel of Matthew (24:14) is unequivocal about Jesus's mission of expansion:

> This gospel of the kingdom shall be preached in the whole world as a testimony to all the nations, and then the end will come.[32]

Christ liberated his message from the Jewish yoke without excluding the Jews; he intended his message to be universal.

While Greek was indisputably the language used by early Christians, Christianity's center was not established in Jerusalem or even in Alexandria, but in Rome. The relocation from Jerusalem to Rome can be perceived when reading the Acts of the Apostles.

Apostles Peter and Paul came to Rome because Jesus Christ asked them to do so. These apostles may also have understood this request simply because the Magic Square is written in Latin.

For Paul, Rome was the preferred location for Christianity. He specified in his epistle to the Romans: "your faith is being proclaimed throughout the whole world. For God, whom I serve in my spirit in the preaching of the gospel of His Son, is my witness as to how unceasingly I make mention of you" (Rom. 1:8-9). Did Paul mean that the Gospel of Christ (i.e., the Sator Square) written in Latin, often reminds him of Roman Christians?

Thus, some might say that the message is written in Latin because the Temple must reside in the city of Rome. Indeed, if the city of Rome is elected as the place to build the Church of Jesus Christ, then a message in Latin, such as the one on the Sator Square, is completely appropriate. Therefore, promoting the importance of Latin was like promoting the importance of Rome. The Roman Catholic Church protects the Latin language; it is known as the Latin Church, after all. As mentioned in Chapter 6, Jerphanion noted that some Eastern Christian monks also ensured the preservation of the five Latin words of the Magic Square. The monks undeniably had a great interest in the Latin artifact and the Latin language. For example, Evagrius Ponticus, a monk who lived in the Egyptian desert at the end of the fourth century, was able to refer to a rich collection of Latin monastic terms when translating his writings.[33]

The arguments I have raised in this chapter are also supported by Origen of Alexandria:

> God preparing the nations for His teaching, that they might be under one prince, the king of the Romans, and that it might not, owing to the want of union among the nations, caused by the existence of many kingdoms, be more difficult for the apostles of Jesus to accomplish the task

enjoined upon them by their Master, when He said, "Go and teach all nations."[34]

This passage shows the deep and indissoluble link between the Gospel of Christ and the grouping of nations. This grouping is made under a single Roman establishment, and under one language— Latin. Also, the passage claims that the unification of the Roman Empire helped the apostles to preach their message. Indeed, during this period, the Romanization or Latinization of the Roman Empire could certainly have helped Christians teach the Latin message of the Magic Square.

The transition of Western Christianity from Greek to Latin took place gradually over many centuries. Finally, the belief that Jesus Christ spread his Gospel only in Greek is a limited and short-term perspective. If Jesus truly advocated a paradigm shift by communicating his message in Latin with the Magic Square, as an *a posteriori* examination shows that the results speak for themselves. This possible strategy of writing the divine message in Latin not only conformed to the divine will outlined in the Old Testament; it also bore tremendous fruit in the long term. I am the first to admit that a Latin message written directly by Jesus Christ is, to say the least, unusual and unexpected; however, it is possible that this surprising outcome largely contributed to the success of keeping the secret under wraps for two thousand years. Thus, according to this proposition, the rule of not divulging that the universal language of the Gospel of Christ is Latin is very likely part of the *Disciplina arcani.*

In summary, it is quite plausible that the Roman Church solidified its privileged Christian status at the world level because of the Latin stone that was given to Peter. We can now understand the scope of the enigmatic inscription *Roma tibi salus ita* that was written immediately before the inscription of a Rotas Square on a tile in Budapest (Aquincum). The inscription means "Rome your salvation, here it is!"[35]

THE PROPHECY OF ST. MALACHY: *PETRUS ROMANUS*

One day I happened to watch a documentary on the "Prophecy of the Popes,"[36] also known as the "Prophecy of St. Malachy." A short document, written by a twelfth-century Irish archbishop and discovered in 1595, announces the coming of Pope Celestine in 1143. It briefly describes the 110 popes who would succeed him. The conclusion of the prophecy text predicts an apocalyptic scenario, such as the end of the papacy or the end of the world. Many experts have expressed doubts about the identity of the author and about the exact date of the prophecies. Some believe that the prophetic evidence concerning the identities of the popes is accurate. According to the documentary, many high-ranking individuals in the Vatican have taken these prophecies very seriously.

Many people find the document disturbing. According to one of its passages, after the reign of the last pope, who many people believe will be Benedict XVI, a certain *petrus romanus* will arrive and pasture the sheep until the end; then, the "city of the seven hills," likely Rome, will be destroyed and Judgment Day will come. What does *petrus romanus* mean? Does it refer to Peter the Roman? To Pope Francis? I am afraid not. It soon dawned on me that *petrus romanus* does not mean "Peter the Roman" but rather "the Roman rock" or better yet—"*the rock written in Latin.*"

The petrus romanus *that heralds the end of the world must be the Sator Square.*

Whether or not one believes this prophecy, the author was certainly aware of the Sator Square. By announcing that after the reign of the last pope, the divine stone will pasture the sheep till the end, the author means that it will be harvest time—or Judgment Day—as reflected indirectly in the Sator Square. The Roman Catholic Church must fully understand these prophecies, since it knows the identity of the *petrus romanus*. Does the institution currently believe that the end is coming? What exactly is "the end"? Does unveiling the Sator Square to all indicate that the stone will shortly be used as the foundation of a Renewed Church, or a New Church? Or does it announce that the end of the Roman Church and the end of the world are near? In examining this prophecy, we may wonder whether the stone that was used to build the Roman institution will also destroy it.

AFTERWORD

What is this? What just happened to me?" These were the questions that popped into my mind right after my religious conversion, which I shared at the beginning of the book.

THE QUESTIONING PROCESS

After my "what" questions, the process continued with a second set of questions that started with "why." I think those were the hardest to answer.

The first "why" question was, "Why me?" I have yet to answer this crucial and painful question. I am no more deserving of this experience than the next person; I can think of many others who would be more worthy. I had not dedicated my life to religion and theology was not my initial field of expertise. In the beginning, I thought it must be some kind of mistake, and I often found myself looking up to the sky, thinking: "Lord, I am not worthy that you should enter under my roof."

I became deeply convinced that I had a mission to write about the Sator Square. This led me to "Why do I have to write a book?" I knew that doing so would require a great deal of study and research, as well as significant time and resources. In addition to these sacrifices, I was also fully cognizant that religion is a sensitive topic that is subject to a great deal of criticism and debate. Christians who have limited views on Christianity and believe that they hold the only truth may find the content of the book scandalous and even un-Christian. Also, I am aware that this field is often considered to be saturated and ruled by a handful of scholars; new findings could create a stir.

Some people might think that the whole thing is foolish; they may try to disprove the content of the book, or attempt to prove that the artifact is of dubious origin. I acknowledge all of this, and I accept it.

In short, I fear that Christians and non-Christians today will perceive the artifact the same way that Jews and non-Jews perceived it two thousand years ago, as mentioned in the first epistle of Paul to the Corinthians 1,23: "To Jews [to Christians] a stumbling block [a scandal], and to Gentiles [to non-Christians] foolishness."

When I realized that the artifact has most likely been preserved within the Christian world, another question came to mind: "Why do I have to reveal this secret message *outside* of Christianity?" In fact, even though the content of the enigma may have been protected by highly-placed ecclesiastics, it is obvious that in certain periods of Christian history, many other devotees knew how to decipher the artifact. For instance, some Magic Squares are displayed for all Christians to see at Roman military sites such as Dura Europos. No matter who knew the secret, it seems that the artifact was always intended to be hidden within the Christian world. My question remains unanswered, but I find comfort every now and then when I read the following passage in the three synoptic gospels, where Jesus says:

> For nothing is hidden that will not become evident, nor anything secret that will not be known and come to light.[1]

It became clear that these "why" questions would remain unanswered—or perhaps even unanswerable—and that I had to let go and find the confidence to move ahead without a safety net. When I finally realized that the biblical phrase "Lord, I am not worthy that you should enter under my roof" is completed by "but only say the word and my soul will be healed," I felt that an enormous weight had been lifted from my shoulders.

Even though the questions remained at the back of my mind, I knew that I had to move on to the "how" questions, including, "How will I complete this mission?"

FAMILY VISITS

One day, while attending a university theology course on ecumenism—a movement favoring the union of all the Christian churches under one Church—I unexpectedly received a clear, though partial, answer to my question about why I had to write this book. *The Secret Gospel of Jesus* is aligned with the ecumenical movement and I modestly hope that it will prove helpful, when the time comes, in reuniting all Christians under one universal Church in whatever form.

As part of my studies, I attended a service and interviewed a pastor from three different denominations: Methodist, First Baptist, and Evangelical. I must admit that before entering the churches, I was beset by a fear of the unknown. However, in all three situations I was warmly received and my fears were soon allayed.

Encountering these three denominations made me realize that we all have one thing in common: we all praise and worship Jesus Christ. I felt a spiritual communion in a familiar environment, as if I were a member of an extended family.

There were points of divergence, of course, but at the end of the day, as a Christian, I came away with numerous benefits. The impact of the meetings went beyond my university studies; it broadened my horizons. Being open to and learning about various perspectives creates great richness and, in my view, should be strongly encouraged.

ONE CHRISTIAN PATH, MANY WAYS TO FOLLOW IT

The Sator Square reveals a simple divine message—the truth. Christians must follow a single path with the divine and adhere to a single truth.

Although all Christians, no matter their denomination, must stay on the path and respect its blueprint, Jesus Christ left a message that is open to different interpretations. As mentioned previously, the Apostle Paul and the apologist Justin Martyr both noted that people can be Christians even if they have more than one interpretation of the divine message, as long as they follow the divine blueprint. Also, Augustine of Hippo wrote on numerous occasions that a variety of interpretations is possible if the interpretations respect the faith.[2] Thus, in my opinion, the most important step is to obtain consensus among Christians on what is considered to be the original content of the deposit of faith (i.e., the content of both the sacred Scripture and the fixed sacred tradition), rather than a consensus on the interpretation of the content.

MEMBERS OF THE BODY OF CHRIST

In Paul's epistle to the Romans, the apostle makes this comparison:

> For just as we have many members in one body and all the members do not have the same function, so we, who are many, are one body in Christ, and individually members one of another (12:4-5).

The comparison also appears in other passages of the epistles of Paul.[3]

The Uniqueness of the Body of Christ

In these passages we can see that *all* Christians are united in *one* mystical body of Christ; a concept seen in the word "sower" on the Sator Square. In the epistle to the Ephesians, Paul clarifies the metaphor by specifying that the Church is the body of Christ (Eph. 1:22-23). Each Christian denomination forms just one part of the universal body of Christ. Therefore, each denomination needs the others to be unified in the body of Christ.

The Diversity of the Members

In the first epistle of Paul to the Corinthians, the apostle shows once again that the body of Christ is made up of a diversity of members. This metaphor ultimately represents the different interpretations and denominations that exist among Christians (1 Cor. 12:12-20). These different interpretations do not exist outside the body of Christ; instead, they are an integral part of it.

Each Christian denomination, regardless of its prominence and reason for being, is a member of the body of the universal Church and contributes to the body of Christ (1 Cor. 12:27), as long as it follows certain established norms outlined in the divine blueprint. Paul notes, for instance, that those who are part of the members of the body of the Church must agree that there is "one Lord, one faith, one baptism" (Eph. 4:5).

Thus, those who claim to be Christians must give priority, not to a particular denomination (a member of the body), but to Jesus Christ and the universal Church (the entire body of Christ). Each denomination must work in close cooperation and coordination with the others and must fit together, as does each member of the body. As for me, I am first and foremost a Christian who wants to be in Jesus Christ through the universal Church.

Building the Foundation of the Temple or Church of Christ

The question of what exactly is this universal Church of Christ is a thorny one, to say the least. Even though this book shows that Jesus Christ wanted to build his foundation in Rome, the New Testament also stresses that this foundation, like the body of Christ, is not made up of a single component, but of various materials. The following passage describes how the foundation of the Temple should be built:

> Now no man can lay a foundation other than the one which is laid, which is Jesus Christ. Now if any man builds on the foundation with gold, silver, precious stones, wood, hay, straw, each man's work will become evident; for the day will show it because it is to be revealed with fire, and the fire itself will test the quality of each man's work (1 Cor. 3:11-13).

The term "various materials" in the figurative sense means that other opinions and interpretations are not only accepted, but encouraged in order to build the foundation; they will be judged at fair value. The Apostle Paul also says that only God has the right to judge: "each will receive his own reward according to his own labor" (1 Cor. 3:8).

Above all, the universal Church must be a community of all Christians who follow Tradition and the Scriptures. Many may question whether the foundation is *actually* built with *various* materials.

ECUMENICAL MOVEMENT

The contemporary ecumenical movement began in the early 20th century and has continued its efforts ever since to bring together Christians of all denominations in order to promote Christian unity.

In 1950, the World Council of Churches, which comprises some 350 Christian churches around the world, adopted the *Toronto Statement*. This document states that the churches that have *vestigia Ecclesiae* (vestiges), or predetermined elements, can be considered to be members of this group. As such, each member church acknowledges the other member churches, and therefore the diversity of the Church of Christ. While the Roman Catholic Church is not a member of this group, it has attended meetings.

In 1964, the Second Vatican Council of the Roman Catholic Church issued a decree on ecumenism, *Unitatis Redintegratio*, in which it states the desire to restore Christian unity. It lists a series of ecclesiastical elements required for unity, including "the written Word of God, the life of grace, faith, hope and charity, other internal gifts of the Holy Spirit and other visible features."[4] It also recognizes that these ecclesiastical elements that are necessary for solidifying the Church of Christ can also be found outside the Roman Catholic Church.[5]

In the ecumenism decree, the Council distinguishes two major groups of churches outside of the Roman Catholic Church: Eastern Churches and ecclesial churches and communities.

The Council considers the Eastern Churches to be closely linked and independent, because they have *the apostolic tradition*.[6] The interpretations of the divine message of both the Eastern and Western

Churches are considered to be supplementary and not in conflict with each other.

The second group, ecclesial churches and communities, became separated from the Roman Catholic Church at the end of the Middle Ages. Considering the large number of members in this group (including Lutherans and Anabaptists) and their significant differences with the Catholic Church, the latter has invited each of them to initiate a dialogue and to begin a process of reconciliation.[7]

The Roman Catholic Church subsequently held several bilateral meetings and entered into numerous agreements with members of this second group, which demonstrates a certain level of reconciliation, despite some persistently contentious issues. One of the most remarkable agreements is the *Joint Declaration on the Doctrine of Justification,* signed in the Bavarian city of Augsburg in 1999, which indicates, on the one hand, a welcoming climate that encourages common prayer, respect and active listening, and on the other, the possibility of reaching consensus on certain elements, while recognizing certain differences. These remarkable efforts should be continued.

Within the Denomination

Up to this point, we have only discussed the process of unification between Christian denominations. However, in reality, the tensions and divisions that currently exist are mainly within the denominations, not between them.

Within a denomination, we can frequently see a diversity of ideologies, often influenced by political and economic pressures. As such, the challenge of obtaining some form of unity is even greater today in an environment of increasing diversity. The Christian groups can only accomplish unification if they fully focus on Jesus Christ and his *core* message.

Christians can gain a better understanding of the divine message by attentively listening to various interpretations that are consistent with the deposit of the faith; this allows them to see the message from a different angle. These interpretations deepen their Christian faith and solidify Christian unity in diversity, which represents a huge growth potential for Christianity. Finally, in all of this, I humbly believe that Jesus Christ deliberately issued a great challenge to all his followers to implement his commandment to love their neighbors as themselves.

One day, which may come soon, Jesus Christ will return to this earth. Finding all Christians in harmony, united in diversity, would be an unmistakable sign of gratitude for all that God has done through His Son Jesus Christ.

APPENDIX I

AFTER NICAEA

T his appendix outlines the positions of two renowned Christian authors and the Catholic Church on the seven key themes of the Sator Square. All these positions were issued after the Council of Nicaea.

A. AUGUSTINE'S POSITION

Divine grace and free will were such important and controversial principles that Augustine saw fit to clarify his position on these topics in documents dealing with grace, such as *On Rebuke and Grace, On Nature and Grace, On the Grace of Christ and On Original Sin,* and *On Grace and Free Will.*[1] Let us examine his position through the perspective of his debate with the semi-Pelagians, including John Cassian.

The Initium fidei

The *initium fidei* or "the beginning of faith" is the most contentious issue between Cassian and Augustine. It has to do with which comes first in the process of salvation: the grace of God or human will.

On one hand, Cassian firmly believes that even if people are under sin, they can begin to believe on their own and thus receive divine grace in return. Like the Eastern Orthodox Church, Cassian relies above all on Christian anthropology, according to which human beings are basically created in the image of God and have been given free will. Cassian also maintains that human beings require grace as their faith grows, but not necessarily at the "beginning of faith" or *initium fidei* stage.[2]

The Doctrine of Original Sin

Conversely, Augustine believes that human beings cannot choose to do good, because they are corrupt. He upholds his view by developing the doctrine of original sin, a sin that is handed down to human beings at birth following Adam's disobedience of God. Therefore, human freedom is limited; human beings cannot choose to do good without the help of grace and so they cannot save themselves. However, God can save them by bestowing divine grace on them. According to Augustine, the divine grace called "operating" or "prevenient" grace, which corresponds to the initial grace revealed in the two sentences of the Sator Square, comes before human will; it begins the process of salvation and influences the person.

A basic question arises: At what point does God's grace influence human beings? Does divine influence irrevocably reduce or eliminate free will?

The 16th-century Protestant Reformation—particularly Calvinism—, basing itself on the Scriptures and its own interpretation of the doctrine presented by Augustine, promotes "monergism," which means "to act alone." Devotees of monergism maintain that God controls everything and is solely responsible for the salvation of every human being. In their view, the total depravity of human nature prevents humans from choosing good on their own; they are mired in evil. When humans do good, it is only because God has strengthened human will.

However, other interpreters believe that Augustine leaves a bit of room for free will in human salvation, despite the clear predominance of God's grace. Is Augustine significantly downplaying human effort in salvation to properly counterbalance Pelagians' arguments?

The Doctrine of Predestination

If human beings are influenced or subjugated by receiving divine grace, then why do many of them not answer the call? In Augustine's view, quite simply, it is because God does not invite everyone—only those who will be saved.

Thus, Augustine presents a disputed doctrine, that of predestination: God alone predestines some people to eternal salvation; those who do not receive divine grace will not obtain salvation. The offer of grace is not preceded by individual merit.

Augustine's doctrine cannot have pleased Cassian or other monks like Vincent de Lérins, because it threatened the fundamental pillar of the monastic institution so cherished by those monks.[3]

Nuns and monks dedicated their lives to God and wanted to live by God's Ten Commandments in hopes of attaining eternal life, without lessening the importance of God's grace in their lives. These people often isolated themselves from the outside world and expended an enormous amount of effort on trying to lead a virtuous life while fighting temptation. They must have found Augustine's doctrine radical and even hostile to their way of life.[4] According to Augustine, only God knows and chooses those who will be saved. This means that even the most virtuous person would not necessarily be saved. The doctrine might also suggest that some people are condemned from birth not to be saved, no matter what they do throughout their lives. Augustine felt the need to clarify that God knows everything, so he already knows who will receive salvation. This means that God only invites and influences those people, knowing that they will answer his call.[5]

In short, Augustine's view is that God's operating grace moves human will toward faith. The person will be largely influenced in his freedom to believe and to act. However, in that context, many people question whether the freedom to believe and to act truly exists. According to the Eastern Orthodox Church, an operating grace calls to human beings. The Holy Spirit introduces this grace into the person's heart so that the person moves toward the Holy Spirit.[6]

However, as emphasized by the fourth-century Desert Father Macarius of Egypt, the divine call is neither coercive nor authoritarian: "When the grace comes to the person, it does not have the possibility to shackle the person's will ... rather, it bows before the person's free will."[7] Grace certainly influences the person, but it undeniably leaves the person free to decide.

B. THOMAS'S POSITION

A close reading of three passages from the *Summa Theologica* reveals a striking resemblance to the seven key themes.

The first passage, which is quoted below, illustrates the two ways in which grace acts on a person:

> First, inasmuch as man's soul *is moved* by God *to know or will or do* something... Secondly, man is

> *helped* by God's *gratuitous* will, ... does He move them to their natural acts, but He bestows upon them certain forms and powers, which are the principles of acts, in order that they may themselves be inclined to these movements, ... whereby they may be moved by Him sweetly and promptly to acquire eternal good.[8]

Comments: All the themes related to divine grace are included. It is universal, free, omnipresent and persuasive. With respect to predestination, Thomas clarifies that grace is offered to everyone, but that God only breaks off the relationship with those who do not accept divine grace, thereby refusing the invitation.[9] The second passage focuses on human actions that are led by grace in the process of salvation:

> First, there is an interior act of the will, and with regard to the act of the will is a thing moved, and *God is the mover*; and especially when the will, which hitherto willed evil, begins to will good.... we speak of *operating* grace. But there is another exterior act; .... And because God *assists* us in this act, both by strengthening our will interiorly so as to attain to the act, and by granting outwardly the capability of operating, it is with respect to this that we speak of *cooperating* grace.[10]

Comments: Thomas goes back to the categories of grace—operating and cooperating—that were previously presented by Augustine. He also repeats most of the themes of grace found in the Sator Square. On one hand, he shows the importance of God, who holds the plow. God is the only mover. Without God, the plow simply does not move. Operating grace breathes internal will into human beings, who then begin their path to salvation. On the other hand, Thomas presents a cooperating grace that moves the person to act and to follow God along the way, to turn with and toward God. There could not be a better word than "moving" in these passages to reflect the action of the sower taking to the path and walking.

Finally, the third passage from *Summa Theologica* invokes humans' freedom to choose:

> Now the reason why it is possible not to choose, or to choose, may be gathered from a twofold power in man. For man can will or not will, act or not act; again, he can will this or that, and do this or that.[11]

Comments: In this passage, we find the themes related to free will. In Thomas's view, human beings on one hand have the freedom "to will" (to believe), seen in the first sentence of the artifact, and on the other hand, the freedom "to act" (to work) from the second sentence.

Thomas's explanations in the three passages from his work correspond precisely to all seven themes found in the enigmatic Sator Square.

C. THE CATHOLIC CHURCH POSITION

The Catholic Church waited until 529, during the Second Council of Orange, to issue its comments on the doctrines outlined by Augustine. On original sin, the Roman Catholic Church stated that each human being, being a descendant of Adam, is born of original sin and requires the help of Christ at baptism to be forgiven for this sin. Although baptized people retain an inclination toward evil, they are not totally corrupt.[12] On the subject of predestination, the Church specified that God wants salvation for all.[13] Through his omniscience, God knows absolutely everything, including the future, and knows in advance who will follow Him and who will accept the grace that was initially offered to everyone. In the Church's view, God does not predestine anyone to evil;[14] people are solely responsible for their bad decisions and evil deeds.

The Church was obviously following the plan of the tradition or, in my view, the Sator Square, but it also relied on the Scriptures to clarify certain points concerning Augustine's interpretation on grace and free will.

A thousand years after the Second Council of Orange, the Church, very much against its wishes, had to return to these subjects and define them in more detail to counter the pressures of the Protestant Reformation.

The Roman Catholic Church organized the Council of Trent (1542-1563) chiefly to respond to the repeated theological attacks of the Protestant Reformers and to disclose the doctrine that it had always preserved. As their influence grew, the Protestants launched a frontal attack on some of the doctrinal foundations upheld by the Roman Catholic Church.

At the sixth session in 1547, the Council of Trent clarified the Catholic position on justification by issuing a decree. The decree held that the primary purpose of a Christian is to become righteous before God. The Roman Catholic Church held that justification was a process, and in explaining it, the

Church once again seemed to be referencing the two sentences of the Sator Square. The Council of Trent established that justification begins when an individual freely accepts the invitation of operating divine grace to follow God (to convert) and to work with God through Jesus Christ.[15] Grace is the very first step in justification and so it precedes faith, which remains a main factor throughout the process of salvation. Justification is not limited to a single, one-time, narrowly defined event; it is also present in an active Christian spiritual life in an ongoing relationship with God. Thus, gradual justification develops on a daily basis in Christians who have faith, and who do good work in close cooperation with the divine. The interior sanctification of the soul happens during the justification process. The person hopes to be righteous before God.

The text from the Council of Trent specified the need for "freely assenting to and cooperating with that said grace,"[16] exactly like the two human freedoms required for salvation that are indicated in the artifact, namely "to believe" and "to work with God." Once again, the description of the process corresponds perfectly with the content of the Sator Square.

The Councils of Orange and Trent stated that the grace offered by God precedes any merits and the human will to want God.[17] The Church's position was explicit: the gift of grace bestowed on a person does not first depend on that person's merit. However, with cooperating grace, human effort is absolutely required in the process of salvation.

With respect to synergism—cooperation between human will and divine grace—and integration in Jesus Christ, we should never confuse the necessary level of participation with the power of each entity. Both human and divine wills work fully together, but there is no doubt that in the process of salvation, the transcendent (divine) power is immeasurably superior to the power of a mere human being. Yet however small the power of a person's will, that person's contribution is an indispensable element of their salvation.

APPENDIX II

BEFORE NICAEA

This appendix covers the positions taken in the period before the First Council of Nicaea in relation to the seven key themes of the Sator Square. We will look at the positions taken by the ante-Nicene Church Fathers and the authors of the New Testament.

A. THE ANTE-NICENE CHURCH FATHERS' POSITION

The following three ante-Nicene passages encompass some of the seven key themes.

- Origen of Alexandria (*c.* 230 A.D.)

    We are not to suppose either that those things which are *in our power can be done without the help of God*, or that those which are in God's hand can be brought to completion without the intervention of our *acts*, and desires, and *intention*; because we have it not in our own power so to will and to do anything, as not to know that this very faculty, by which *we are able to will or to do*, was bestowed on us by God.[1]

- Clement of Alexandria (*c.* end of the second century A.D.)

    God ministers eternal salvation to those who *co-operate* for the attainment of knowledge and good conduct; and since what the commandments enjoin are *in our own power*, along with their performance, the promise is accomplished.[2]

- Irenaeus of Lyon (*c.* end of the second century A.D.)

    Nor did He stand in need of our service when *he ordered us to follow Him*; but thus bestowed salvation upon ourselves. *For to follow the Saviour* is to be a partaker of salvation, and to follow light is to receive light... For as much as God is in want of nothing, so much does man stand in need of *fellowship with God*.[3]

Indeed, the above passages contain many themes extracted from the artifact, such as grace that is present, that calls to, provides advice to and influences a Christian. They also exhibit the human freedoms to believe and to work, as well as the need for a Christian to co-operate with divine grace to obtain salvation.

B. Jesus Christ's Position in the Four Gospels

The seven key themes can also be found in Jesus Christ's teachings.

1) God's grace

As outlined in Chapter 2, the fundamental principle of God's grace relates to the first four key themes found in the Sator Square. To Jesus Christ, divine grace is necessary for leading people to their eternal salvation. His Parable of the Growing Seed (Mk. 4:26-29) teaches that a good harvest results primarily from the grace of God and not from the efforts of the human being.

Jesus Christ often spoke of salvation; he provides the opportunity to enter the Kingdom of God, which is not of this world but is present in our midst. Thus, the divine call in the Sator Square challenges human beings to immediately take part in this new world, as part of their daily lives. It is a call to take action—immediately—to embark on the path of life with Jesus Christ. Some may believe that Christians often focus too much on the ultimate goal of eternal life, thereby overlooking the privileged opportunity to walk every day with hope and to grow in Jesus Christ.

Theme 1: Initial (Operating) Grace Is Offered to Everyone

The message of the Sator Square is that grace is not restricted to chosen people from a particular ethnicity, social class, or gender. Jesus Christ confirms this point, as demonstrated in the following passages:

> For God did not send the Son into the world to judge the world, but that the world might be saved through Him (Jn. 3:17).

> And I, if I am lifted up from the earth, will draw all men to Myself (Jn. 12:32).

> The field is the world (Mt. 13:38).

Theme 2: Initial Grace Is Free

There are no specific requirements in the Sator Square for receiving the gift of this initial grace. Jesus confirms that initial grace is freely bestowed; it is not awarded for merit. In fact, even sinners and tax collectors can have this grace—which is of particular importance to me as a former tax collector! God gives everyone a chance, even those who are judged or excluded by the reigning religious authority, as Jesus said:

> If you knew the gift of God (Jn. 4:10).

> He causes His sun to rise on the evil and the good, and sends rain on the righteous and the unrighteous (Mt. 5:45).

> Several statements made by Jesus about sinners or tax collectors (Lk. 7:34, 7:47-50, 18:14, Mk. 2:17, Mt. 9:12)

Theme 3: Grace Is Constantly Present

God's grace, whether operating or cooperating, is omnipresent from the beginning to the end of a Christian's life. Jesus emphasizes cooperating grace in the following passages:

For where two or three have gathered together in My name, I am there in their midst (Mt. 18:20).

I am with you always, even to the end of the age (Mt. 28:20).

Theme 4: Once Initial Grace Is Accepted, God Guides and Provides Advice

As discussed in Chapter 3, grace, whether operating or cooperating, guides human beings, as Jesus confirmed:

I am the Light of the world; he who follows Me will not walk in the darkness, but will have the Light of life (Jn. 8:12).

I am the good shepherd (Jn. 10:11).

2) Human free will

Let us look at the two fundamental human freedoms that are present in Jesus' teachings.

Theme 5: Freedom to Believe

As outlined in the artifact, humans need divine support to obtain salvation. If someone does not believe, then there is no walking, no plowing, and no access to the Kingdom of God.

Although God occasionally uses His coercive power, His love and kindness are abundant. Jesus Christ lovingly invites us to believe in him—and in God—and to follow him, as seen in the following extracts:

> Do not let your heart be troubled; believe in God, believe also in Me (Jn. 14:1).

> All things are possible to him who believes (Mk. 9:23).

> He who has believed and has been baptized shall be saved; but he who has disbelieved shall be condemned (Mk. 16:16).

> For God so loved the world, that He gave His only begotten Son, that whoever believes in Him shall not perish, but have eternal life (Jn. 3:16).

> For this is the will of My Father, that everyone who beholds the Son and believes in Him will have eternal life, and I Myself will raise him up on the last day (Jn. 6:40).

Theme 6: Freedom to Work

Those who plow must not only believe; they must roll up their sleeves and work hard throughout their journey to achieve their goal, as Jesus said:

Why do you call Me, Lord, Lord, and do not do what I say? Everyone who comes to Me and acts on them, I will show you whom he is like (Lk. 6:46-47).

But the one who has heard and has not acted accordingly, is like a man who built a house on the ground without foundation (Lk. 6:49).

Therefore beseech the Lord of the harvest to send out workers into the harvest (Mt. 9:38).

3) Interaction Between Free Will and God's Grace

The final theme concerns the interaction between the two principles.

Theme 7: Human Freedom Cooperates with the Grace of God for Salvation

Lastly, Jesus wants everyone to be with him—and to work in concert with him—to obtain salvation, as stated in the following passages:

The kingdom of God is like a man who casts seed upon the soil; and he goes to bed at night and gets up by day, and the seed sprouts and grows—how, he himself does not know... But when the crop permits, he immediately puts in the sickle, because the harvest has come (Mk. 4:26-29[4]).

Truly, Truly, I say to you, he who believes in Me, the works that I do, he will do also; and greater works than these he will do; because I go to the Father (Jn. 14:12).

He who abides in Me and I in him, he bears more fruit (Jn. 15:5).

In short, these passages, scattered throughout the four gospels, cover all the key themes found in the two sentences of the Sator Square. All the above quotes come from the heart of Jesus Christ's teachings—directly from his lips. This is crucial, because all the divine statements in the New Testament, like those of the Old Testament, are much more significant than any made by a mere human being.

C. THE POSITION OF THE NEW TESTAMENT AUTHORS (EXCEPT FOR THE FOUR ÉVANGELISTS)

The seven key themes are also found in the New Testament books, other than the four gospels. Table 4.1 provides examples for each theme.

TABLE 4.1 Passages from New Testament Books (other than the Four Gospels) that are related to the seven key themes from the Sator Square.

The Seven Themes	Passages from Pauline epistles	Other than the Pauline epistles
Grace of God		
1) Initial (Operating) Grace Is Offered to Everyone	Rom. 5:18; Col. 1:23; 1 Tim 2:4.	Acts 10:45; 17:26-27; Jas. 1:5.
2) Initial Grace Is Free	Rom. 5:15; 6:23; 11:6 ; 2 Cor. 9:14-15.	Acts 8:20; 10:45; Jas. 1:17.
3) Grace Is Constantly Present (Omnipresence)	Rom. 14,11; 1 Thess. 5:10.	Heb. 7:25; 13:5; 1 Pet. 4:2; 5:10, Rev. 4:8.

4) Once Initial Grace Is Accepted, God Guides and provides Advice	2 Cor. 5:14; Eph. 1:18; 5:8; 1 Thess. 3:1.	Heb. 12:2; 1 Pet. 2:9; 2 Pet. 1:19; 1:21; 1 Jn. 2:27; 5:20; Rev 7:17.

Human Free Will

5) Freedom To Believe	Rom. 10:9; 1 Cor. 15:12-14.	Acts 16:31; 1 Jn. 5:1; 5:10.
6) Freedom To Work or To Turn	1 Cor. 6:11; 2 Cor. 9:6; Gal. 5:21.	Jas. 1:22-25; 2:14-26; 1 Pet. 3:11-12; Rev. 22:12.

Interaction Between Free Will and Grace of God

7) Human Freedom Cooperates with the Grace of God for Salvation	1 Cor. 3:9; 15:58; 2 Thess. 1:12; be "in Jesus Christ": Rom. 3:22; 8:9-11; Gal. 3:22; Eph. 4:21; Phil. 1:26.	Heb. 3:14; 1 Jn. 1:6; 2:5; 4:13; 14:16-17; Jude 1:1; Rev. 1:9; 3:20.

Note: For the purposes of this table, Paul is not considered to be the author of the epistle to the Hebrews.

NOTE

Preface

[1] Simcha Jacobovici, Director and Producer, The Roman Army's Secret Christians (Season 1, Episode 6) [Television documentary series episode] in Decoding the Ancients, Produced by Associated Producers in association with History Television Canada and The History Channel US, 2010.

[2] Unless otherwise indicated, the word "Christian" generally refers to any person who believes that Jesus Christ is the Messiah, whether or not the person is of Jewish origin.

[3] Larry A. Angus explains some of this questioning in The Hidden Message of Jesus: How the Gnostic Gospels Change Christianity (Shelbyville, KY: Wasteland Press, 2012), pp. 76-78.

[4] Irenaeus of Lyon, Against Heresies, I, Preface, 2.

---

[5] See, among others: Irenaeus of Lyon, Against Heresies, I, Preface, 1; Justin Martyr, First Apology, 58, 1; Tertullian, The Prescription Against Heretics, 4 and Against Praxeas, 1.

[6] Alister McGrath, Heresy: A History of Defending the Truth (New York, NY: HarperOne, 2009), p. 202.

[7] A bishopric was certainly a coveted position, if we think of Valentine, who formed his own school of Gnosticism following his unsuccessful candidacy for the position of bishop of Rome (Tertullian, Against the Valentinians, 4).

[8] Irenaeus of Lyon, Against Heresies, I, 10, 1-2.

Chapter 1

[1] Jérome Carcopino, *Études d'histoire chrétienne, le Christianisme secret du carré magique, les fouilles de Saint-Pierre et la Tradition* (Paris: Albin Michel, 1963), pp. 21-23.

[2] Archeologist Guillaume de Jerphanion mentions that Della Corte could have found another Rotas Square in 1925 on a wall of the house of P. Paquis Proculus. *La voix des monuments: études d'archéologie chrétienne*, Nouv. Sér. (Roma: Pontificio Istituto orientale, 1938), pp. 78-79 and Jérôme Carcopino, *Études d'histoire chrétienne*, p. 66.

[3] Jérôme Carcopino, *Études d'histoire chrétienne*, p. 28.

[4] Ibid., p. 96.

[5] Alison E. Cooley and M.G.L Cooley, *Pompeii: A Sourcebook*, 2nd ed. (New York: Routledge, 2004), p. 76. Cf. Mary Beard, *Pompeii: The Life of a Roman Town* (London: Profile, 2008), p. 302.

[6] Rose Mary Sheldon, "The Sator Rebus: An Unsolved Cryptogram?" *Cryptologia*, vol. 27, no. 3 (July 2003), p. 286.

[7] Felix Grosser, "Ein neuer Vorschlag zur Deutung der Satorformel," *Archiv für Religionswissenschaft* (1926), pp. 165-169.

[8] Is it really pure coincidence that a Swedish scholar made the same discovery in the same period as Grosser and another scholar claimed to have made the identical discovery two years before Grosser? (See Rose Mary Sheldon, "The Sator Rebus," p. 247.) After reading this book, some people may suspect that this was a deliberate and orchestrated diversion with the intent to hide the secret message of the Magic Square.

[9] William Baines, "The Rotas-Sator Square: A New Investigation," *New Testament Studies*, vol. 33, no. 3 (1987), 469-476.

[10] Pierre Chompré, *Dictionnaire abrégé de la fable, des poètes, des tableaux et des statues, pour l'intelligence dont les sujets sont tirés de l'histoire poétique* (Paris: Lebigre, 1833), p. 392.

[11] Walter O. Moeller, *The Mithraic Origin and Meaning of the Rotas-Sator Square* (Leiden: E. J. Brill, 1973), p. 8.

[12] Rose Mary Sheldon, "The Sator Rebus," p. 242.

[13] Abbé Doublet, *Jésus-Christ étudié en vue de la prédication dans saint Thomas d'Aquin*, 6e éd., Tome 3 (Paris: Berche et Tralin, 1881), p. 8.

[14] This method was proposed by Ludwig Diehl according to C. W. Ceram, *The March of Archaeology* (New York: Knopf, 1971), p. 30.

[15] Ibid.

[16] John T. Cullen, *Sator Enigma, Ancient Roman Mystery Solved* (California: Smashwords: 2010), Ch. 5. For more information about his discovery, refer to Cullen's book. Note that he uses the conjunction "but" to connect the two sentences. While this conjunction is widely used in these kinds of statements, it is not directly indicated in the five words of the Sator Square. The terms "and" or "and then" could also be used to link the two sentences. Despite this, John Dominic Crossan notes that the importance with this kind of compound statement lies in the power of their interaction created by the parallelism, see *In Fragments: The Aphorisms of Jesus* (Eugene, OR: Wipf and Stock Publishers, 2008), p. 78.

[17] John T. Cullen, *Sator Enigma*, Ch. 5.

[18] Joachim Jeremias, *The Parables of Jesus* (London: SCM Press, 1963), p. 195.

[19] John T. Cullen, *Sator Enigma,* Ch. 11.

Chapter 2

[1] Mt. 13:1-23; Mk. 4:1-20; Lk. 8:4-15.

[2] However, it could be argued that the celestial assistance is intended only for readers who are able to decode the Sator Square hidden message.

[3] Sabine Baring-Gould, *The Origin and Development of Religious Belief,* Part 1, *Polytheism and Monotheism* (London: Rivington, 1884), pp. 219-220; cf. Bart D. Ehrman, *Misquoting Jesus: The Story Behind Who Changed the Bible and Why*, 1st ed. (New York: HarperSan Francisco, 2005), p. 19.

[4] John T. Cullen, *Sator Enigma,* Ch. 11.

⁵ In fact, several other disputes on these principles occurred between these two major debates as indicated by Alexander Y. Hwang, *"Prosper, Cassian, and Vincent: The Rule of Faith in the Augustinian Controversy"* in *Tradition & the Rule of Faith in the Early Church,* ed. Ronnie J. Rombs and Alexander Y. Hwang (Washington, D.C.: The Catholic University of America Press, 2010), p. 84.

⁶ Owen Chadwick, *John Cassian* (Cambridge: University Press, 1968), pp. 126-127.

⁷ See also John Cassian, *Conference* 13.2.

⁸ Owen Chadwick, *John Cassian*, p. 7.

⁹ John Cassian, *Institution,* 10. 7; cf. A. M. C. Casiday, *Tradition and Theology in St John Cassian* (Oxford: Oxford University Press, 2007), p. 119.

¹⁰ John Cassian, *Conferences,* 18.5.

¹¹ Owen Chadwick, *John Cassian,* pp. 20, 52.

¹² Vincent of Lérins, *Commonitorium*, 10.

¹³ Ibid., 6.

¹⁴ Ibid., 22.

¹⁵ Vladimir Lossky, *Mystical Theology of the Eastern Church* (London: James Clark & Co, 1957), p. 198.

¹⁶ Justin Popovitch, *Les voies de la connaissance de Dieu: Macaire D'Égypte, Isaac Le Syrien, Siméon Le Nouveau Théologien* (Lausanne, Suisse: l'Âge d'Homme, 1998), p. 69.

¹⁷ See 1 Cor. 4:15; Gal. 2:4; Eph. 2:6, 2:13; Col. 1:2. This notion is also found in Jn. 15:1-9; 17:21-26.

¹⁸ Such as Vladimir Lossky, *Mystical Theology of the Eastern Church*, p. 198.

¹⁹ Panagiotis Bratsiotis, *The Greek Orthodox Church* (Notre Dame: University of Notre Dame Press, 1968), pp. 18; 26.

²⁰ Guillaume de Jerphanion, *La voix des monuments*, p. 47.

21 Richard Pietschmann, "Les inscriptions coptes de Faras" in *Recueil de travaux relatifs à la philologie et à l'archéologie égyptiennes et assyriennes*, ed. G. Maspero, XXI (Paris: Librairie Émile Bouillon, 1899), p. 134; Guillaume de Jerphanion, *La voix des monuments*, pp. 49-50.

22 Guillaume de Jerphanion, *La voix des monuments*, p. 54.

23 Various inscriptions from the early centuries A.D. were discovered with the same kind of transposition—from Latin letters to Greek letters. See Barbara Frale, *Le suaire de Jésus de Nazareth* (Montreal: Novalis, 2011), pp. 255-256. Transposition should not be confused with transliteration (a process of switching letters that helps language pronunciation of foreign words).

24 Guillaume de Jerphanion, *La voix des monuments*, p. 48.

25 Owen Chadwick, *John Cassian,* p. 161 and Columba Stewart, *Cassian the Monk* (New York: Oxford University Press, 1998), p. 5.

26 For example, Panaiotis Tzamalikos proposed in that the nickname was used to differentiate two people named Cassian, *The Real Cassian Revisited: Monastic Life, Greek Paideia, and Origenism in the Sixth Century* (Leiden: Brill, 2012), p. 235.

27 As suggested by Colomba Stewart, *Cassian The Monk,* p. 5.

28 Christine Mohrmann, *Études sur le latin des chrétiens,* vol.4, *Latin chrétien et médieval* (Roma: Edizioni di storia e letteratura, 1962), p. 12.

29 Ibid., 297.

Chapter 3

1 Cf. Augustine of Hippo, *On Baptism, Against the Donatists,* 4. VI. 10; XXIV. 32.

---

[2] E. I. Watkin, *The Church in Council* (London: Darton, Longman & Todd, 1960), p. 40.
[3] Augustine of Hippo, *On Grace and Free Will,* XVII. 33.
[4] Augustine of Hippo, *The Predestination of the Saints,* 1. XIV. 29 et seq.
[5] A. M. C. Casiday, *Tradition and Theology in St. John Cassian,* p. 70.
[6] Augustine of Hippo, *The Predestination of the Saints,* 1. I. 2.
[7] Ibid., 1. IV. 8.
[8] Ibid., 1. III. 7.
[9] As proposed by Guillaume de Jerphanion, *La voix des monuments*, p. 89 and John T. Cullen, *Sator Enigma,* chap. 1.
[10] There is no denying that having a tailor-made tradition in Latin during the Council of Nicaea would have been quite convenient for the Roman Church as it was seeking to build and solidify its structure and its leadership position in the world of Christianity.

Chapter 4

[1] Until John T. Cullen's discovery in *Sator Enigma,* 2010.
[2] This apostolic tradition is of divine origin. There are probably other apostolic traditions transmitted orally that come directly from the apostles. See Yves Congar, *Tradition and Traditions, An Historical and a Theological Essay* (London: Burns and Oates, 1966), p. 307.
[3] Paul Berry, *The Christian Inscription at Pompeii* (Lewiston, NY: Edwin Mellen Press, 1995), p. 1.
[4] Ibid., p. 9.

[5] See Bruce W. Longenecker, *The Crosses of Pompeii: Jesus-Devotion in a Vesuvian Town* (Minneapolis: Fortress Press, 2016).

[6] Emidio De Albentiis et al., *Secrets of Pompeii: Everyday Life in Ancient Rome* (Los Angeles: J. Paul Getty Museum, 2009), p. 87.

[7] Tertullian, *The Apology*, 40. Specifying that Christians were not present "in the days" that Vesuvius erupted actually indicates that there were some before these days (this period).

[8] In *The Apology*, Tertullian outlines in the same chapter that there were no Christians in Campania, and yet Paul met people in Puteoli (in the Campania region) around the year A.D. 60 (Acts 28:13-14).

[9] Paul Berry, *The Christian Inscriptions at Pompeii*, p. 2.

[10] The calculation takes into account that the estimated total number of Christians was between 2,000 and 3,000 in the A.D. 60 to 70 period. See Table 1.1 data of Rodney Stark, *The Rise of Christianity: How the Obscure, Marginal Jesus Movement Became the Dominant Religious Force in the Western World in a Few Centuries* (San Francisco, CA: HarperSanFrancisco, 1997), p. 7.

Chapter 5

[1] Council of Trent, 4th session, *Decree Concerning the Canonical Scripture*; First Vatican Council, *Dogmatic Constitution on the Catholic Faith*, third session, Chap. 2 and Second Vatican Council, *Dei Verbum*, 9.

[2] Other contentious doctrines are listed in E. I. Watkin, *The Church in Council*, p. 184.

3 In Luther's time, the monetary contributions aimed at earning indulgences financed such works as the rebuilding of Saint Peter's Basilica in Rome.

4 Alister E. McGrath, *The Intellectual Origins of the European Reformation,* 2nd ed. (Oxford: Blackwell, 1987), pp. 44, 146-147.

5 Ibid., p. 144.

6 We will see that material from the Tradition, if it is the Sator Square, is indeed not found, word by word, in the Scriptures.

7 Council of Trent, 4th session, *Decree Concerning the Canonical Scripture.*

8 Second Vatican Council, *Dei Verbum,* 9.

9 Ibid., 10.

10 Norman Tanner, *Vatican II: The Essential Texts* (New York: Image Books, 2012), pp. 79-80.

11 Second Vatican Council, *Dei Verbum,* 9.

12 John Paul II, *Encyclical Letter Fides et Ratio of the Supreme Pontiff John Paul II to the Bishops of the Catholic Church on the Relationship Between Faith and Reason* [14 Sept. 1998], 10-11 and Second Vatican Council, *Dei Verbum,* 2.

13 Divine Revelation should not be confused with personal experiences or personal revelations; cf. CCC 67.

14 Vincent of Lérins, *Commonitory,* 22.

15 Ibid., 23.

16 John Paul II, *Encyclical Letter Fides et Ratio,* 13.

17 Ibid., 11.

18 Vincent of Lérins, *Commonitory,* 23.

19 Ibid.

20 Ibid.

---

21 In *Commonitory*, 2, Vincent of Lérins concisely establishes three criteria for determining the truth: *Id teneamus quod unique, quod semper, quod ab omnibus creditum est* [we hold that faith which has been believed everywhere, always, and by all].

22 Second Vatican Council, *Dei Verbum*, 10.

23 Yves Congar, *Tradition and Traditions*, pp. 287-288.

24 Ibid., 8.

25 Second Vatican Council, *Dei Verbum,* 12 briefly outlines the Church's position on this.

26 Robert Murray, *Revelations (Dei Verbum)*, ed. Adrian Hastings, *Modern Catholicism: Vatican II and After* (London: SPCK, 1991), p. 78.

27 Gabriel Flynn, *Yves Congar, théologien de l'Église* (Paris : Édition du Cerf, 2007), pp. 110-111.

28 George H. Tavard, *Holy Writ or Holy Church: The Crisis of the Protestant Reformation* (Westport, Conn.: Greenwood Press, 1978), p. 196; cf. Council of Trent, 4th session, *Decree Concerning the Canonical Scripture.*

29 Cyprian of Carthage, *Epistle* 73.10.

30 Peter Hebblethwaite, *John XXIII: Pope of the Century*, Abridged ed., Rev. by Margaret Hebblethwaite (London: Continuum, 2000), p. 131.

31 Patrick Campbell Rodger and Lukas Vischer, *The Fourth World Conference on Faith and Order, Montreal 1963: The Report*, 43 (London: SCM Press, 1964), p. 52.

32 Second Vatican Council, *Dei Verbum*, 10.

Chapter 6

1 Clement of Alexandria, *The Stromata*, I. 12; cf. John Chrysostom, *Homilies on the Acts of the Apostles*, 1. 1.

2 Origen of Alexandria, *Against Celsius,* I. 3. 7.

3 Ibid., I. 7.

4 Ambrose of Milan, *On the Mysteries*, 9. 55.

5 Guy G. Stroumsa, *Hidden Wisdom: Esoteric Traditions and the Roots of Christian Mysticism* (Leiden: Brill, 2005), p. 29.

6 Everett Ferguson, "Paradosis and Traditio: A Word Study," in *Tradition & the Rule of Faith,* ed. Ronnie J. Rombs & Alexander Y. Hwang (Washington, D.C.: The Catholic University of America Press, 2010), pp. 28-29.

7 Jaroslav Pelikan, *The Christian Tradition: A History of the Development of Doctrine, 1. The Emergence of the Catholic Tradition (100-600,)* (Chicago: University of Chicago Press, 1971), p. 117; Everett Ferguson, "Paradosis and Traditio," p. 29.

8 Ibid., p. 117.

9 As explained by Everett Ferguson, *"Paradosis and Traditio,"* p. 3; cf. George H. Tavard, *Holy Writ or Holy Church*, p. viii.

10 This content can be found in teaching supports, such as Christian letters and apothegms (anecdotes or precepts stated by distinguished individuals).

11 There are some people who were aware of the secret but did not hold Episcopal office. For example, my research shows that Yves Congar was clearly familiar with the content of the Sator Square well before he was appointed as a cardinal shortly before his death.

12 Second Vatican Council, *Dei Verbum*, 10; First Vatican Council, third session, *Dogmatic Constitution on the Catholic Faith,* 3. 10 and Council of Trent, 4th session, *Decree Concerning the Canonical Scripture.*

---

[13] My observations are based only on the Christian authors who are aware of the Sator Square secret.

[14] Irenaeus of Lyon, *Against Heresies,* III. 3. 3.

[15] See, for example, Second Vatican Council, *Dei Verbum*, 9.

[16] Basil of Caesarea, *De Spiritu Sancto*, 66.

[17] See, among others, Clement of Alexandria, *The Stromata*, I. 1. IV. 18; VI. 7; VI. 15; Eusebius of Caesarea, *Church History*, II. 15. 3; cf. George H. Tavard, *Holy Writ or Holy Church,* pp. 59, 127, 132, 134, 145, 215.

[18] Yves Congar, *The Meaning of Tradition*, transl. by A. N. Woodrow (San Francisco: Ignatius Press, 2004), pp. 14, 20.

[19] John. E. Thiel, *Senses of tradition: Continuity and Development in Catholic Faith* (Oxford: Oxford University Press, 2000), pp. 32-33.

[20] Council of Trent, 4th session, *Decree Concerning the Canonical Scripture.*

[21] In the Council of Trent texts, the Church uses the word "traditions" in the plural, while later on, Vatican II uses the term "sacred tradition" in the singular.

[22] Yves Congar, *The Meaning of Tradition*, pp. 14, 20.

[23] Ibid.

[24] This topic is dealt with in the "Living Tradition" section of the previous chapter.

[25] Second Vatican Council, *Dei Verbum*, 8.

[26] In Mt. 7:6, Jesus asks that what is holy not be given to dogs; cf. 1 Cor. 3:1-2; Heb. 5:12-14.

[27] Pierre Batiffol, *Étude d'histoire de la théologie positive*, 2e éd. (Paris: Librairie Lecoffre, 1902), p. 38.

[28] Origen of Alexandria, *Against Celsius*, I. 7; Basil of Caesarea, *De Spiritu Sancto*, 66.

[29] Guy G. Stroumsa, *Hidden Wisdom*, p. 33.

[30] Pierre Batiffol, *Étude d'histoire de la théologie positive*, p. 6.

[31] Irenaeus of Lyon, *Against Heresies,* III. 4. 2.

[32] Lk. 2:19; Jn. 12:40; Acts 8:22 and Rom. 1:21.

[33] Mary J. Carruthers, *Le livre de la mémoire: une étude de la mémoire dans la culture médiévale* (Paris: Macula, 2002), p. 363.

[34] Guillaume de Jerphanion, *La voix des monuments*, pp. 54-55.

[35] Clement of Alexandria, *The Stromata*, V. 7. 10.

[36] Birger Gerhardsson, *Memory and Manuscript: Oral Tradition and Written Transmission in Rabbinic Judaism and Early Christianity* (Grand Rapids, Michigan: W. B. Eerdman, 1998; Cf. James D. G. Dunn, *Jesus Remembered: Christianity in the Making,* vol. 1 (Grand Rapids, Michigan: W. B. Eerdman, 2003), pp. 197-198.

[37] A number of texts have been written on this subject, including Terence C. Mournet, *Oral Tradition and Literacy Dependency: Variability and Stability in the Synoptic Tradition and Q* (Tubïnger: Mohr Siebeck, 2005), pp. 63-67 and Bart D. Ehrman, *Jesus Before the Gospels: How the Earliest Christians Remembered, Changed, and Invented Their Stories of the Savior*, (New York: HarperCollins, 2016), pp. 66-71.

[38] James D. G. Dunn, *Jesus Remembered,* p. 198.

[39] Christine Mohrmann, *Latin chrétien et médiéval*, pp. 16-17.

[40] Such as John Cassian, *Conference* 13. 3 and 7; Augustin of Hippo, *On Grace and Free Will,* X. 10. 3.

[41] Benedict XVI, *General Audience on the Apostolic Tradition of the Church*, Wednesday, 3 May 2006.

---

⁴² Benedict XVI also refers to the four Gospels of the New Testament.

⁴³ Yves Congar, *Tradition and Traditions*, p. 301.

Chapter 7

¹ John Paul II, *Encyclical Letter Fides et Ratio*, 16-17.

² Irenaeus of Lyon, *Against Heresies,* I. 24. 4.

³ Everett Ferguson, *Backgrounds of Early Christianity,* 3rd ed. (Grand Rapids, MI: Wm. B. Eerdmans, 2003), p. 308.

⁴ Ibid., p. 113.

⁵ John Denham Parsons, *The Non-Christian Cross: An Enquiry Into the Origin and History of the Symbol Eventually Adopted as That of Our Religion* (Charleston, SC: BiblioBazaar, 2007).

⁶ In addition to these writings, there is the *Alexamenos graffito,* drawn by a non-Christian, which depicts a crucified man with a donkey's head. On the lower left of the graffito, there is a second person who is lifting his left arm while looking at the crucified man. Below that is a caption: "Alexamenos worships [his] God."

⁷ Justin Martyr, *Dialogue with Trypho,* 40; see also by the same author: 11 and 90; *The First Apology*, 35 and 55; cf. Tertullian, *Ad Nationes,* 1. 12.

⁸ Richard Viladesau, *The Beauty of the Cross: The Passion of Christ in Theology and the Arts, from the Catacombs to the Eve of the Renaissance* (Oxford: Oxford University Press, 2006), p. 21.

⁹ George Henry Lane Fox Pitt-Rivers, *The Riddle of the "Labarum" and the Origin of Christian Symbols* (London: George Allen & Unwin, 1966), p. 80.

[10] Ibid., p. 22.

[11] Frédérick Tristan, *Les premières images chrétiennes : du symbole à l'icône: IIe-VIe siècle* (Paris: Fayard, 1996), pp. 34-35.

[12] One exception is the Jewish letter *tav* in the form of an "X," which will be discussed in Chapter 11.

[13] Robert E. Van Voorst, *Jesus Outside the New Testament: An Introduction to the Ancient Evidence* (Grand Rapids, MI: Wm. B. Eerdmans, 2000), p. 8.

[14] Ahmed Osman, *Christianity: An Ancient Egyptian Religion* (Rochester, VT: Bear & Company, 2005), p. 243.

[15] Robert Eisenman, *James the Brother of Jesus: The Key to Unlocking the Secrets of Early Christianity and the Dead Sea Scrolls* (New York: Penguin, 1997), p. xxv.

[16] Jean-Louis Bernard, *Apollonius de Tyane et Jésus*, éd. de la Maisnie (Paris, Guy Trédaniel, 1994), p. 108; cf. Richard Carrier, *On the Historicity of Jesus: Why We Might Have Reason for Doubt* (Sheffield: Sheffield Phoenix Press, 2014), p. 291.

[17] Richard Carrier, *On the Historicity of Jesus*, p. 291.

[18] Kersey Graves, *The World's Sixteen Crucified Saviors: Christianity before Christ* (Boston: Colby & Rich Publ., 1876), p. 30.

[19] Maurice Casey, *Jesus: Evidence and Argument or Mythicist Myths?* (London: Bloomsbury Academic, 2014), see pages 10, 26, among others; cf. Everett Ferguson, *Background of Early Christianity*, pp. 298-299.

[20] Everett Ferguson, *Background of Early Christianity*, pp. 298-299.

21 Earl Doherty, *The Jesus Puzzle: Did Christianity Begin with a Mythical Christ?* (Ottawa, Canada: Canadian Humanist Publications, 1999), see, for example, p. vii.
22 Rom., 1 Cor., 2 Cor., Gal., Phil., 1 Thess. and Philem.
23 The "Q" source, from the German *Quelle*, or "source," is a hypothetical document from which some passages were taken by evangelists Matthew and Luke, but not by Mark. The passages that are common to both evangelists are known as the Double Tradition.
24 The material common to all three evangelists is called the Triple Tradition.
25 Suetonius, Book VI (*Nero*), 16.
26 Ibid., Book V (*Claudius*), 25.
27 Publius Cornelius Tacitus, *The Annals,* 44.
28 Pliny the Younger, *Letters*, X. 96.
29 Flavius Josephus, *The Antiquities of the Jews,* XX. 9. 1.
30 Ibid., XVIII. 3. 3.
31 As outlined in many publications, including that of Alice Whealey, *Josephus on Jesus: the Testimonium Flavianum Controversy from Late Antiquity to Modern Times* (New York: P. Lang, 2003), p. xiii and Robert E. Van Voorst, *Jesus Outside the New Testament*, p. 88.
32 John P. Meier, *A Marginal Jew: Rethinking the Historical Jesus, 1. Origins of the Problem and the Person* (New York: Doubleday, 1991), p. 68.
33 We have seen that the oldest artifacts discovered are Rotas Squares. In addition, the artifact can be considered a "document" since it provides information, once read in the proper order.
34 Indeed, this would signify that the two Rotas Square of Pompeii were created up to eight months before the

eruption of Vesuvius (i.e. between January 1 and August 24, 79).

[35] As explained by Robert E. Van Voorst, *Jesus Outside the New Testament*, pp. 7-8.

[36] Harry Y. Gamble, *Books and Readers in the Early Church: A History of Early Christian Texts* (New Haven: Yale University Press, 1995), p. 71.

[37] See the father of the documentary hypothesis, Julius Wellhausen, *Prolegomena zur Geschichte Israel,* 1878.

[38] Walter C. Kaiser Jr., *The Old Testament Documents: Are They Reliable & Relevant?* (Downers Grove: InterVarsity Press, 2001), p. 164.

[39] Kim Haines-Eitzen, *Guardians of Letters: Literacy, Power, and the Transmitters of Early Christian Literature* (Oxford: Oxford University Press, 2000), p. 85.

[40] Bart D. Ehrman, *Misquoting Jesus*, p. 44.

[41] See, Rufinus of Aquileia, *Apology of Pamphilus for Origen.* However, Rufinus adds that these controls were missing in Origen's time, before the mid-third century.

[42] Origen of Alexandria, *Against Celsius*, III. 44.

[43] Ibid., I. 27; III. 18.

[44] William V. Harris, *Ancient Literacy* (Cambridge, MA: Harvard University Press, 1989), p. 22.

[45] Chris Keith, *The Pericope Adulterae, the Gospel of John, and the Literacy of Jesus* (Leiden, Boston: Brill, 2009), p. 55.

[46] Harry Y. Gamble, *Books and Readers in the Early Church*, p. 3.

[47] Cf. Chris Keith, *The Pericope Adulterae,* pp. 57-59.

---

[48] H. Gregory Snyder, *Teachers and Texts in the Ancient World: Philosophers, Jews, and Christians* (London: Routledge, 2000), pp. 210-211.

Chapter 8

[1] Arland J. Hultgren, *The Parables of Jesus: A Commentary* (Grand Rapids, MI: Wm. B. Eerdmans, 2000), p. 1.
[2] Joachim Jeremias, *Unknown Sayings of Jesus*, transl. by Reginald H. Fuller (London: SPCK, 1964), pp. 18-19.
[3] Based on his studies on the words of Jesus, Jeremias believes that the four New Testament gospels do cover all of the teachings of Jesus Christ; *Unknown Sayings of Jesus*, p. 121.
[4] Ibid., p. 6.
[5] Jean Delorme, *Les paraboles évangéliques: perspectives nouvelles, XIIᵉ congrès de l'ACFEB, Lyon, 1987* (Paris: Éditions du Cerf, 1989), pp. 173-174, 389.
[6] Joachim Jeremias, *The Parables of Jesus*, p. 12.
[7] James Breech, *Jesus and Postmodernism* (Minneapolis: Fortress Press, 1989), p. 25.
[8] James L. Bailey and Lyle D. Vander Broek, *Literary Forms in the New Testament: A Handbook* (Louisville, KY: Westminster John Knox Press, 1992), p. 106.
[9] David Stern, *Parables in Midrash: Narrative and Exegesis in Rabbinic Literature* (Cambridge, MA: Harvard University Press, 1991), p. 5.
[10] John Dominic Crossan, *In Parables: The Challenge of the Historical Jesus* (New York: Harper & Row, 1973), pp. 19-21; cf. Rudolf Bultmann, *The History of the Synoptic Tradition*, transl. by John Marsh (Oxford, England: Basil

Blackwell, 1963), p. 59; other differences were cited by
Jean Delorme, *Les paraboles évangéliques*, p. 77.

[11] Excluding two comparisons made in the first century B.C.
by Hillel the Elder, the first rabbinic parables originate
from the year A.D. 80 according to Joachim Jeremias, *The
Parables of Jesus* (London: SCM Press, 1976), p. 12; cf. David
Instone-Brewer, "Rabbinic Writing in the New Testament
Research," in *Handbook for the Study of the Historical Jesus*,
ed. Tom Holmén and Stanley E. Porter, vol. 2 (Leiden: Brill,
2011), pp. 1707, 1719.

[12] Cf. Howard Clark Kee, *Jesus in History: An Approach to the
Study of the Gospels* (New York: Harcourt, Brace & World,
1970), p. 19.

[13] To explain these disparities, writers produced theories
suggesting that Jesus introduced the variations to explain
different points in his teachings, cf. David Wenham, *The
Parables of Jesus: Pictures of Revolution* (London: Hodder &
Stoughton, 1989), p. 220.

[14] C. H. Dodd, *The Parables of the Kingdom* (London: J.
Nisbet and Co., 1935), p. 29.

[15] Joachim Jeremias, *The Parables of Jesus*, pp. 42-45.

[16] Ibid., pp. 25-26.

[17] Rudolf Bultmann, *The History of the Synoptic Tradition*,
p. 6.

[18] Ibid., p. 370; the form-criticism method of Bultmann does
not focus on the historical fact of Jesus of Nazareth, but
instead on his preaching, meaning the authentic divine
kerygmatic content being conveyed, based on his death and
Resurrection.

[19] John Dominic Crossan, *In Parables*, pp. 7-8.

[20] Gerd Theissen and Annette Merz, *A Historical Jesus: A Comprehensive Guide* (Minneapolis: Fortress Press, 1998), p. 109.

[21] According to Rudolf Bultmann's classification, *The History of the Synoptic Tradition;* cf. John Dominic Crossan, *In Parables*, p. 55.

[22] John Dominic Crossan, *In Parables*, pp. 23-27.

[23] John Dominic Crossan, *In Fragments*, p. 12.

[24] Robert W. Funk and the Jesus Seminar, *The Acts of Jesus: The Search for the Authentic Deeds of Jesus* (San Francisco: Harper San Francisco, 1998), p. 9.

[25] Collin Brown, *"The Quest of the Unhistorical Jesus and the Quest of the Historical Jesus"* in *Handbook for the Study of the Historical Jesus*, ed. Tom Holmén and Stanley E. Porter, vol. 2 (Leiden: Brill, 2011), p. 871.

[26] John Dominic Crossan, *In Fragments*, p. viii.

[27] John T. Cullen, *Sator Enigma,* Ch. 6.

[28] Ibid., p. 14.

[29] John Dominic Crossan, "Parables" in *The Anchor Bible Dictionary*, ed. David Noel Freedman (NY: Doubleday, 1992), 5:149; cf. James L. Bailey, *Literary Forms in the New Testament*, p. 100.

[30] John Dominic Crossan, *In Fragments*, p. 78.

[31] David Wenham, *The Parables of Jesus*, p. 218 and Charles W. Hedrick, *Many Things in Parables*: Jesus and His Modern Critics (Louisville, KY: Westminster John Knox, 2004), p. 26.

[32] Mt. 13:13; Mk. 4:12 and Lk. 8:10

[33] Andreas J. Köstenberger and Richard D. Patterson, *Invitation to Biblical Interpretation: Exploring the Hermeneutical Triad of History, Literature, and Theology* (Grand Rapids, MI: Kregel Publications, 2011), p. 429.

[34] See Lk. 11:5; 17:7; Mt. 18:12.

[35] A number of texts discuss this topic, for example, Andreas J. Köstenberger and Richard D. Patterson, *Invitation to Biblical Interpretation,* p. 441.

[36] Amos N. Wilder, *Eschatology and Ethics in the Teaching of Jesus*, Rev. Ed. (Westport, CT: Greenwood Press, 1979), p. 106.

[37] C. H. Dodd, *The Parables of the Kingdom*, p. 178; cf. Joachim Jeremias, *The Parables of Jesus*, p. 119.

[38] See, for example, Norman Perrin, *Jesus and the Language of the Kingdom: Symbol and Metaphor in New Testament Interpretation* (Philadelphia: Fortress Press, 1976), p. 202 and C. H. Dodd, *The Parables of the Kingdom,* p. 175.

[39] C. H. Dodd, *The Parables of the Kingdom,* p. 178.

[40] Concile Vatican II, *Lumen Gentium,* p. 5.

[41] Arland J. Hultgren, *The Parables of Jesus,* pp. 129-130.

[42] André Lemaire, "Wisdom in Solomonic Historiography," in *Wisdom in Ancient Israel: Essays in Honour of J. A. Emerton*, ed. John Day et al. (Cambridge: Cambridge University Press, 1995), p. 110.

[43] A. A. Macintosh, "Hosea and the Wisdom Tradition: Dependence and Independence," in *Wisdom in Ancient Israel*, p. 130.

[44] Arland J. Hultgren, *The Parables of Jesus,* pp. 10-11.

[45] Charles W. Hedrick, *Many Things in Parables*, p. 67; cf. Andreas J. Köstenberger and Richard D. Patterson, *Invitation to Biblical Interpretation,* p. 441.

[46] A.A. Macintosh, "Hosea and the Wisdom Tradition," p. 131; cf. Gerd Theissen and Annette Merz, *A Historical Jesus,* p. 374.

[47] Howard Clark Kee, *Jesus in History*, p. 20.

[48] Gerd Theissen and Annette Merz, *A Historical Jesus,* p. 336.

[49] James Breech, *Jesus and Postmodernism,* p. 66.

[50] Mt. 13:1-23; Mk. 4:1-20; Lk. 8:4-15.

[51] See, for example, Éric Edelmann, *Jésus parlait araméen* (Gordes, France: Les Éd. Du Relié, 2000), p. 385; cf. Robert Winterhalter and George W. Fisk, *Jesus' Parables: Finding Our God Within* (New York: Paulist Press, 1993), p. 33.

[52] Clement of Alexandria, *The Stromata,* I. 12; Denise Kimber Buell, *Making Christians: Clement of Alexandria and the Rhetoric of Legitimacy* (Princeton, NJ: Princeton University Press, 1999), p. 76.

Chapter 9

[1] Mt. 26:25; 49; Mk. 10:51; 11:21; Jn. 1:38; 1:49; 3:2; 4:31; 8:2; 11:8.

[2] Publius Cornelius Tacitus, *Annals of Tacitus,* transl. by A. J. Church and W. J. Brodribb (London: Macmillan & Cie, 1876), p. 59. Having to pay taxes to Rome reinforced the feeling of oppression.

[3] For example, the Roman general Pompey dared to enter the exclusive area of the Temple of Jerusalem (Flavius Josephus, *The Antiquities of the Jews,* XIV. 4. 4), and Roman general Crassus did not hesitate to rob the Jewish treasury of 2,000 gold talents (Flavius Josephus, *The Antiquities of the Jews,* XIV. 7. 1).

[4] See Chapters 7 and 12 of this deuterocanonical book.

[5] Flavius Josephus, *The War of the Jews,* II. 8. 11; 14.

[6] Sanhedrin 10.1.

[7] The fact that Paul cleverly raised the issue of resurrection to create discord among the Sanhedrin group composed of

Sadducees and Pharisees shows that it was a timely and heated topic for the Jews (Acts 23:6-8).

8 See, among others, Ps. 1:6 and Prov. 2:20. Chapter 12 of the book of Daniel refers to other criteria, such as being recorded by God in the book of Life, being intelligent and teaching righteousness.

9 Throughout the history of Israel, the salvation of the community was often emphasized, to the detriment of individual salvation. In fact, it was not a question of one or the other, but one with the other.

10 Robert Eisenman, *James the Brother of Jesus*, p. 85.

11 See also the following passages: Isa. 40:9; Ps. 16:10-11; 23:1-3; 86:11; 119:33; 139:24; cf. 1 Enoch 48:1-7.

12 In fact, we will see later in the text that ultimately, Jesus Christ himself is the Redeemer.

13 The *Didache,* Ch. I; IX; X.

14 See also Acts 2:25-28 and the epistle of Barnabas, XVIII to XX.

15 See Jean Rivière, *Saint Justin et les apologistes du second siècle* (Paris: Bloud & Cie, 1907), p. 340.

16 Irenaeus of Lyon, *Against Heresies,* IV. 1. 1.

17 Augustine of Hippo, *Contra Faustum,* X. 2.

18 According to the passage of Thomas More quoted in George H. Tavard, *Holy Writ or Holy Church*, p. 133; cf. Yves Congar, *The Meaning of Tradition,* p. 16.

19 The two Rotas Squares of Pompeii.

20 The Magic Square can be considered a "document" since it provides information once read in the proper order.

21 Irenaeus of Lyon, *Against Heresies,* I. 10. 2.

---

[22] Yves Congar, *The Meaning of Tradition,* pp. 12, 53-54, 114; cf. Jaroslav Pelikan, *The Christian Tradition,* vol. 1: *The Emergence,* p. 7.

[23] Yves Congar, *Tradition and Traditions*, pp. 264-5, 343.

[24] Yves Congar, *The Meaning of Tradition*, p. 114.

[25] Council of Trent, 4th session, *Decree Concerning the Canonical Scripture.*

[26] Yves Congar, *The Meaning of Tradition,* pp. 40, 84

[27] Even after the death of Jesus Christ, people would continue to ask Jesus' followers how to obtain salvation. For example, in the Acts of the Apostles (16:30), the jailer asks Paul and Silas what he must do to be saved.

[28] Eusebius of Caesarea, *Church History*, II. 23.

[29] Another characteristic that could be added to this list is that Jesus of Nazareth led an exemplary moral life.

Chapter 10

[1] Clement of Alexandria, *The Stromata*, II. 12.

[2] George Willard Benson, *The Cross, Its History & Symbolism: An Account of the Symbol More Universal in Its Use and More Important in Its Significance Than Any Other in the World* (New York: Hacker Art Books, 1976), p. 68.

[3] Ibid., p. 42.

[4] Tertullian, *An Answer to the Jews*, 11.

[5] Marcus Minucius Felix, *Octavius,* 29.

[6] Justin Martyr, *First Apology*, 55.

[7] Tertullian, *The Apology,* 16.

[8] See also The epistle of Barnabas, 9.

[9] Clement of Alexandria, *The Stromata*, VI. 11.

[10] John Denham Parsons, *The Non-Christian Cross*, p. 28.

[11] However, in some passages of the Old Testament, God asks people to do things that could be perceived as idolatry. For example, God asks Moses to make and look at a bronze serpent (Nb. 21:9) and to make two cherubim of gold and place them on the Ark of the Covenant (Ex. 25:18-22) or in the Temple of Solomon (1 Kgs. 6:23; 6:28).

[12] See, for example, Justin Martyr, *Dialogue with Trypho*, 89 et seq; Rufinus of Aquileia, *Commentaries on the Apostles' Creed,* 18.

[13] Tertullian, *An Answer to the Jews,* 10; see also Trypho's comment in Justin Martyr, *Dialogue with Trypho*, 89.

[14] See Tertullian, *An Answer to the Jews* or Justin Martyr, *Dialogue with Trypho.*

[15] Publius Cornelius Tacitus, *The Annals,* 44.

[16] George Willard Benson, *The Cross, Its History & Symbolism*, p. 40.

[17] Robert Eisenman, *James the Brother of Jesus,* p. 419.

[18] See, for example, Acts of the Apostles 17 and 18 and the persecution of the early Christians by the Jews, with the participation of Saul.

[19] Justin Martyr, *Dialogue with Trypho*, 89; 90.

[20] Frédérick Tristan, *Les premières images chrétiennes*, p. 556.

[21] Eusebius of Caesarea, *Church History*, III. 1.

[22] Frédérick Tristan, *Les premières images chrétiennes*, p. 72.

[23] See Bruce W. Longenecker's book *The Crosses of Pompeii: Jesus-Devotion in a Vesuvian Town.*

[24] Shimon Gibson, *The Cave of John the Baptist: The First Archaeological Evidence of the Truth of the Gospel Story* (London: Century, 2004), p. 64.

[25] E. L. Sukenik, "The Earliest Records of Christianity" in *The American Journal of Archaeology*, vol. 51, (1947), pp. 351-365; cf. Erwin R. Goodenough, *Jewish Symbols in the Greco-Roman Period,* vol. 1, *The Archaeological Evidence from Palestine,* Bollingen Series XXXVII (New York: Pantheon Books, 1953), pp. 130-131.

[26] Daniel Rancour-Laferriere, *The Sign of the Cross: From Golgotha to Genocide,* (New Brunswick, NJ: Transaction Publishers, 2011), p. 10.

[27] John Denham Parsons, *The Non-Christian Cross*, p. 132.

[28] As explained by James D. Tabor and Simcha Jacobovici, *The Jesus Discovery: The New Archaeological Find That Reveals the birth of Christianity* (New York, NY, Simon & Schuster, 2012), pp. 101-103.

[29] Bruce W. Longenecker, *The Crosses of Pompeii,* p. 217.

[30] Justin Martyr, *First Apology*, 1; 55.

[31] There are also other Magic Squares, as seen in Chapter 1, such as the ones in Dura-Europos, Budapest, Cirencester and Manchester that were all inscribed well before the fourth century.

[32] See, for example, Jean Daniélou, *Primitive Christian Symbols* (London: Burns & Oates, 1964).

[33] Bruce W. Longenecker, *The Crosses of Pompeii*, pp. 69-70.

[34] Jean Daniélou, *The Theology of Jewish Christianity,* translated and edited by John A. Baker, vol. 1, *A History of Early Christian Doctrine Before the Council of Nicaea* (London: Darton, Longman & Todd, 1964), p. 275.

[35] Irenaeus of Lyon, *Against Heresies,* IV. 34. 4.

[36] Jean Daniélou, *Primitive Christian Symbols,* p. 91.

[37] Ibid., p. 100.

[38] Ibid., p. 101.

[39] Daniel Rancour-Laferriere, *The Sign of the Cross*, p. 2.

Chapter 11

[1] Irenaeus of Lyon, *Against Heresies,* IV. 14. 2.

[2] Eusebius of Caesarea, *Church History*, III. 27. In the same chapter, Eusebius specified that there had also been another group with the same name, a group that believed in Jesus Christ's divinity, but not in the pre-existence of the Word or the Wisdom.

[3] See Irenaeus of Lyon, *Against Heresies,* I. 26. 2; III. 11. 7; 21. 1 and Epiphanius of Salamis, *Panarion,* 30.

[4] Epiphanius of Salamis, *Panarion*, 30. 18. 5.

[5] Acts 3:22-23; 7:37

[6] Mt. 16:14, 21:11; Jn. 4:19; 6:14; 7:40, 42; 9:17.

[7] The wisdom of Jesus was recognized, among others, by Flavius Josephus, *The Antiquities of the Jews,* XVIII. 3.3, and even by Mara Bar-Serapion, who was probably a Syrian pagan, in one of his letters dating back to the first century A.D.

[8] If we rely on the gospel of Luke, in which Jesus says: "My mother and My brothers are these who hear the word of God and do it" (8:21) then the word "brother" could refer to anyone who follows the path of life or the blueprint.

[9] The Apostle Paul could have also used the word "brother" to indirectly show that Apollos adopted the position of Jesus's blood brothers, particularly the position of his brother James. As we will see, those brothers followed the same path as Paul, even though with a different interpretation, at least for a while.

[10] 1 Cor. 1:12; 3:22.

---

[11] Let us not forget that the Apostle Peter sometimes showed a deeper knowledge than the other apostles, if we consider his confession in the gospel of Matthew (16:13-20).

[12] Peter realized the universal scope of the message during the baptism of the centurion Cornelius (Acts 10:34).

[13] Acts 2:38, 3:6; cf. 1 Pet. 4:14-16.

[14] Jaroslav Pelikan, *The Christian Tradition,* vol. 1: *The Emergence*, p. 117.

[15] See the pseudonyms in Chapter 6: Secret Rule 2.

[16] 1 Clement, 1; 7.

[17] Irenaeus of Lyon, *Against Heresies,* I. 9. 4.

[18] Cf. CCC 1229 and Augustine of Hippo, *On Baptism, Against the Donatists*, 7. 53. 102.

[19] Using an analysis based on the criterion of historical authenticity, many researchers believe that baptism is an authentic event, because it meets the criterion of ecclesiastical embarrassment over what some saw as Jesus's submission to John the Baptist. See John P. Meier, *A Marginal Jew: Rethinking the Historical Jesus*, vol. 1, p. 168; cf. Rafael Rodriguez, "The Embarrassing Truth About Jesus: The Criterion of Embarrassment and the Failure of Historical Authenticity," in *Jesus, Criteria, and the Demise of Authenticity,* ed. Christ Keith and Anthony Le Donne (London: T&T Clark, 2012), which explains the history, its application, and his conclusions about the criterion.

[20] Tertullian, *On Modesty*, 9, "the sign and seal of baptism."

[21] Although I do not address the baptism of young children in this book, the elements remain essential for all Christians.

[22] Many of Jesus's apostles were former disciples of John the Baptist (Jn. 1:35-39, Acts 1:21-22) and therefore undoubtedly went through that type of baptism.
[23] Mt. 11:7-14; 21:23-32; 11:27-32; Lk. 20:1-8.
[24] Jack Finegan, *The Archeology of the New Testament: The Life of Jesus and the Beginning of the Early Church,* Rev. ed. (Princeton, NJ: Princeton University Press, 1992), p. 347.
[25] Ps. 54:1; Jer. 16:21.
[26] Jack Finegan, *The Archeology of the New Testament,* p. 344.
[27] Jean Daniélou, *Primitive Christian Symbols*, 139.
[28] Rowan Williams, *Arius: Heresy and Tradition* (London: Darton, Longman & Todd, 1987), pp. 106-107.
[29] Alexander of Alexandria, *Letter to Alexander of Constantinople*, 1.
[30] Ibid., 9.
[31] Athanasius of Alexandria, *Discourse Against the Arians*, I. 6.
[32] Ibid., III. 18.
[33] Ibid., I, 9.
[34] R.P.C. Hanson, *The Search for the Christian Doctrine in God: The Arian Controversy 318-381* (Edinburgh: T. & T. Clark, 1988), pp. 109-110.
[35] Rowan Williams, *Arius: Heresy and Tradition,* p. 96.
[36] Lucien Dînca, *Le Christ et la Trinité chez Athanase d'Alexandrie* (Paris: Éd. du Cerf, 2012), p. 131.

Chapter 12

[1] Basil of Caesarea, *De Spiritu Sancto*, 35.

[2] Many people may find it offensive, even blasphemous, to make a connection between Jesus Christ and the serpent, given that the serpent is depicted as evil in the Bible. However, many other Christian writers, such as Justin (*Dialogue with Trypho,* 40), and Tertullian (*Against Marcion,* II, 22), associated the serpent with Jesus Christ. In order to explain the representation of the bronze serpent, Gregory of Nyssa, a fourth-century Cappadocian Father, stated that Jesus Christ took upon himself the sins of all human beings on the cross to liberate them from their sins (*The Life of Moses,* transl. by Abraham J. Malherbe and Everett Ferguson (New York: HarperOne, 2006), p. 40.

[3] This death is a spiritual death that results from the expulsion of Adam and Eve from the Garden of Eden. It represents the state of no longer being in communion with God. Jesus Christ enables human beings' relationship with God to be reestablished.

[4] Rom. 16:20; 24; Eph. 4:7; 2 Cor. 13:13; cf. Jn. 1:14; 17.

[5] Rom. 1:7; 1 Cor. 1:3; 2 Cor. 1:2.

[6] *The Shepherd of Hermas,* Similitude 9, 12; 13; 14; 16; 17; 28.

[7] Acts 2:38; see also 2:36; 10:48.

[8] David Instone-Brewer, "Rabbinic Writing in the New Testament Research," p. 1705.

[9] Mt. 10:38; 16:24; Mk. 8:34; Lk. 9:23; 14:27.

[10] Cf. Frédérick Tristan, *Les premières images chrétiennes,* p. 35.

[11] Jean Daniélou, *The Theology of Jewish Christianity,* p. 330.

[12] Jn. 1:29; cf. Thomas Aquinas, *S. Th.,* II-II, 2, 7, ad. 2.

[13] For example, in *Dialogue with Trypho,* 111, Justin Martyr saw the link with Chapter 12 of Exodus.

---

[14] Erwin R. Goodenough, *Jewish Symbols in the Greco-Roman Period,* vol. 10, p. 131.

[15] It is one of the Jewish religious documents from the Library of Qumrân, discovered in the mid-20th century.

[16] Jean Daniélou, *The Theology of Jewish Christianity*, p. 275

[17] Basil of Caesarea, *De Spiritu Sancto*, 66.

[18] Tertullian, *The Chaplet*, 3.

[19] John Paul II, *Apostolic Letter Divini Amoris Scientia* [19 October 1997], 8; see also: CCC 571; Pope Francis, *Encyclical Letter Lumen Fidei* [29 June 2013], 15 or *Walking with Jesus: The Heart of Christian Life* (London: Darton, Longman & Todd Ltd, 2015), pp. 4, 40; Benedict XVI, *Homily of the Holy Mass for the Opening of the Year of Faith* [11 October 2012]; John Paul II, *Letter to the Priests for Holy Thursday 1995*, 3 and Yves Congar, *Tradition and Traditions*, pp. 10; 20; 32; 340; 431.

[20] The word "stumble" is used in the New King James Version Bible.

[21] See, for example, Gn. 9:12; 9:13; Ex. 12:13; 2 Kgs. 20:8.

[22] Lucien Dînca, *Le Christ et la Trinité chez Athanase d'Alexandrie*, p. 182.

[23] Clement of Alexandria, *Exhortation to the Heathen,* 1.

[24] This idea, so well described by Athanasius, was deepened over the following centuries by, among other things, the doctrine of the two wills.

[25] Athanasius of Alexandria, *Discourse Against the Arians,* III, 20-21.

[26] Ibid., III, 21.

[27] The word *homoousios* was presented by bishops at the First Council of Nicaea. It is a word that is not recorded in the Bible.

---

[28] Athanasius of Alexandria, *Discourse Against the Arians*, I, 4; 16; 34; 61; II, 33; 54; III, 4, 10, 16, 32, 34, 48.
[29] Ibid., II, 41.
[30] Ibid., II, 35; III, 11.
[31] Ibid., III, 11; cf. III, 14.
[32] Thomas Aquinas, *S. Th.*, I, 26, 2, ad 1.
[33] Irenaeus of Lyon, *Against Heresies,* IV. 26. 1.
[34] Mary J. Carruthers, *Le livre de la mémoire*, p. 363.
[35] There are others, such as the Rotas Square of the Santa Lucia Church, Magliano de' Marsi in the Abruzzo region of Italy.
[36] As also mentioned by N. T. Wright, *What Saint Paul Really Said: Was Paul of Tarsus the Real Founder of Christianity?* (Grand Rapids, MI: William B. Eerdmans Publishing Company, 1997), pp. 45-46; 64; cf. Oswald Chambers, *Biblical Ethic*, pp. 86-87.

Chapter 13

[1] Barrie Wilson, *How Jesus Became Christian* (Toronto, Ontario: Random House of Canada, 2008), p. 13.
[2] Jean Daniélou, *The Origin of Latin Christianity*, transl. by David Smith and John Austin Baker (United Kingdom, Darton, Longman &Todd, 1977), pp. 5-8; Classical Latin was used later in many writings by the first Latin Church Fathers according to Christine Mohrmann, *Études sur le latin des chrétiens*, p. 27.
[3] According to Guillaume de Jerphanion, *La voix des monuments*, p. 90.
[4] Eusebius of Caesarea, *Church History*, II. 1.

5 John Taylor, *The Gospel of St. Mark: Greek, Latin, and English Interlinear with Grammatical Notes* (London: Upper Gower Street, 1832), p. 238.

6 The subject has been dealt with in many books, such as N. T. Wright, *What Saint Paul Really Said,* pp. xi, 17-18 and John G. Gager, *Who Made Early Christianity? The Jewish Lives of the Apostle Paul* (New York: Columbia University Press, 2015), pp. 12-15; among the scholars who support this view are Hyam Maccoby, *The Mythmaker: Paul and the Invention of Christianity* (New York: Harper & Row, 1986) and James D. Tabor, *Paul and Jesus: How the Apostle Transformed Christianity* (New York: Simon & Schuster, 2012).

7 In the early centuries A.D., this group was composed of Judeo-Christians who imposed the Law of Moses on other Christians, such as the obligation to practice circumcision.

8 Peter J. Tomson, *Paul and the Jewish Law*, p. 53; cf. James D. G. Dunn, *Jesus Remembered,* p. 176.

9 W. D. Davies, *The Setting of the Sermon on the Mount* (Cambridge: Cambridge University Press, 1963), pp. 353, 366.

10 Cf. Rom. 2:16; 2 Tim. 2:8.

11 Daniel R. Langton, *The Apostle Paul in the Jewish Imagination: A Study in Modern Jewish-Christian Relations* (New York: Cambridge University Press, 2010), p. 110; cf. W. D. Davies, *Paul and Rabbinic Judaism: Some Rabbinic Elements in Pauline Theology*, 4th ed. (Philadelphia, PA: Fortress Press, 1980).

12 Daniel R. Langton, *The Apostle Paul in the Jewish Imagination,* p. 198.

[13] In fact, it was Jesus who disrupted the existing Jewish paradigms of this period.

[14] Irenaeus of Lyon, *Against Heresies,* III. 15. 1; cf. Tertullian, *The Prescription Against Heretics,* 23.

[15] 1 Tim. 6:20; 2 Tim. 1:13-14; 2:2.

[16] See, for example, A. Souter, "Did Paul Speak Latin?" *The Expositor*, 8th Series, I, 1911, pp. 337-342; William M. Ramsay, *St. Paul: The Traveler and Roman Citizen,* rev. ed. Mark W. Wilson (Grand Rapids (MI): Kregel Publications, 2001), p. 240; Stanley E. Porter, "Did Paul Speak Latin?" in *Paul: Jew, Greek, and Roman*, ed. Stanley E. Porter (Leiden-Boston: Brill, 2008).

[17] See, for example, Stanley E. Porter, "Did Paul Speak Latin?" pp. 292-302.

[18] Paul Berry, *The Christian inscription at Pompeii*, p. 8.

[19] See, for example, Robert Eisenman, *James the Brother of Jesus,* p. 128 and James D. Tabor, *Paul and Jesus*, p. 3.

[20] Justin Martyr, *Dialogue with Trypho*, 48

[21] Tertullian, *The Prescription Against Heretics,* 23.

[22] W. D. Davies, *The Setting of the Sermon on the Mount,* p. 357, James D. G. Dunn, *Jesus Remembered,* pp. 239, 502.

[23] Mt. 13:11; Mk. 4:11; 12:14; Lk. 8:10; Jn. 12:50.

[24] Translation from: "Ce sont les noms de vers du Christ" in Chapter 2, Richard Pietschmann, "Les inscriptions coptes de Faras" in *Recueil de travaux relatifs à la philologie et à l'archéologie égyptiennes et assyriennes*, ed. by G. Maspero, XXI, (Paris: Librairie Émile Bouillon, 1899), p. 134.

[25] Among others, Thomas Aquinas deals with the writing of Jesus Christ. The passage *S. Th.*, III. 42. 4. resp., contains many language subtleties and clues that could actually demonstrate that Jesus is the creator.

[26] Yves Congar, *Tradition and Traditions.* 371-372.

27 Mt. 21:42; Mk. 12:10-11; Lk. 20:17; Acts 4:11.

28 See Mt. 21:42-44 where Jesus makes a link between the stumbling block (the one rejected by the Jews) and the cornerstone.

29 Jeffrey J. Bütz, *The Secret Legacy of Jesus: The Judaic Teachings That Passed from James the Just to the Founding Fathers* (Rochester, Vermont: Inner Tradition, 2010), p. 204.

30 As believed by the Roman Church; see Adolf Harnack, *Apostle's Creed, transl. by* Rev. Stewart Means (Eugene, OR: Wipf and Stock Pub., 2001), pp. 11-13.

31 Taylor R. Marshall, *Eternal City: Rome and the Origins of Catholic Christianity* (Dallas, TX: Saint John Press, 2012), pp. 100-101.

32 Ignatius of Antioch, *Epistle to the Romans,* 4; Irenaeus of Lyon, *Against Heresies,* III. 1. 1; 3. 2; 3. 3 and Eusebius of Caesarea, *Church History*, II. 14-15.

33 Eusebius of Caesarea, *Church History*, II. 15.

34 The 21st saying attributed to Jesus in the Greek Oxyrhynchus papyrus 654; Jean Doresse, *The Secret Books of the Egyptian Gnostics: An Introduction to the Gnostic Coptic Manuscripts Discovered at Chenoboskion* (New York: MJF Books, 1997), p. 358.

35 Eph. 2:20

36 Ps. 89:26.

37 When it comes to reading Aramaic and Hebrew vertically, the first letter at the top is the letter on the far right when read horizontally, and so on. Also, when a text is written in more than one column (like the Sator Square), the reader starts reading with the first column on the far right.

38 Mt. 21:42 (New International Version Bible).

Chapter 14

[1] But the initial version of the gospel of Matthew may have been written in Aramaic.

[2] Paul Berry, *The Christian Inscription at Pompeii,* pp. 42-43.

[3] Stanley E. Porter, "Jesus and the Use of Greek: A Response to Maurice Casey," *Bulletin for Biblical Research*, 10.1, 2000, 71.

[4]Tertullian, *Against Praxeas*, 16; cf. Justin Martyr, *Dialogue with Trypho*, 102; 127.

[5] Cf. Lk. 1:51.

[6] Cf. 2 Sam. 7:13.

[7] Jas. 4:6; 1 Pet. 5:5; cf. Prov. 3:33-34; Isa. 2:11.

[8] Ezek. 42,16-20; Rev. 21,16.

[9] 2 Sam. 7:13.

[10] Heb. 9:15; 1 Tim. 2:15; 1 Pet. 2:5.

[11] *The Shepherd of Hermas,* Vision 3, c. 2.

[12] Cf. Isa. 33:19.

[13] Anthony Rich, *A Dictionary of Roman and Greek Antiquities with Nearly 2000 Engravings on Wood from Ancient Originals* 3rd ed. (London: Longmans Green and Co., 1873), p. 46.

[14] Flavius Josephus, *The War of the Jews,* III. 6. 2 and V. 2. 1.

[15] Paul Veyne, *L'Empire gréco-romain* (Paris : Éditions du Seuil, 2005), pp. 201-202.

[16] Paul Berry, *The Christian Inscription at Pompeii*, p. 39.

[17] Stanley E. Porter, *"Did Paul Speak Latin?"* p. 301.

[18] Tore Johnson, *A Natural History of Latin*, transl. by M. D. Sorensen and N. Vincent (Oxford: Oxford University Press, 2004), p. 13.

19 Émile Lombard, *De la glossolalie chez les premiers chrétiens et des phénomènes similaires, étude d'exégèse et de psychologie* (Lausanne : Georges Bridel & Cie, 1910), p. 231.

20 Verses 1 Cor. 14:23; 26 could also be modified.

21 This thankfulness to God, for having been able to learn Latin to complete his destiny, is similar to the Gal. 1:15-16 seen previously, where Paul thanks God for allowing him to learn Latin from a very young age.

22 See, for example, Lk. 24:45.

23 Émile Lombard, *De la glossolalie chez les premiers chrétiens,* p. 17; translated by author.

24 See the discussion between the American preacher Charles Perham and his students in John L. Sherrill, *They Speak With Other Tongues* (Old Tappan, NJ: F. H. Revell Company, 1973), pp. 36-37.

25 See, for example, John XXIII, *The Apostolic Constitution "Veterum Sapienta" on the promotion of the study of Latin* [22 February 1962] and Pius XI, *Apostolic Letter "Officiorum Omnium"* [1 August 1922], both of which deal with some of these points.

26 Taylor R. Marshall, *Eternal City*, pp. 15-19.

27 Cf. Irenaeus of Lyon, *Against Heresies,* III. 21. 7 and Acts 7:48.

28 Guillaume de Jerphanion, *La voix des monuments*, p. 60.

29 Origen of Alexandria, *Against Celsius*, V. 45.

30 Panaiotis Tzamalikos, *The Real Cassian Revisited*, p. 238.

31 Dio Cassius, *Roman History*, LX. 17. 4.

32 Cf. Mk. 13:10; Lk. 2:31; Jn. 3:7.

33 Christine Mohrmann, *Études sur le latin des chrétiens*, p. 297.

34 Origen of Alexandria, *Against Celsius,* II. 30.

35 Jérôme Carcopino, *Études d'histoire chrétienne*, p. 100.
36 François Barré, Director, *La prophétie des papes*, France: FBI Production - System TV, 2014.

Afterword

1 Lk. 8:17; cf. Mt. 10:26; Mk. 4:22; Lk. 12:2.
2 Everett Ferguson, *The Rule of Faith: A Guide* (Eugene, OR: Cascade Books, 2015), p. 79.
3 As in 1 Cor. 6:15; Eph. 4:25; 5:30.
4 Second Vatican Council, *Unitatis Redintegratio,* 6.
5 Second Vatican Council, *Lumen Gentium*, 8.
6 Second Vatican Council, *Unitatis Redintegratio,* 14-17.
7 Ibid., 19.

Appendix I

1 For the purposes of this book, the study of Augustine is limited to the key themes drawn from the Sator Square.
2 Justo L. González, *A History of Christian Thought: From Augustine to the Eve of the Reformation* (Nashville: Abingdon Press, 1971), pp. 58-61.
3 William Harmless, *Desert Christians: An Introduction to the Literature of Early Monasticism* (Oxford: Oxford University Press, 2004), p. 399; cf. Aaron J. Kleist, *Striving with Grace,* p. 151.
4 Aaron J. Kleist, *Striving with Grace: Views of Free Will in Anglo-Saxon England* (Toronto: Toronto University Press, 2004), p. 285, n. 13; cf. Columba Stewart, *Cassian the Monk,* p. 19.

5 Augustine of Hippo, *The Predestination of the Saints,* 1. III. 7.
6 Vladimir Lossky, *Mystical Theology of the Eastern Church,* p. 201.
7 "Lorsque la grâce vient vers lui [c'est-à-dire l'homme] elle n'a pas la possibilité d'enchaîner sa volonté ... mais elle s'incline devant son libre arbitre," Justin Popovitch, *Les voies de la connaissance de Dieu,* p. 70.
8 Thomas Aquinas, *S. Th.,* I-II. 110. 2.
9 Thomas Aquinas, *Summa contra Gentiles*, III. 159.
10 Thomas Aquinas, *S. Th.,* I-II. 111. 2.
11 Ibid., I-II. 13. 6.
12 Second Council of Orange, Canon 19 and, more specifically, the Council of Trent, 5th session, *Decree Concerning Original Sin*, 5; cf. CCC 1264; 1701-15.
13 Second Council of Orange, Conclusion and Second Vatican Council, *Sacrosanctum Concilium*, 5.
14 Second Council of Orange, Conclusion.
15 Council of Trent, 6th session, *Decree on Justification*, 5 to 10.
16 Ibid., 5.
17 Second Council of Orange, Canon 18 and Conclusion; cf. Council of Trent, 6th session, *Decree on Justification*, 5.

Appendix II

1 Origen of Alexandria, *De Principiis*, Latin Version, III. 1. 22.
2 Clement of Alexandria, *The Stromata*, VII. 7. 48. 4.
3 Irenaeus of Lyon, *Against Heresies,* IV. 14. 1.
4 Cf. Gerd Theissen and Annette Merz, *The Historical Jesus*, p. 376.

SCRIPTURE INDEX

NEW TESTAMENT

INDEX OF NAMES

Author's Note

Thank you for reading this book. I hope you're as fascinated by the Sator Square as I am. If you have a moment, please consider posting a quick review of my book on online book review platforms, such as Amazon, Apple Books, Kobo, and on Goodreads. I would be truly grateful for your feedback.

www.ingramcontent.com/pod-product-compliance
Lightning Source LLC
Chambersburg PA
CBHW070858120626
46546CB00001B/47